For Joey:
With best wishes
for beauty and
abundance

Dig
Yarb

BEAUTIFUL AND ABUNDANT

BEAUTIFUL AND ABUNDANT

Building the World We Want

Bryan Welch

B&A Books
2040 West 31st Street, Suite G #127
Lawrence, Kansas 66046-5164

Visit our Web site at
www.beautifulandabundant.com

First Edition: November 2010

ISBN 978-0-615-42129-2

Library of Congress Control Number: 2010917218

Photographs by Bryan Welch
Book design by Matthew T. Stallbaumer
Hard case design concept by Laura Perkins

Printed in the United States of America

Beautiful and Abundant

BEAUTIFUL AND ABUNDANT

INTRODUCTION

Beautiful and Abundant

We are unique and brilliant creatures.

Humanity has expanded into every corner of the planet. With our extraordinary tools, we are stronger and faster than any other species. And we are improving. We are more powerful and more mobile than any previous generation. We can circumnavigate the Earth in 90 minutes. We travel to outer space and plumb the depths of the oceans. We accumulate information. We build on the knowledge of our ancestors. We record our ideas in colorful and astonishing forms.

We are the brightest, loudest, most powerful living things.

We are the most creative and potent creatures in the universe, so far as we know.

Generation after generation we have visualized–and then realized–one astonishing invention after another. Wheeled vehicles. Agriculture. Sailing ships. Automobiles. Aircraft. Smartphones. Every day entrepreneurs bring a new idea to market that supersedes a million previous good ideas. It seems that each generation can visualize some previously unimaginable goal, and reach it.

Humanity needs that entrepreneurial energy today more than ever. We face a definitively human challenge that is testing human ingenuity. We are the only species that can conceptualize its own impact on its habitat. Today we are becoming increasingly aware that the planet's capacities are limited. As our population has expanded we have also developed technologies that consume natural resources at unprecedented rates. These converging forces are damaging the natural systems on which we, and all other living things, depend. Common sense tells us our expansion can't go on forever, but no species has ever intentionally limited its own growth. No species has ever conceptualized the limits of its habitat and adjusted its behavior to live within those limits. If we are to change our course before some natural calamity forcibly curbs our expansion, the solution will be delivered by human ingenuity.

Human ingenuity gets its energy from visualization. We need to visualize a successful human future on this planet before we can create that future.

Recent global discussions of humanity's future have been preoccupied with the immediate challenges we face. The environmentalist's attention has been trained mostly on negative visualization. Conversations about the environment orbit around one prospective catastrophe or another. We don't have a positive vision for our future, but we can picture a lot of different ways in which things may go badly for us and for the planet.

This lack of a positive vision seems particularly dangerous to me because we so often realize what we visualize, and right now a lot of people are visualizing disaster.

The scale of humanity's immediate challenges is daunting, to be sure. It's difficult and counterintuitive to look past the immediate problems. Considering the scale of those problems, this discussion of positive visions might strike some people as a trivial distraction. But right now our obstacles–resource depletion, population expansion and economic malaise–effectively block our view forward. We're making very little progress against species loss, deforestation, desertification or global warming. The human population continues to grow with astonishing speed. And when we stabilize our population, as we inevitably must, economic growth will stall.

With these big obstacles in our way, we collectively find it difficult to picture a beautiful, abundant world for our grandchildren to live in. To visualize that future, we need a new perspective. To gain that perspective we need to move forward. It's time to engage, to move forward not just *against* the phenomena damaging our habitat, but also *toward* a sustainable *and* prosperous way of life.

We need to engage the passionate human imagination, that great engine of creativity, and challenge it to go beyond its anxious contemplation of environmental disaster to envision the world we desire–vigorous, verdant and enduring. Once the human imagination visualizes a brilliant future, the human intellect can achieve what previously seemed impossible. The human imagination and the human intellect have, together, achieved countless astonishing things in the past. I believe they can do so again and again.

Human beings invented flying machines because we were entranced by the idea of flight. We didn't need to fly but we were thrilled by the prospect. We've joyfully tinkered with wheeled machines, making automobiles and motorcycles faster and more comfortable, generation after generation. We didn't need to propel ourselves around at 70 miles per hour, but once we had the idea in our head we couldn't wait to press that accelerator pedal. We assembled the Internet in a spirit of giddy discovery with a collective vision of global knowledge made ubiquitous and free. Our collective enthusiasm for fairness has, in the past 30 years, redefined civil rights in our global society.

We don't need a disaster to motivate change. A great, contagious idea or two can create all the motivation we need.

Every major human realization was assembled from the discoveries of lots of different people, each pursuing an individual vision and building on each other's work. Our collective visions are always constructed from a bunch of individual visions. Our achievements are shared achievements.

The biggest and most successful component in my business is the magazine *Mother Earth News*. Since 1970 the principal source of energy at *Mother Earth News* has been the contagious idea – organic gardening ideas, homemade renewable energy ideas, ideas for homesteading and natural health and self-reliance. The magazine has prospered because these ideas have kindled millions of imaginations and engaged them in a spirit of mutual exploration. With our readers we have explored many, many different optimistic visions for humanity's future on earth. That's our passion, and our business.

I hope this book will stimulate your imagination. I wrote it, in part, to stimulate my own and to give myself a framework for ongoing invention in my own life. Our collective vision will be synthesized from billions of individual minds engaged in imaginative aspiration and intellectual problem-solving.

To get the conversation started, I'm going to suggest some steps that may help direct our imaginations and our intellects down the right paths.

STEP ONE: IDEALIZE THE DESTINATION. (DON'T BE REALISTIC!)

The Olympic downhill skier prepares for her race with an exercise in visualization. Eyes closed, hands clenched around imaginary poles, the athlete traces every contour and turn in her mind. Finally, she visualizes her triumphant finish, a world record and a gold medal celebration.

During the race her conscious attention is trained down the mountain on the gates ahead. Her reflexes are taking care of the present obstacles. She has visualized the run dozens of times. Her mind is trained on future challenges two or three gates down the course and, ultimately, on victory.

High achievers in every realm of endeavor engage in some version of positive visualization. World-class athletes, successful entrepreneurs and groundbreaking inventors don't reach those pinnacles by imagining realistic outcomes. The Olympic skier knows there are dozens of talented people in the race. Even if she's highly ranked, victory is unlikely. She plans for victory anyway. The entrepreneur knows hundreds of companies are competing with him for capital and customers. Still, he visualizes his company's eventual market dominance and writes that accomplishment into the business plan. Investors aren't looking to fund average companies planning for marginal success. They are looking for visionaries with victory in mind. Savvy investors know that unless the entrepreneur plans for great things, great things will not be achieved. Maybe the gold medal is unlikely. But if the athlete isn't aiming for a gold medal, then it's nearly certain that her destiny will not include a turn on the winner's podium.

This is not a book about my own idealized vision for humanity's future. This book is about the process of forming and nourishing a collective vision. Yes, I have my own idealized vision as I suspect most people do. My vision is informed by all my quirks, my unique social conditioning and my prejudices–just as every person's vision is a product of their unique background and biological makeup. The world we will realize in subsequent generations will be an unpredictable aggregate of myriad individual visions and real-world circumstances.

If you're curious about the beautiful and abundant world I,

as an individual, visualize in our future and you're not patient enough–or charmed enough–to read this book through to the end, you can skip forward to the Epilogue where I lay it out.

Humanity has the technological and intellectual capacities to preserve for our great-grandchildren a world teeming with life and human prosperity. Why would we plan for anything less?

Step Two: Acknowledge the Challenges

My wife and I love watching our land flourish. Raising livestock in a natural way on our little piece of native prairie has enmeshed us in a web of relationships with the millions of living things that share our property. With careful management, keeping the livestock on pasture, we have seen the soil improve each year as the animals help stimulate the natural processes that make the native prairie one of the most productive biological systems on earth. Previous owners cut hay and hauled the nutrients and energy off the land. Since we began grazing it, the land has become much more fertile. A pasture that four cows grazed off in five weeks a few years ago has this summer carried 15 full-grown animals for four months and the forage is still excellent, probably good for another four to six weeks.

"Watching grass grow" metaphorically defines boredom for a lot of people but if you're a rancher and that grass supplies your sustenance, watching grass grow gets a lot more interesting.

And watching it die–destroyed by overgrazing–can be devastating.

The main thing a rancher manages is population.

Conscientious ranchers maintain intricate, attentive relationships with their habitats. Temperature, precipitation, sunshine and many other variables affect our pastures. Properly husbanded, the prairie is perpetually productive. Natural prairie can survive extended periods of drought, floods, snow cover and sub-zero temperatures. But its health can be destroyed by a few weeks of acute overpopulation. Overgrazing devastates grasslands in ways that can take decades to repair, even with expert human intervention. In arid regions overgrazed grasslands become deserts.

Every natural system is vulnerable. Every habitat has limits. Balanced ecosystems evolve over millions of years. When ecosystems fall out of their natural balance the consequences for their dependents are profound.

The global human population has doubled during my lifetime. Our habitat is either in serious trouble now, or it will be, probably soon. Our powerful technology aggravates the damage caused by our expansion. Technology makes us more potent, but it has magnified our impact on the planet. We mine carbon from the earth and deposit it in our atmosphere. We concentrate toxins and release them into the air and water. We cut down forests and despoil the oceans. We can debate the symptoms but we can't reasonably deny that our habitat is limited and our expansion is testing its capacity. Eventually we must manage our impact, our consumption and our population.

It's not going to be simple. No living thing has ever recognized the limits of its habitat and consciously chosen to curb its own expansion. In fact only one species in the universe, so far as we know, is capable of conceptualizing its own impact on its habitat. That's us. We would be the first ever to consciously limit ourselves. So it's a little hard to imagine.

But sooner or later we must stabilize our population. Then we're going to have to design an economy that creates prosperity without a perpetually expanding human population.

The global economy is built on population growth. In 2009 global economic output shrunk by about half a percentage point.[1]

Global financial markets read that as a catastrophe and world trade volumes shrank by more than 11 percent. What would happen if we had 1 percent fewer customers and 1 percent fewer workers every year for a few years in a row?

The scale and complexity of this economic dilemma are intimidating. Evidence of habitat damage is alarming, and that evidence is visible everywhere. Resource depletion, population expansion and economic vulnerability are enormous obstacles and they form a barrier that effectively blocks our view of the future. Even if we dream up a beautiful and abundant vision for our future, can we see the path from where we are today to that future past these big obstacles?

How do you see past an obstacle? You have to climb over it or travel around it. Either way, you have to move. You need to begin climbing to gain a prospect. But how do we pick a direction? For that we need some criteria to direct our first few steps.

Step Three: Define Criteria (Don't Be Practical!)

The Religious Society of Friends, known popularly as "Quakers," has practiced pacifism and economic simplicity for 350 years. Quakers have traditionally tried to avoid dogma, which they believe would alienate them from other faiths. They want to connect with other people, spiritually, and so they express their beliefs in the humblest manner and the most general vocabulary possible.

Instead of a creed, the Quakers rely on "queries," questions that shape their daily behavior without blocking out people who don't share all their beliefs. Quaker queries include things like, "Is your home clean enough that you feel comfortable offering hospitality to anyone who might stop by?" "Do you strive to be truthful at all times?" Or, "Do you seek employment consistent with your beliefs and in service to society?"[2] The answers to these queries shape the Quaker vision of a spiritual way of life. The individual Quaker's answer to any particular query is almost never an unqualified "yes," because the questions describe goals to be strived for. The Quaker queries chart a path toward an ideal.

I'm offering four very simple, very general queries as criteria that I hope will help you shape your own personal enterprises and lead you toward a new perspective on our future as a species. Imagine using these criteria to guide your plans for your yard, your Sunday-school class, your farm, your neighborhood or your business. Imagine the ways in which the criteria might shape your efforts. Imagine the ways in which those efforts might change the outcomes.

If we ask the right questions, they could guide us down a new path so that we arrive at a better place, a place from where we can hopefully see the path to a better future.

The queries:

Is It Beautiful?
Does It Create Abundance?
Is It Fair?
Is It Contagious?

Is It Beautiful?

Beauty should be a primary ingredient of every human endeavor.

Beauty is a critical component of your vision for your home, your business or anything else you care about. Why would we envision a human future without beauty? If we did, would anyone want to go there?

The Sydney Opera House resonates with its setting on the coast of eastern Australia by evoking the beauty of the Chambered Nautilus, a Pacific Ocean cephalopod whose shells are exquisitely beautiful. The opera house covers 4.5 acres with concrete, plywood and glass. It is difficult to heat and cool. Built before the idea of "green design" was conceived, it's not energy-efficient. The building is not, explicitly, a tribute to nature. Yet it metaphorically places humankind—opera, ballet, great theater—in nature. It reminds human beings throughout the world of the beauty and vulnerability of the Pacific Ocean and Australia's Great Barrier Reef.

The Sydney Opera House makes a compelling statement for conserving natural resources without any literal reference to conservation.

Many of the greatest achievements in conservation during the 19th and 20th centuries were motivated by beauty. The National Parks of the United States–from Acadia in Maine to Yosemite in California–were chosen for their beauty. Artists disseminated that beauty. How many of us first encountered Yosemite through the lens of the photographer Ansel Adams? Or first saw Yellowstone in the brush strokes of the painter Albert Bierstadt?

If art reflects the human mind, if beauty represents aspiration, then beauty must be a part of our vision for the future.

Does It Create Abundance?

The human sense of wellness depends on surpluses. People need to feel that they will have at least a little more than they need, and if possible most of us would like to have the potential for achieving slightly more than we desire. The possibility of the occasional jackpot stimulates the mind. Efficiency alone doesn't complete our happiness equation. A meal may be filling if it supplies the required calories but it is only abundant only if it exceeds our desires for flavor and nutrition. A feast may even require good conversation to be part of the experience if it is to be defined as a truly *abundant* feast.

The definition of abundance includes at least three variables we may be able to control.

The first and most obvious is the supply of resources. Can our society create more food? Better, cheaper housing? Faster, more efficient transportation? Efficiency is the simplest ingredient in any recipe for abundance. If a system can make more with less, then resources are more abundant–both the raw materials and the final products. Anyone who wants to create abundance must care about efficiency. Historically, civilization has created abundant resources for humanity–food, shelter and transportation–by improving efficiency through the use of new technology. When one thinks about abundance, we generally think about improved technology that gives us access to expanded resources: industrial agriculture, central heating, modern medicine, automobiles and airplanes.

The second variable under human control is the demand for resources. Individuals can live more frugally and efficiently. How much of your driving is unnecessary? How often do you take more food than you can eat? Should we think about stabilizing or decreasing the human population of the planet? We have powerful tools for controlling our demand for resources, as well as the supply of resources, and we can have an equivalent impact on either end of the equation.

The third variable is less concrete but equally profound. Human beings can control their desires.

And by controlling our desires, we can reduce the demands we place on the planet.

In his book, *Voluntary Simplicity*[3], Duane Elgin explores, in detail, the benefits of managing desires. Jesus of Nazareth, Gautama Buddha, the Prophet Muhammad, Aristotle, Plato, Mahatma Gandhi, Albert Schweitzer, Simone de Beauvoir, Martin Buber, Joseph Campbell, Meister Eckhart, Ralph Waldo Emerson, Elise Boulding, Buckminster Fuller, Soren Kierkegaard, Lao-Tzu, Linda Breen Pierce, Charles Mingus, Pablo Picasso, Thomas Aquinas, Henry David Thoreau and Frank Lloyd Wright are all referenced in support of his argument: By managing our desires human beings can conserve natural resources, improve the human condition and enhance their enjoyment of life.

Elgin distinguishes between "ascetic simplicity,"–ritualistic deprivation–and "aesthetic simplicity," a celebration of simple pleasures. He advocates a new aesthetic that exalts the humble: smaller houses, common clothes and self-reliance.

When my wife and I were raising our children we heard a lot of parental chatter about "quality time." The idea was that, since we were so busy, we should spend our few hours with our children reading books and playing intellectually stimulating games. That way, we could be great parents even if we worked 50-hour weeks and exercised two hours a day.

In our experience, quality time was a fraud. Although some family activities were clearly superior to others, what really counted, the thing that deepened our relationships, was "quantity time," long uneventful hours in the car or on a walk or even washing up after dinner.

Consider the things you love in the world. Now consider how many of them were created from abundance. Consider whether you could appreciate them if you had no extra time, no extra money or only enough food to survive.

Abundance is not a luxury. Abundance is necessary to health and wellbeing. We need time to rest. We need a few extra vitamins and nutritious calories to stave off infection. We need quiet, reflective moments when we're not required to be productive.

In business, capital is the medium of abundance. Many enterprises start on a shoestring. The entrepreneur figures a way, by hook or by crook, to get up and running. For the business to thrive, however, nearly every entrepreneur eventually requires capital. Capital is "extra" money generated somewhere in the economic system and then made available for investment. Some group or individual, somewhere, must have built up enough wealth so that they are willing to risk part of it on the entrepreneur's initiative.

If no business or individual generates surpluses then there is no capital available to risk. Creativity dries up. Entrepreneurial spirit dies out. Abundance is a critical element in our economic and financial systems.

The same might be said for all human enterprises, whether they involve money or not. In contemporary society we often measure value with money, but abundance can be measured in any unit of value. We need surpluses to be creative. And we need to be creative to survive. If we have only enough arable land to support ourselves, then we can't experiment with new techniques or innovative crops. If our employers provide us with only the resources necessary to attend to today's business, then our enterprise will be blindsided by tomorrow's challenges. We need extra time, space and money to brainstorm, to innovate, to invent. Abundance is necessary.

Few achievements in the history of our species have been accomplished in the absence of abundance. Science, technology, literature and art spring only from societies in which the surpluses enable some people to live reflective, inventive lives free of the daily necessity of securing adequate food, water and shelter.

Certainly busy, hungry people have invented remarkable things out of necessity. The conversation contained in this book has, in fact, been motivated by my own sense of urgency. I believe we need to change our perspective soon. I believe we're up against a deadline. But the time it takes to write a book, to invent a new crop, to conceive of any new piece of technology is our most precious resource, and it is symptomatic of abundance. Perhaps the recipe for innovation could be described as the combination of a sense of urgency with the resources necessary to address the problem.

If we train our ingenuity solely on efficiency, we stunt our potential. A lot of people are promoting conservation and efficiency as though they provide some kind of solution to our resource limitations. They are squandering valuable time and energy by reacting to the symptoms of habitat damage rather than addressing its root causes. In light of the growing human population, conservation is only a stopgap.

The most chilling implication of a mania for efficiency is the prospect of zero-sum societies. A zero-sum environment is one in which no new resources are available. An individual can only expand his or her resources at the expense of another individual. Zero-sum environments utilize resources very efficiently, because they are so scarce. However, since an individual can only gain if another individual loses, they also tend to reward ruthless behavior. You may have worked in a zero-sum professional environment, or known someone who has. It can be a very unpleasant experience. Countries where resources are strained approximate zero-sum environments. Because there's no practical way of increasing the society's prosperity through cooperative efforts, people turn to various forms of corruption or even violence as tactics for taking resources from their fellow citizens. It is, tragically, a logical choice.

In their purest philosophical essences both conservation and hyper-efficiency lead to the same dreary destination, a world that has maximized its human population at the expense of beauty and creativity. We need space and capital to realize our potential as a species. We should plan for abundance.

Is It Fair?

Fairness is among the most subjective of standards. Its definition changes from one place to another and from one moment to the next. It's a fluid and powerful concept. The group defines fairness. It's the product of consensus.

Justice is sometimes confused with fairness. Justice is not fluid. Justice forms the foundation of legal systems. It is represented by a rigid, written code that supports the activities of our courts and prisons.

The international economic systems that make some people rich and some people poor based merely on the fact of where they were born are, in some formal sense, just. They are legal. But are they fair?

Fairness is defined in the moment. When someone feels a rule has been broken, at work or in school or on the ball field, it often precipitates a conflict. The rules are interpreted by one side, then the other. People argue. When a person appeals for fairness, on the other hand, it implies the opportunity for a negotiation. We search for a solution that restores the group's sense of fairness. That process of consensus-building decides, case by case, whether something is fair or not.

A sense of fairness is necessary for an enterprise to harness joint efforts among diverse people. North American sustainable-forestry practices, although good as far as they go, can't be fairly applied in Brazil until Brazil's timberlands are no longer needed for grazing and crops. So long as Brazilian farmers depend on deforestation for their survival we can't, in fairness, call for a halt to deforestation in the Amazon. It's difficult for conservation organizations funded by wealthy Westerners to protect Africa's mountain gorillas if their human neighbors in central Africa perceive that the gorillas have a higher standard of living than the local villager's.

Individuals are willing to make a personal sacrifice for the greater good if, and only if, they feel that the greater good includes their group. If any influential society on any part of the globe feels that the world's power institutions are unfair, then we won't be able to effectively address our global problems. In Guatemala, a country divided by a 36-year civil war and isolated from the growing economies of surrounding countries, huge tracts of rain forest are being burned to provide new ranchland, squatters have occupied the former Maya Biosphere Reserve and drug traffickers rule much of the countryside.[4] Habitat preservation is not a high priority in Guatemala right now, and it won't be until the Guatemalan people are safer and better fed.

As individuals, we can't be expected to do the right thing unless doing the right thing has positive implications for our individual lives or our children's lives. Bluntly, how can we expect poor people to stop cutting down trees for firewood while the affluent drive 5,000-pound automobiles dozens of miles a day just for fun?

Global fairness is, obviously, a cumbersome project. It can only be assembled from fairness exercised in billions of transactions around the world across the decades. But we can begin cultivating a sense of fairness by imposing fairness as a standard in our own homes, our churches, our schools, our towns, our governments and our businesses. We can shop for products that have been created with a sense of fairness, wherever they are manufactured. We can openly discuss the notion of fairness with our leaders, at work and in government. Maybe we can set a groundwork on which a global sense of fairness might be built.

Is It Contagious?

Anyone can initiate small positive changes by creating beautiful things and enterprises that foster abundance, and by focusing on fairness in their daily affairs.

To create major change, however, we need ideas that are contagious.

In his book *The Tipping Point*, Malcolm Gladwell demonstrates that, "Ideas and products and messages and behaviors spread just like viruses do."[5] Gladwell compares HIV and a recent fashion craze for Hush Puppies shoes. When a virus–or a shoe–catches on it can spread across the globe almost instantaneously.

Footwear might seem like a frivolous example but fashion provides us with an excellent model for the creation of contagious ideas. Fashion is an ideal technical example of how one develops a collective human vision. From year to year, human beings around the world collectively alter their vision of beauty. Millions of individuals suddenly subscribe to a new idea and implement it in their own lives, sometimes at great expense. The mavens of *haute couture* are global experts in the art of forming–and reforming–collective vision.

Our ideas, if they are to be effective, should be epidemically contagious like a new style of blue jeans or a new way of wearing classic products like Hush Puppies or Converse Chuck Taylor All-Stars.

If our concepts are beautiful and fair, if they create abundance, then they have an excellent chance of achieving contagiousness, especially if we work at making them contagious.

I used to go backpacking with a friend who drilled holes in his toothbrush handle to decrease its weight. With his goose-down sleeping bag, dehydrated food and plastic utensils, he could tell you within an ounce exactly what his pack weighed. His obsession was entertaining, at first. The conversation was interesting for an hour or two. Then it became tedious. Another friend loved campfire-grilled steaks and would hit the trail with 10 or 15 pounds of beef in his backpack. Sometimes he brought fresh potatoes, too, and some whiskey. We relished the smell of cooking meat in the mountain air. He strapped an old guitar to the top of his pack.

For a camping companion, I preferred the steak-and-whiskey friend. He helped me appreciate nature; both the natural world and my human nature.

We environmentalists have drilled a lot of metaphorical toothbrushes over the years. Conservation invites a fundamentalist approach to sustainability. Too many environmental commandments begin "Thou shalt not…" Our negativity has prevented our ideas from catching on. Conservation, as an ethic, is not particularly contagious. So even when we've been right, we have not inspired action.

If we want to involve people in the process of forming a collective vision, we need a different approach.

We will not engage the great engines of human creativity with a vision of pure frugality.

We need to plan for beauty and abundance.

Step Four: Take the First Steps (Be Realistic, Practical and Optimistic!)

How do we gain perspective? How do we gain a prospect from which we can visualize a beautiful, abundant long-term future beyond the obstacles? We need to climb.

For 40 years the magazine I publish, *Mother Earth News*, has started millions of people down the first paths of this journey toward a beautiful and abundant human future. The magazine publishes stories about sustainability achieved mostly through the medium of self-reliance. *Mother Earth News* teaches people how to raise their own food, how to generate clean, renewable energy and how to find joy in a simple lifestyle designed to conserve natural resources. This approach has made *Mother Earth News* the most widely read, popular and profitable voice for sustainability in the world.

My own life on our little organic farm is a reflection of the *Mother Earth News* approach. My wife and I grow much of our own food. We cut our own wood to provide part of our household heat. We're not "off the grid" but we do use solar energy for electricity and hot water. We live on a healthy, pretty and copious patch of tall-grass prairie that provides sustenance for us and thousands of other species.

The farm also provides a prism through which my family and I can focus our larger aspirations for the planet. We might donate a few hours a week toward one worthy environmental cause or another, but we're happy to spend hours *a day* working in our gardens and pastures. The time we spend on our treasured little piece of the earth enriches our affection for the planet as a whole. We've focused our daily attention on these 50 acres and in the process we've reinforced a conviction that we want to help make the entire planet healthier and more beautiful. That's an exciting possibility. It's the sort of project that should ignite the passionate human imagination.

Human beings could plan and manage this planet as a beautiful, abundant garden.

Once our bodies and our imaginations are engaged, the incremental change begins. Then it gets easier and easier to envision humanity occupying this planet–this beautiful, abundant planet–

far into the future. We can climb on top of the immediate obstacles to a place where we can see the broad horizon of our destiny.

Climb Over the Obstacles

Most people talking about protecting the environment have trained their attention on what they perceive as looming disasters. As the evidence of habitat destruction mounts, the voices become more strident, "We have to stop living this way!"

The volume and urgency of these warnings make it more and more difficult to discuss positive outcomes. Imagining a positive vision of the future strikes the alarmed mind as a trivial distraction.

We learned a long time ago that we couldn't attract an audience for our magazines unless we gave our readers tools they could use to improve the world personally. A backyard organic garden is the perfect symbol of positive vision and personal commitment. The gardener visualizes the short-term satisfaction of tending a lovely and productive little piece of the earth, and in the process preserves resources for humanity's future. The gardens we describe in the pages of *Mother Earth News* make the world more productive and beautiful today, while they preserve resources and help sustain the world for the next generation. Our audiences come to us for ingenuity, creativity, inspiration and beauty: elements that enhance in their lives. We describe ways people can live more sustainably through personal initiative.

Our readers get a kick out of brewing homemade beer and wine. They generate their own power using the sun, the wind, and homegrown ingenuity. We think they make some pretty important positive contributions in the world. It's obvious that they have a lot of fun.

In the same way that *Mother Earth News* readers have imagined, then realized, their gardens and homesteads, I believe we can imagine on a larger scale. We should picture our communal home, the planet, as we want it to be. We can visualize a global garden, as it were, that reflects human aspiration and the human aesthetic, complete with the profusion of life God put here.

We can plan a really, really big garden.

The Farm as Mandala

I write this during the most bittersweet of our seasons. It's either late fall or early winter depending on my mood and the weather. Tomorrow it might be 20 degrees and driving sleet or it might be 70 and sunny.

It's the time of year when we kill the animals–the cattle, sheep and goats–we will eat next year.

Just a few months ago they were the blithe spirits of spring, filling the pastures with the joyful, bouncing exuberance of new life. Soon their meat will be in my freezers, and my friends', on our tables and, quite literally, part of us.

My wife and I raise most of our own food and earn a little income from our farm. But it's more art than business. We draw a frame around our 50 acres of prairie. Nature fills it with color and motion. Every day brings new pigments, new images and new performances. Every hour of the year is a revelation. The colors change. Some wild creature makes a sound we've never heard before. The sky delivers endless, vivid surprises on the grandest scale possible. New players cross the stage–wildlife and our closest associates, the cattle, sheep, goats and chickens.

Some farmers may never stop to consider their animals as anything other than livestock–literally their inventory, their stock in trade.

To us they are partners, friends, entertainers and something close to family. And then, of course, they are food.

People often ask, "How can you eat animals you knew?" Sometimes it's a sincere question, meant to explore the emotions associated with raising sentient beings for meat. Often I think it's more of an accusation: "How can you be so callous?"

I might respond, "How can you be so thoughtless as to eat animals without knowing them? Without knowing how they lived? Without making sure they were treated with respect while they were alive?"

My father, both my grandfathers and all my great-grandparents were grass farmers. By that I mean that their vocation, for at least part of their lives, was to raise or find forage to sustain the livestock that provided their livelihood. It's quite possible that every generation of my family since prehistoric times has followed a herd of grazing animals–either domesticated or wild–down its nomadic path across the ages. We have lived in direct contact and in a kind of kinship with the animals that end up on our table. I believe it's a "natural" relationship in the deepest and most profound sense of that word.

I don't mean to suggest that everyone should raise their own meat. But it's perverse, isn't it, that people in our society seem to consider it more civilized to eat animals they never even see? Meanwhile, industrial agriculture treats meat animals as cogs in a machine, without regard for their health or happiness except as it affects production.

Relatively few people these days enjoy the privilege of knowing the creatures they eat, or of experiencing the miraculous transformation of their energy into our own vitality. Few people take personal, emotional responsibility for the consequences of existence: In order for us to live, other creatures must die.

Vegans take a similar kind of responsibility. They make a conscious sacrifice for a principle, and that's admirable. But the cultivated fields where our grain and vegetables are raised become biological deserts where very, very few creatures can actually live. The soybean field displaces and destroys native plants, microbes and animals. Our natural pastures, on the other hand, teem with natural life. Every day we see rodents, ground-nesting birds, snakes, frogs and myriad insects. Every night we hear the owls and the coyotes. If you look only at the number of creatures displaced or destroyed by a meal of soybeans versus the number of creatures who pay, in one sense or another, to provide us with a grass-fed, pasture-raised steak dinner, the steak could very well win the humanitarianism contest based on that criterion. Millions of wild animals can live on the pasture occupied by our cows, and will happily live there with the cows, sheep and goats. Our grass-fed meat diet consumes some animals, but preserves the habitat for others.

While I'm proud of the natural, healthy lives our domesticated animals live, I still sometimes feel a profound twinge of sadness as I look out over the pastures. My computer, when it's idle, displays a slide show of my personal photos–many of them pictures of animals we have raised over the years. Most of them are, of course, gone. I feel a particular sadness I've gradually learned to embrace, a melancholy that embodies the transience of our individual existence. When I kill our animals for food, I sense the implication for my own fate. I'm forced to consider my own life and death as well as the sturdier, less ephemeral living network that includes us and our food.

This sadness I feel is associated, somehow, with life's astonishing richness and vitality. It's a sadness associated with mortality. It's a sadness human beings feel as we consider the impermanence of everything on this planet, everything mortal we hold dear; the sadness that makes life poignant and sweet.

My melancholy brings with it a profound feeling of gratitude.

This exercise of raising my own food forms the bedrock of my love and concern for the planet. I certainly care about *the rainforests of Malaysia and the Amazon, but I care* for *this small piece of Kansas prairie, which in turn cares for me. It's a very personal, very intimate form of stewardship. My concern for the world's coral reefs and alpine tundra is informed and enhanced by my stewardship of the grasses and forbs that carpet the black-dirt prairie around my home. In the act of bringing our nourishment directly from the earth I think I've developed a deeper emotional attachment to the planet as a whole.*

One chilly day I was working on a fence far out in a new pasture and I kept smelling food. I checked my pockets for old sandwich wrappers. I checked the toolbox for neglected snacks. I smelled the cuffs of my work coat. Then I realized I had been sitting in the wild onions that sprout green among the brown grasses all the way through the Kansas winter. They smelled like hamburger fixings.

Like any artistic medium, nature rewards people who've studied its methods and its innate character. For the farmer, that study is part of a vocation. It's a vocation that, at its best, can deepen our appreciation of nature profoundly. The fact that we must destroy life to create life is a subject that farmers seldom discuss, but we must understand the contradiction implicitly.

I don't believe its possible to fully appreciate life without that understanding.

The sheep and goats eat the green onion shoots. Sometimes I can smell onion on their breath. I enjoy watching the goats eating the dry seed-heads off sunflowers. In late summer they work the edges of the pastures with their heads stretched high over their backs, crunching one protein-rich nugget after another. I puzzle over the way sheep like to trim the grass down to a slick butch, like the manicured greens on a golf course, favoring the new growth next to the ground between the big lush clumps of mature grass. Cattle, on the other hand, seem to enjoy a nice big, leafy mouthful.

Twenty-five years ago I was an avid hiker and backpacker. A skier and a climber. I probably spent 45 days a year in the outdoors. I slept outside five or six nights a year. I knew I was missing a lot, about 360 nights every year.

Now I'm outside nearly every night, checking on the livestock and closing the chicken house. I see the ice crystals in a halo around the moon. I watch the sun come up nearly every day. I know what's blooming and which birds are traveling through. What the soil smells like as the seasons change. How it feels to be outside on the worst night of the year watching a coyote try to open the latched door of the henhouse. I think I have an inkling of what it must feel like to have an empty belly on a cold night and to smell all those warm, plump hens just a few feet away. I watched one coyote trying to slip a paw under the swinging door. I consider whether I would let him take a meal if he prevailed. I probably wouldn't, but I admired his enterprise.

I see much more of nature than I did when I was outdoors purely for recreation. Now when I go on a fishing trip or take a long hike, I think I see nature more clearly and notice details I wouldn't have before I came to see the natural environment from the farmer's perspective. I've appreciated more of the natural world as I've come to know it better.

For me the difference between hiking and farming is the difference between listening to music and playing music. As a hiker, I enjoy the dramatic rhythms and splashy vistas of the mountains. As a farmer, I actually get to play this dense, vigorous prairie music.

I get a lot of blood, dirt and manure on my hands and my

clothes these days. I get calluses and scars. I get a lot of laughs watching my animals figure out their lives and I feel very sad when it's time to kill them.

I have a lot more death in my life than I did before I began farming.

And, paradoxically, that's part of the reason I feel like I have a lot of life in my life.

CHAPTER ONE

The "Destination Fixation"

In July 2007 I nearly killed myself. I didn't do it intentionally, but I almost died from a case of poor visualization.

That's right; I almost died for lack of a positive vision of my own immediate future.

The motorcycle and its rider can form a beautiful partnership between human and machine. In motion they are graceful, yet their movement defies physical intuition. When a motorcyclist navigates a corner the rider intuitively solves a ridiculously complex equation involving speed, gravity, the road, the tires and a thousand other elements that allow the motorcycle to lean into the curve at an angle that appears–in video or photographs–perfectly impossible. Until a new rider gets used to it, it doesn't feel much more plausible than it looks.

In the mountains, especially, curves are not always symmetrical. You may enter a curve with a gentle arc and discover that the arc gradually becomes smaller. That contour is called a decreasing-circumference curve and it is the bane of the inexperienced rider. It presents a serious problem when you enter the curve too fast and then discover it tightening down on you. It's the classic rookie error, and I made it.

There's only one way out. Slowing down is not an option. To brake a motorcycle in a high-speed curve is disastrous. You'll lose traction and drop the machine on its side. So the experienced rider leans deeper into the irrational angle and holds his intent. He concentrates on the curve's exit and visualizes a successful outcome. He experiences the exhilaration of successfully testing his courage and skill against the limits of physics.

I, on the other hand, lost my nerve. Rather than visualizing myself–and the motorcycle–carving our way through the curve and out of our predicament I became trapped in a tentative state of mind in the middle of the turn. I let fear take over. Even though I was following two riders who had successfully negotiated the corner, even though logic dictated that I could follow those other riders, I lost my confidence. I just couldn't see myself completing that turn at that speed. I didn't have a clear vision of a good outcome and I started making decisions that led to an undesirable consequence–a wreck. Instinctively, I tried to slow the motorcycle down. In an automobile that would have been precisely the right answer. On the motorcycle it was a bad decision and could have been fatal. The motorcycle and I bounced off a propitious guardrail and went down in the middle of the road at about 50 miles per hour.

I walked away after ruining a good helmet and about $1,000 worth of excellent protective clothing.

Well, "walked" might be inaccurate. I hobbled away. It was about a year before I healed completely.

Naturally I did a lot of reflecting about how the accident could have been avoided.

The most obvious answer to that question is, of course, "Don't ride motorcycles." My wife and a number of friends have brought this simple solution to my attention. Duly noted.

But as I considered the lessons I took from the experience–

while massaging the deep bruises on my legs, arms and torso–it dawned on me that our species is, in a manner of speaking, right in the middle of a decreasing-circumference curve. There's a growing worldwide sense that if we don't make dramatic changes to our lifestyles we may soon begin to feel the painful effects of damage we are doing to our habitat.

At the moment we have our attention trained on conservation, effectively the middle of the curve. Instinctively, we want to slow down our personal consumption. For many people, cutting back on personal consumption is undoubtedly appropriate. Abundance is healthy; excessive consumption for consumption's sake is a kind of pathology. But looked at from a global perspective, conservation alone cannot be the solution because the rate of human population growth and our growing global appetite for technologies that consume energy make conservation almost immaterial. No matter how much we conserve, environmental damage will continue to accelerate unless we stabilize–or reduce–our numbers. Between 1965 and 2005, worldwide energy consumption increased by about 2.5 times, expanding a little faster than the human population, which grew from about 3.4 billion to about 6.7 billion over the same time frame.[6] [7] While we invented more and more efficient appliances and vehicles, the savings were offset by the spread of energy-consuming technologies to developing nations, where the rate of population growth accelerates energy consumption. And we are expected to add another 2.5 billion people over the next 40 years, most of them in developing nations where the numbers of cars, trucks, computers and refrigerators are expanding rapidly.

A wreck is imminent if we just follow our instincts. Conservationists are calling for us to slow down. But we're in the middle of a bunch of phenomena we don't know how to interrupt. Natural resources fuel economic growth. In fact, the first decline in energy consumption in 30 years was recorded during the economic slowdown of 2009.[8] If we slow economic growth it could inhibit innovation just when we need that innovation the most. By focusing most of our efforts on conservation we distract ourselves from more complex and critical puzzles involving economics and population.

We are training our attention in the wrong place. Motorcyclists, mountain-bikers, skiers and steeplechasers all learn the same lesson: When you are moving forward with a lot of momentum you have to focus beyond the short-term challenges. You need to be thinking ahead. You need to picture yourself past the coming obstacles. You have to visualize the successful outcome. Then your reflexes can take care of the short term.

A friend who races mountain bikes calls it "the destination fixation."

If you focus on the intermediate obstacle, you're likely to collide with that obstacle. Just like I did on that mountain road. I focused on the guardrail. I hit the guardrail. I was lucky. I survived. But it hurt. Abrasions, deep bruises, a cracked pelvis and a huge repair bill all for lack of a positive vision.

Idealize the Destination (Don't be Realistic.)

It's relatively simple to imagine a motorcycle navigating a curve on a mountain road. To imagine humanity emerging, successfully and gracefully, from the present era into a beautiful, abundant future is a more complex exercise in visualization. To start, it seems to make sense to keep it simple. Let's not try to get too realistic, or too specific. What are the basic components of a terrific future?

It will be beautiful. Beauty is, of course, in the eye of the beholder. Since we are not there, in the future, we can only work on beauty here and now, according to our own tastes. We'll leave the job of defining future beauty to the people who will be there to see it.

But the aspiration toward beauty and the preservation of beautiful things require attention and energy from every generation.

My friends Randy and Debra run an investment firm in a medium-sized Midwestern city. A few years ago they outgrew their rented space in an office tower and started looking for new digs. The easy and obvious choice was to rent another floor in the same nondescript high-rise. But they had noticed a 140-year-old three-story building nearby. Plastered and patched, it didn't look like much but the ceramic brick façade was intact and the original limestone walls were visible inside where the plaster was missing. The purchase price was reasonable. The cost of renovation was daunting. They bought it anyway. They stripped the limestone interior walls, put in skylights and sanded the hardwood floors. In the process, they exposed the architectural ambitions of seven generations. Then they hung art, mostly impressionistic paintings by local artists chosen to evoke the regional landscape. Their office is not only beautiful, it is a working reminder of the aesthetic ambitions of previous generations, and the natural beauty of the land where they live. Their office is beautiful, and it promotes beauty.

On every continent you can see beautiful art, buildings and landscapes preserved over the centuries by people who cared for them. In every city and town around the world people are creating beautiful new things today – buildings, gardens, paintings and sculpture. Beauty, as we define it, is often the product of human aspiration. In our offices, our homes, our farms or on the balconies of our apartments, we have opportunities to invest a little time and energy in beauty every day. That investment earns dividends today in the form of our own appreciation and preserves beauty for the future. Why be satisfied with any office, farm or factory that isn't beautiful?

Our collective vision should incorporate the aspiration toward beauty in every human community around the world. Our cities can preserve their connection to nature while preserving beautiful historic buildings and creating exquisite new structures where they are needed. Why not plant gardens in our vacant lots and across our rooftops?

By planning for beauty we acknowledge the importance of the work of artists, and implicitly promise our support for the arts. New information technologies give human beings access to all the music, all the painting, all the sculpture and nearly every form of aesthetic ambition in the world. We enhance our ability to aspire together, plan together and build together. If our communities are not beautiful, then we need to talk.

Why settle for anything less than beauty?

Of course people only create and preserve beauty when they have the necessary time and materials, and preferably a little money. To create beauty, a degree of prosperity is necessary. The slums metastasizing around many of the world's largest cities today are the antithesis of beauty. If we want to create a beautiful future, then we need to plan for abundance as well.

Resources will be abundant. The two primary elements in a plan for abundance are, obviously, supply and demand. Since we invented agriculture we have, ingeniously and continuously, increased supply. Human beings have maintained a remarkably abundant existence through several thousand years of population growth by utilizing natural resources with increasing ingenuity.

Logically, as we exhaust some of our resources and draw nearer the limits of our planet's capacity to support us, expanding supply becomes more difficult. Conservation becomes more important. Ideas for improving our conservation of natural resources increasingly provide better solutions as it becomes more difficult to find new resources to exploit. Conservation, while not a complete solution to our resource issues, is a key strategy for creating abundance.

In California, Jules Dervaes and his family are demonstrating, on a personal level, the creation of abundance through conservation[9]. Just a mile from downtown Pasadena behind their 1,500-square-foot home they've devoted one-tenth of an acre – about half their property – to a spectacular garden where more than 350 varieties of vegetables, fruits, berries and herbs grow in abundance. In their best year, they say they harvested more than 6,000 pounds of food from the garden. Based on a painstaking technique Jules Dervaes dubbed, "Square-Inch Gardening," the "Path to Freedom" garden thrives on close human attention. Jules and his grown children, Justin, Anais and Jordanne, tend the plants and soil obsessively. They raise a few chickens, ducks and rabbits and keep two goats and a beehive. The results are stunning: Four adults effectively supporting themselves on a 4,350-square-foot "farm." Jules Dervaes and his kids are conservation experts. They take a minimum of natural resources, add ingenuity, and create abundance. Through the prism of their garden they depict an abundant human future.

About 7,000 miles south of Pasadena, Doug and Kris Tompkins are securing the planet's abundance in a different way. Doug and Kris got rich in business. Doug co-founded the North Face outdoor-equipment company and the Esprit fashion dynasty. Kris was CEO of Patagonia, Inc., the adventure-apparel company. In 1991 Doug bought 42,000 acres of temperate rain forest at the end of an isolated fjord in Chile.[10] He started the Conservation Land Trust, a nonprofit set up to protect the land permanently. Then he and Kris went about acquiring–or convincing other people to acquire–a total of about two million acres of wilderness in Chile and Argentina to protect it, forever, from development. Their projects include the 700,000-acre Pumalin Park that grew out of their first 42,000-acre ranch; the 726,000-acre Corcovado National Park in Chile; and the ambitious Patagonia National Park project that seeks to connect national parks in Chile and Argentina to protect wilderness at the southern tip of South America. The land is purchased by private individuals, protected by private nonprofits and managed by the governments of Chile and Argentina. Once the parks are established, they are open for the public to enjoy, presumably forever.

Jules Dervaes experiences abundance in the cramped, leafy profusion of his Pasadena backyard. He's proud to support his family on about $40,000 a year. Kris and Doug Tompkins find abundance in the vast wildernesses of South America. They invest hundreds of millions of dollars to preserve it. They are inspired by similar visions, but different definitions, of abundance in humanity's future.

We'll keep on striving toward fairness. It's impossible to visualize a world in which all human beings agreed on a definition for fairness. Human affairs bubble with controversy.

I realize that if I provide an example for the pursuit of fairness in the world I will be inviting dissent. Any real-world example of the ideal of fairness will, no doubt, be contradicted by someone who has been marginalized.

But maybe an idealistic endeavor, an endeavor like the international Fair-Trade movement, can at least illustrate the aspiration toward fairness, even if we'll never have a perfect consensus regarding its definition.

Fair Trade certifies the fairness of certain businesses by illuminating the supply chain all the way from original producers–usually farmers–to the ultimate consumers. Fair-Trade agencies certify that products were grown in ways that were humane and environmentally friendly, that original producers and their employees were paid fairly at values higher than commodity prices and that the products were transported by the most conscientious means possible.[11] Fair-Trade certifications are currently available for dozens of products including coffee, fruits, vegetables, wine, soccer balls, tea and herbs marketed in about 50 countries.

In 2008, Fair Trade labeling organizations worldwide reported a 22-percent increase in sales, worldwide, to just over $4 billion. It appears that fairness, as a marketing strategy, may already be demonstrating its value.

The Gardener as Magus

Tim Posey lived in a former barracks bought surplus from the U.S. Army at Fort Bliss, Texas, and moved a few miles into the dusty, unpaved village of Anapra, New Mexico in the late 1950s. Most of Tim's 10 acres was devoted to his business–the Posey Trailer Park. But at the center of his property, surrounded by the trailers and the vast Chihuahuan Desert, the Posey homestead teemed with life. Milk goats bleated under a shed. Chickens scratched in the shade. Miraculously, two dozen kinds of vegetables grew in the sand behind the horse stable. A big man past middle age, suntanned and stiff with arthritis, Tim spent most of his time on a kitchen chair under one or another of the awnings he had built onto his barns. He watched the animals, sharpened his tools and chatted with his tenants when they stopped by. I remember him in dark prescription sunglasses. I almost never saw him indoors.

I was 9 when Mr. Posey "hired" me. My family lived about a quarter-mile away. The livestock and the garden drew my attention. I was fascinated. Once I was certain he wouldn't chase me off, I started spending nearly every spare moment there. He asked me if I wanted to learn how to milk the goats. Then he asked me if I was willing to do it every day. He paid me in produce, eggs and goat's milk. My dad paid me cash for the food.

It was my first job, and I loved it.

There are places on the continent more barren than southern New Mexico, but not many. Creosote and mesquite bushes dot the sand hills. Most of the plants have spines or thorns. We called the surrounding landscape "hills," but they were more like dunes. If you leave a junked car on the downwind side of a hill there, the hulk will disappear under the drifting sand in a few months.

Mr. Posey boarded horses. He raised chickens, guinea fowl, milk goats and honeybees.

I don't know how long he had been moving manure from the chicken pens and horse corrals into the vegetable garden, but he had created a marvel there. Watermelons grew huge and dark green in the tangles of vines. On the ground between the rows of corn was a moist wonderland of dappled light buzzing with insects.

It's hard to describe the emotional impact of encountering all that life in the context of our garbage-strewn village in the middle of the desert. Tim Posey had taken a small plot of land, raked out the broken glass and old bleach bottles, added manure and created a small, earthly paradise. It captured my heart.

I helped Mister Posey mix a potent fertilizer from chicken manure and water in a 55-gallon drum, a slurry that could be mixed with the irrigation water he pumped into the garden. I gathered the eggs. I milked the goats. I don't remember many sweeter moments in my life than the walk from my home to the goat pens in the cool early morning, smelling the creosote bushes, then the goats, then the sugary aroma of cracked corn and the warm, delicious odor of new milk. Sometimes we let the goats out into the open desert where they browsed blue grama grass, mesquite beans and acacia leaves. I loved watching them shop among the plants for those they found most appetizing. The technical term for the way a goat eats is "browsing," and it's a perfect description. They are like shoppers in a supermarket, and even in the desert they seemed to find plenty of goods. While the goats were out of their pen and the gate left open, the chickens and guinea hens moved in and, scratching and clucking, found a feast of their own. I could never tell exactly what they were eating. They probably found scraps of grain and alfalfa, maybe insects or worms attracted by the animals and the manure.

From the chicken pen to the garden to the watermelons, from the mesquite beans to the goat's udder to my breakfast cereal I became an eyewitness to a form of alchemy that struck me then–and strikes me now–as magical.

I thought of Tim Posey as a sort of magician whose rituals of feed, fertilizer and irrigation created numinous transformations. I wanted to learn how to practice that magic.

CHAPTER TWO

Acknowledging the Challenges (What a Great Time To Be Alive!)

When I did an Internet search for the phrase, "a vision for the Earth's future" recently the first two results referred to NASA's predictions of massive floods and the rest on the first page are religious sites, most of them offering various descriptions of the apocalypse. Evidently when it comes to visualizing our future, a lot of people expect the worst and are inclined to leave it up to God.

It is up to God, of course, but God gave us two eyes in the front of our heads to look forward and prepare for what's to come.

As far as we know, there is only one species in the universe capable of conceptualizing its own impact on its habitat. That's us. Our peculiar objectivity is the character trait that makes us human.

If we are defined by our capacity for objective thought, then we are now living in one of the definitive moments in human history. Our ability to conceptualize our own role in nature defines us as human beings. Our capacity for creating solutions to complex problems is the primary factor in our success as a species. In the Judeo-Christian Bible we define ourselves as human beings when we eat the fruit of the "Tree of Knowledge" and spontaneously realize we are naked. In a phrase, we become self-aware. The most striking evidence of that self-awareness is not our modesty, however. The fig leaf is not what makes us truly unique. Our awareness of our own nudity is a symbol of our capacity for perceiving ourselves objectively–our ability to visualize ourselves from a perspective outside ourselves. Our definitive quality is our capacity to conceptualize events outside the sphere of our own momentary self-interest. We make decisions based on chains of cause-and-effect that stretches across decades–maybe centuries. No other living thing does this.

So today we face the challenge of solving what might be the definitive human riddle. We are aware that we have an impact on the environment. We are aware that our population has been growing exponentially. We are perfectly aware that no species can expand infinitely on this finite planet. With this awareness comes responsibility. We are capable of moderating our impact on the planet. We are capable of conceptualizing a sustainable human habitat and executing a plan to create that habitat. In fact, we could create a beautiful and abundant habitat built to last for millennia if we set our minds to it.

Yes, we face very complex problems. But we've solved complex problems before. We like solving puzzles.

Perhaps the most vexing puzzle we now face is how to defeat our biological programming–the programming that, in the words of the Judeo-Christian Bible, tells us to "go forth and multiply." That's the instruction branded on the first cell in the smallest living thing and on every subsequent cell of every living thing. It is hard-coded into every particle of our being: "Propagate your genes."

But that's an absurdly simple-minded interpretation of the biological imperative. Our biology motivates us to survive and to prosper. What if our prosperity and our very survival were dependent on limiting the rate at which we multiply?

We know how to curb global warming and stabilize the human population. We've already invented practical alternatives to wood heat and fossil fuels. We've already invented birth control. These challenges are just variations on the standard, logical decision to make short-term sacrifices to avoid longer-term catastrophes. But we don't yet know how to reach consensus, as a species, to take on this project before a crisis forces us into action. What we need, first, is a philosophical or perhaps spiritual revelation that helps us see ourselves and our role in a new way. We need a belief system that reinforces environmental stewardship in the same way our existing major religions value compassion. Humanity needs a new way of seeing itself in the planetary context, a new perspective that helps us assign appropriate value to our habitat so that we understand our incentives for preserving it.

It's a good thing we enjoy solving puzzles.

Now is the moment when our uniquely objective perspective and our enterprising intellect are engaged in what may be the most important challenge faced by our species so far. If human beings are defined by their objectivity, then we are now facing the definitive challenge of all human history.

We could restore the astonishing garden into which we were born–the Earth.

I can't think of a more inspirational goal.

It's a terrific time to be human. We're here just in time to meet our biggest challenge so far–bigger than bipedal locomotion; bigger than the domestication of plants and animals; bigger than the invention of the wheel. It's time to confront our essential nature, which has been telling us to keep reproducing and expanding.

If you could view the entirety of human experience from the dawn of our evolution to the present, if you could pick the human century you'd like to witness first-hand, you might choose this one. I think I would. I would want to watch us tackle this problem. I would want to take part.

The suffering, if we don't get it right, will not be humanity's alone. We've already destroyed thousands of species of birds, mammals, insects, reptiles, amphibians, plants and fish. In just the last few years Africa's Western Black Rhinoceros, Europe's Pyrenean Ibex, Costa Rica's Golden Toad and North America's Pearly Mussel have, so far as we can tell, passed into oblivion as humanity has destroyed their habitats. This planet hasn't seen the current rate of extinction since the demise of the dinosaurs 65 million years ago. Scientists are comparing the impact of human population expansion–on the global environment–to the impact of the asteroid that destroyed the dinosaurs.

We continue extinguishing species at a horrifying rate. Since the total number of species on earth can only be guessed at, the exact rate of species loss is difficult to measure. We're probably losing between 50 and 150 species per day. Extinction is normal, but the rate of extinctions today is very far from normal. The current rate is at least 10,000 times greater than the natural rate of species extinction, according to the United Nations Development Programme, and it's the result of human activities. By 2100, according to current trends, two-thirds of species alive in 1900 will have gone extinct.[12]

It's no great tragedy that any particular species becomes extinct (unless of course it's us.) Extinction is natural. Each extinction opens opportunities for other species.

The greater tragedy is the fact that we're taking a healthy, resilient and rich natural habitat–the only planet we know where life thrives–and degrading its vitality. New species can't evolve fast enough to replace the diversity we're destroying even if we restore the habitat. We've inherited the best planet in the known universe and squandered it. Even if we reversed the process of extinction tomorrow, it would take hundreds of thousands of years to replace the species that have been lost. Evolution is not quick.

And if we don't change course soon, the planet could very well end up unfit for human habitation or at the very least damned uncomfortable.

We could take this philosophically, I suppose. Mankind won't live forever. A few millennia after we disappear there will probably be a healthy planet here. We could look at it fatalistically. The damage we are doing is part of a natural process. Our awareness doesn't change that essential fact. We can salve our guilty consciences by looking at it all from the geologic perspective. Eventually this planet will suffer some sterilizing galactic calamity. Scientists tell us our sun will, eventually, burn out.

We can put our faith in a divine being and, like faithful children, believe the all-knowing deity has a plan we can't understand. But isn't that a waste of the awareness our creator gave us? In a way, it insults God when we refuse to engage the logic and self-awareness we've been given.

The threat that confronts us now is not a supernova or some other impersonal cosmic Armageddon. The Earth's looming environmental crisis is our fault and our responsibility.

Even though we find it difficult, as a species, to accept that responsibility we should still be able to agree that a clean, healthy, verdant and prosperous planet is worth working for. We know how, physically, to preserve and enhance our planet. Just as we once visualized the first irrigated field, invented the first wheeled vehicle and dreamed of machines that fly, we can visualize the earth as a beautiful and productive garden where millions of species thrive. We can, in effect, invent the planet where we want to live. We can restore, to some extent, the garden God gave us.

Imagine an environment as clean, productive and resilient as God–or Nature–can build. Imagine our biological diversity recovering, the fisheries rebuilding themselves, the tropical rain forests growing back and repopulating themselves with the Javanese rhino, the gorilla and the orangutan. Imagine the restoration of the polar ice caps and the great alpine glaciers of the world. All these things are within reach.

We've just begun conceptualizing a long-term model for stewardship. We've just started thinking about our responsibilities. Now that we've dominated the planet we are called upon to care for it. Our species is capable of maintaining a planet based on these fledgling ideals of environmental health and sustainability. Perhaps that's our destiny, as a species. Why not aspire to that destiny?

We can visualize that global garden. We can design it. Then we can build it.

I think it's time for us to start visualizing the future we desire. I'm not pretending it will be easy to get there.

The First Mountain

I believe we have three tall mountains to climb. Right now those mountains block our view forward.

Conservation is, indeed, the first, least imposing mountain. We need to forestall the effects of global warming and habitat destruction as much as possible while we get our act together. Conservation dampens the effects of human population growth. Beyond that, it's an engaging spiritual discipline. If we accept that our own consumption inevitably displaces other living things, then its fundamentally compassionate–fundamentally virtuous–to avoid waste.

Unfortunately this simple ethic, like many others, leads to misery if followed to its logical conclusion. When I say, "avoid waste," you may logically interpret that as "consume as little as possible." I believe that would be a mistake. Without surplus–without waste–without extra food and extra energy–we would be a species using all its resources just to stay alive. There would be no art. There would be no invention. So we must be careful to maintain our surpluses, while protecting the superb biological machine that provides them.

Still, conservation will always be an important ethical principle. It's the most elementary of moral imperatives not to squander resources. We've got that much figured out. We're on the lower slopes of the first mountain.

THE SECOND MOUNTAIN

The next climb is longer and steeper. Population control is perfectly unavoidable. I raise livestock. My pastures are pretty good examples of the natural prairie that's thrived across the center of North America for millennia. I try to keep track of the plants growing in my fields and I adjust the numbers of cattle, sheep and goats to protect the health of this little piece of nature on which my family depends. If I let the animal population grow beyond what's sustainable, overgrazing can do long-term damage to the health of the prairie and its ability to support us. One year of overgrazing can create damage that lasts for decades. I've seen it. No natural environment can support an infinite population. Every living thing is part of the natural balance and when one species throws the balance off various natural forces exert pressure to restore equilibrium. Eventually, we must control human population or we'll make a mess of the habitat and then nature will take the control we've abdicated.

We don't need to forcibly restrict anyone's reproduction. That wouldn't be right, and it wouldn't work. We could however, if we focused on it, help people throughout the world understand that their lives can be improved by limiting our population. If parents, worldwide, had access to adequate food and health care, if infant mortality rates were moderated and parents worldwide had decent prospects for raising and educating two healthy children we could, perhaps, create an international consensus that a healthy family of four people is the ideal. Maybe we would decide to provide incentives. We could provide simple birth-control supplies worldwide, for free.

If we formed an international moral consensus that each human being should reproduce himself or herself once–two children per couple–populations would shrink. I understand that this is a huge philosophical hurdle for many people. The notion of taking control of our own reproduction has bedeviled and divided societies since we invented birth control. From a certain perspective, the fundamental division between the United States' two primary political parties is drawn along this philosophical fault line. The depth of the divide proves the significance of this debate.

A declaration like this–that we can reverse human population growth by talking about it–strikes a lot of people as unrealistic and simple-minded. Clearly this book doesn't contain a solution. No one person has the solution. Millions of tiny innovations created by millions of individual human beings lie between us and that solution.

Inventors were sketching flying machines 400 years before the Wright brothers lifted off at Kitty Hawk. Until the 20th Century, none of them flew. However, each of those hare-brained ideas contributed, in some small way, to the jet aircraft in which we routinely circle the globe today.

I must admit that when I started writing about population for *Mother Earth News* and the *Utne Reader* a few years ago I was naïve. I thought the problems were fairly clear and I believed our readers–because they are environmentalists–would readily agree with my premise. I discovered that the deep emotional divide that runs through American politics cuts right through society and into our readership. I received hundreds of letters, many of which I've included in the appendix to this book. First they came in a tidal wave from people who reacted with outrage to the very idea of discussing population control. Hundreds of readers immediately jumped to the conclusion that the only way of controlling population is through draconian laws that limit personal freedoms. "Outraged" is not too strong a term to describe the tone of the first surge of correspondence. Nearly all of them promised to cancel their subscriptions if we ever mentioned population stabilization again. When we published those letters in the magazines and on the websites we received a similarly strong reaction from the other side. We had, obviously, hit a nerve. We haven't reached anything like a consensus, even among the relatively homogeneous readers of progressive North American magazines.

The population discussion is subverted by genetics. We are biological creatures and deep in our natural psyches we want our personal genetics to prevail over our neighbor's. If any countries, races, tribes or ethnicities are not engaged then no consensus will exist. Instinctively, we would resist limiting our own reproduction if other groups refused to limit theirs. Whether we like it or not our success as a species on this planet depends on consensus. Consensus depends on the fair distribution of the benefits of success. Every nation–and every socioeconomic category–needs to see a clear payoff.

Unfortunately, we can't argue about this forever. While we struggle with the issues species die out, forests and grasslands disappear and the planet's capacity for supporting life is degraded every day.

After conservation, population is the second mountain we

have to climb. We have the practical tools we need to control our own reproduction, but we'll likely have to negotiate some very difficult routes through social and political consensus-building to reach the top.

The Third Mountain

I'm optimistic that we'll reach both of the first two goals. We already have the physical resources we need. As the evidence mounts, agreement will be easier to reach. That leaves the third, and tallest, mountain.

As our economies are now structured, we depend on population growth to support economic growth. This rule is so deeply ingrained in our economics that it's seldom acknowledged. As population grows, so grows the demand for housing, food, automobiles, refrigerators, furnaces, Tupperware, movie theaters, restaurants, airplanes, hotels, computers, toys, clothing, shoes and jewelry. If population was shrinking and the laws of supply and demand remained relevant, then demand for all those things would decline and the value of housing, food, automobiles and just about everything else would fall. Imagine a world in which gold, for instance, was more common and less valuable with each passing generation. That's how a world with a shrinking human population would work. Every city would have to deal with abandoned housing. If population stabilizes, then each generation might be able to sustain some kind of economic equilibrium. But zero economic growth is a profound negative signal in contemporary economies, the way we measure them today. Negative growth is worse. It is the literal definition of economic recession.[13] If population shrinks, so will demand. If demand for all goods and services were shrinking, values of all goods and services would also, based on our economic models, be declining.

Imagine a world in which demand for all the fundamental human necessities–food, shelter, sports memorabilia, etc.–were shrinking every year. Imagine a world in which, let's say, 5 percent of all houses on the market had no buyers because 5 percent fewer families lived in your city. There are a few places in the world today where you can see this economic phenomenon in action, including small towns in my own home state of Kansas. It's not a pretty picture. There aren't enough strong young people to keep local enterprise running. The aging population finds it more and more difficult to maintain amenities. The community's infrastructure falls into disrepair. Incomes shrink. Vacant houses collapse Local business shrivels up.

The mere fact that the phenomena of population decline are so hard to witness in real life is a powerful testament to the fact that we're probably unprepared to deal with it. We've never seen a broad decline in human population and we don't have the means, yet, of creating prosperity in such an environment. To sustain our population at lower, healthier levels while providing the benefits of a functional modern society, we'll have to invent a human economy that creates prosperity without growth. We will need brand new economic tools.

We Love to Climb

But the first step in our journey toward true sustainability is relatively simple. If we are to form the global consensus we will need to support sea changes in human attitudes, economics and culture, then we need to visualize–as individuals and as a species–successful outcomes. Agriculture, the Industrial Revolution, automobiles, airplanes, space exploration–all these achievements have been the product of human dreams. Dreams have provided the incentive for every great human achievement, every great company, every timeless work of art. When we engage the human imagination we can accomplish astonishing things. But every achievement starts with a vision. And most visions start out as dreams.

The effort to restore our planetary health can't be undertaken by any particular country or group of countries. This can't be a pet project of the rich, pursued in our spare time. The problems are global. The effort must be urgently undertaken on a global scale. So far the global discussion has been preoccupied with fairness. One country blames another for lax regulation and overpopulation. The second country, in turn, blames the first for extravagance and waste.

To engage humanity we have to make sure humanity understands the problem, sure, but it may be more important that human beings understand the payoff. The benefits of our efforts must be felt throughout the world. Otherwise, people won't share in the consensus and we won't achieve lasting improvements.

I'm not talking about socialism, communism or any other obsolete social system. Frankly, I don't know how we're going to pull this off. But we are naïve to think that we can create a bright future for our grandchildren without addressing the issue of global poverty. The poor of the world will inevitably be a threat to the security of the rich. It's true on a day-to-day basis in the world's great cities right now. It's true in the world at large. If the world population of poor people continues to grow much faster than the ranks of the rich[14], social unrest will pose a greater and greater risk. And if the natural resources are depleted in the poorest parts of the world the pressure on the global social fabric will increase. Social justice and economic opportunity–across the globe–are critical components in a sustainable human future.

I think we're looking for something new that rewards human innovation without requiring human expansion. Our new economic systems will require unprecedented cooperation across cultural, class and political barriers. The rich will have to find new, more productive ways of sharing what they have with the poor. Today the relationship between wealth and reproductive rates is almost perfectly inversely proportional across the countries of the world. Generally, birth rates decline as affluence grows.[15]

I think we have the tools to halt climate change and reduce the human population. But the economic tools we'll need to secure our societies during a population reduction have yet to be invented.

Can we create economic tools that distribute the benefits of a healthy planet fairly? We can probably conceptualize a plan. Can we execute it? We'll have to if we're to convince our global neighbors to join us in our effort to create a sustainable, healthy habitat.

If we are to cooperate, as a species, in forming a positive vision for our future then the disenfranchised must be enfranchised. It's a global problem whose solution must be a global consensus, or something very close to it.

About 2,000 to 3,000 years ago monotheism became the dominant system of belief across the globe just as our species was experiencing a sudden surge of population growth. This may not have been a coincidence. When every small nomadic clan had its own network of ethnocentric gods we were generally pretty comfortable, when we felt the impulse, crossing the hill into the next valley, killing our neighbors and taking their stuff. It proved our gods were stronger than their gods. But once we began relying on crop-based agriculture, wars threatened to damage our precious food-production infrastructure. To maintain our grain mills and irrigation systems we needed continuity. As monotheism spread it discouraged the traditional raiding and looting and allowed adjacent communities to cooperate and trade. Over the course of just a few centuries most of humanity converted to brand new systems of belief–either Judeo-Christian, Islamic or Buddhist. As religious people we resist the notion that our faith may have been, in some degree, a reaction to sociological change. The coincidence of this timing is, however, remarkable. Could it be that our major religions emerged in part to help us deal with our neighbors more compassionately? Is it possible that there is some pragmatic basis for that evolution in an era when we had much more frequent contact with our neighbors and a greater need for cooperation?

I believe that we are at another turning point and that the vision we need today is, at its root, a spiritual vision. Since we're the only species that perceives its impact on the habitat, we have a sacred responsibility to protect it for our own sake as well as the sake of the biological system as a whole. The gospels of monotheism–Christian, Jewish and Muslim–place this "responsibility" on us, frequently translated as "dominion."[16] Gradually, we are accepting this responsibility. If we are to fulfill our duty, we're going to need a new vision of the future.

And we're going to need it soon.

Maybe a second "green revolution," is sprouting now. In my newspaper on the morning I write this, the CEO of GE and the CEO of Wal-Mart are both featured, in separate stories, talking about their companies' environmental policies. Who would have imagined, just 10 years ago, that the most powerful business leaders in the world would ever publicly proclaim their environmental concern? "Green" has evolved from a color, to a metaphor for fecundity, to a symbol for environmental health. Now we talk about "green" technologies and "greening" our homes. The word is a color, a verb and a noun denoting a certain kind of person. Marketers and politicians pragmatically discuss how to appeal to "the greens"–that is, people who are very concerned about protection of the environment.

The word, as an adjective, is used mainly to denote the negative. A "green" car is not a car that creates something, literally, "green." Nor is it usually painted green. It's a car that consumes less fuel and produces less pollution. A "green" house is not a house with a fine garden. It's a house that uses less energy. Our various green initiatives–political, civic, social and corporate–moderate the damage we are doing. They don't, generally, eliminate it.

Let's say we created a sort of worldwide, per capita reparation index where a person's lifestyle was assigned a number that coincided with the environmental cost of that lifestyle. The number 1,000 symbolizes the most egregiously excessive lifestyle of the California trust-fund billionaire with seven enormous homes, two personal jets, eight children, a bunch of big cars, horses, yachts, you name it. The number 10 symbolizes the ascetic Tibetan monk growing enough food for his own simple diet of lentils and greens in the plot below his mountainside temple.

Everybody gets a positive number. Every human life (and any other kind of life for that matter) contributes, in at least a small measure, to the consumption of the planet's resources. The Tibetan monk's lifestyle is as "green" as a human lifestyle gets, but the monk's net effect on the world's resources is still a negative.

The good news is, the miraculous biological machine we call the Earth is making more natural resources with each passing minute. We are, by the laws of nature, entitled to be here and a lot of us can live here as long as the temperature remains relatively stable and the atmosphere remains intact. We can live here because the sun keeps on showering energy on the planet–energy we convert into life. The sun represents the most powerful natural entity in our realm of experience. We can conceptualize bigger stars, supernovas and black holes, but every morning our brightest beacon rises over the eastern horizon. With its help, we can maintain a comfortable equilibrium on this planet for the foreseeable future.

Religions from the dawn of recorded history worshiped the sun. Solar energy is the source of all life. Petrochemicals are created from solar energy and carbon dioxide banked millions of years ago from plants that captured sunlight and photosynthesized useful carbohydrates. Plants died in oxygen-depleted water where they couldn't decay, for lack of oxygen, and were eventually absorbed into the earth's crust where over a long period of time the pressure and temperature transformed them into crude oil and natural gas. When you burn a piece of wood in the fireplace, you're releasing solar energy stored by the tree. Our varied diets are basically made up of solar energy stored in a variety of forms—meat, vegetables, energy bars and fruit juice–by plants and animals who originally accumulated that energy for their own use.

The energy in oil, like the energy in corn, like the energy in Chicken McNuggets, like the energy in coal, originated in the sun.

Solar energy defines abundance. Only a minute fraction of our sun's energy reaches our little planet. And the natural processes that harvest that energy are inefficient. In nature the most efficient transformation of solar energy into life occurs when plants photosynthesize sunlight to create carbohydrates. Under ideal circumstances, scientists figure that a plant might be capturing 6 percent of the available energy in sunlight.[17]

And the sun keeps shining, showering the earth with useful energy. All living things benefit.

In the sunlight, I believe we can see those three mountains pretty clearly from here.

MEDITATION

Are We Courageous Enough to Care?

I came home one day to find five sheep dead, piled in a corner of their shed. It took me a couple of hours to dig a hole big enough to bury them. Two days later I found six more ewes in the same spot. Five were dead, one moved when I touched her. I pulled her out of the pile and she staggered away to recover.

This was my worst moment in farming.

We were pretty sure the dead sheep were the victims of dogs because so many were killed and none of them had been eaten. Coyotes kill one animal at a time and eat it immediately. Coyotes are all business. And they almost never hunt in the daytime. We guessed our own dogs were to blame because the sheep had no wounds. Other dogs would have bitten them. Border collies are bred to herd sheep without touching them.

Mop had been our primary sheepdog and a fine farming partner for four years. Pitch, her mate and partner, had been around for about two years and was a dependable ally as well. Chico was their pup. The other four pups from the litter had been sold but we planned to keep Chico.

I stayed home for a day to see if I could discover the cause of the carnage. I was pretty sure I knew the culprits. Sure enough at midmorning, about an hour after I would normally have left for work, our border collies crawled under a fence, rounded up the sheep and brought them into the pen, crowding them into a corner of the shed.

We discourage the dogs from working sheep by themselves but a certain amount of self-study is good for a sheepdog. They teach themselves by practicing. In moderation, it is a productive exercise. If a border collie is not fascinated by livestock it doesn't make a good stock dog. The dogs learn to move the herds of cattle and flocks of sheep because they love the work.

The two older dogs mostly stayed back, darting this way and that to watch the way the clump of sheep moved in response. Chico, was a pup about five months old, and he was much more aggressive than his parents. He darted into the flock and pawed the sheep. He barked and ran at them. I went out and called the dogs off. Then I brought Chico inside and started looking for someone who wanted a free border collie. Some nice family with no sheep.

Sheep dread physical contact with a predator. To sheep, noth-

ing is more upsetting. As Chico harassed the ewes, they would have packed themselves more and more tightly into the corner of the shed until they knocked each other down and climbed over the fallen. Eventually those on the bottom died of suffocation or panic.

Was it Chico's aggressive personality that caused the deaths of all those sheep? Was it the chemistry of three dogs together, a dog-pack chemistry, that tipped the balance?

We don't know. But when Chico went away to live with a new family–a family without livestock–our problem was solved.

That was the worst livestock catastrophe we have seen on our farm. However, there have been others. A visiting dog–a friendly, likeable dog–killed about 30 chickens. A neighbor's pit bulls killed a mother and two baby goats one evening just after sunset. They maimed and nearly killed a fourth goat, "Mr. Big," our ancient pet angora who somehow recovered.

Another time I failed to notice a heifer calving in a remote pasture. The calf died in the birth canal and the mother became septic. She died soon after in the veterinarian's corral.

I should have watched Chico more carefully around the sheep. The chickens died because we left the visiting dog unattended. The goats were killed because I had separated them, temporarily, from the mule who normally watched out for them. We keep mules and donkeys with our goats and sheep because they naturally become members of the flocks and, by instinct, protect them from predators.

The heifer and her calf died because I accidentally let her breed too young and then I wasn't attentive when she went into labor.

There have been other fatalities over the years. Chickens and turkeys, mostly. Poultry has a genius for suicide-by-predator. Or, rather, every predator on earth recognizes poultry as an easy, delicious meal. Every dog has to be trained not to kill the chickens and turkeys. In fact, our dogs had to be trained to ignore the chickens and then, when we expanded into turkeys, they had to be taught that turkeys were also not on the canine menu. Hope springs eternal. On the other hand, the dogs help keep the raccoons, opossums and skunks out of the chicken house. The cat, who lives in the coop, had to be taught not to eat the baby chickens. Once we had assisted the hens in teaching him that lesson, he provided another line of defense against the opossums and skunks and eliminated our mouse problem.

Every time one of my mistakes has caused a creature to die, I've thought about selling all the animals and pulling out the fences. I care about each animal personally. When nature takes one of them, I can be philosophical. When they die because I failed to do my job correctly, I'm miserable.

I'm not emotionally detached when it comes to the livestock. I name nearly every creature. Some people–even in my own family–consider this ghoulish. After all, we're going to eat some of them and sell most of the others to people who will eat them.

But I relish their presence. The names help me keep track of them and I enjoy socializing with them. I chat with them while I'm working around the farm. They are, in a very real sense, my constant companions. They might even be called friends.

Of course this makes the process of taking them to slaughter both painful and poignant. But, again, that's nature. All prey animals die, by nature, in the jaws of predators. And our methods are, generally, more humane than the ways other predators kill.

I believe my sense of kinship with the animals, the sense of loss when they are slaughtered and the eventual enjoyment of the food they provide are all primal aspects of human experience. They only seem contradictory if we've isolated ourselves from nature. For me, the farm illustrates the transience and poignancy of life. Each spring the babies are born, the new mothers love them and care for them, then eventually push them away to find their own social stations within the flocks. By late fall many of them are in our freezers, or our customers' freezers. The mothers are munching hay and feeling new life stir inside them.

There is pain–and joy–in the normal cycle of life on the farm. It's a completely different, much worse sort of pain I feel when one of my constant companions is killed as the result of my bad judgment, my lack of attentiveness or my laziness.

We take satisfaction in the opportunity of raising our own meat with a sense of humanity and conscience. Our animals are raised in their natural families in a nutritious environment where they can enjoy good health, companionship, clean air, fresh water and generally as much space as they desire. When our animals accidentally get out of their fenced pastures, they usually hang around until we show up to put them back in. They have family, friends, health and a sense of home here.

Every living thing should be so lucky.

Industrial agriculture cannot spare the time or the space to provide so many amenities. So the animals we raise are sparing some other creatures whose lives would be crowded, lonely, chaotic and often unhealthy.

We believe that the lifestyle we provide for our livestock is humane. Their well-being is a personal concern for us, day in and day out. We really care.

And that's what hurts.

With conscience comes responsibility.

Raising animals for food forces us to confront nature's own tough logic. Raising healthy creatures on a specific amount of property while allowing them to reproduce more or less naturally, we need to harvest more animals than we keep each year. If we fail to harvest enough of our annual crop of babies, pastures are soon damaged and animals become sick from malnutrition. If any of our animal-care systems fails, or if we temporarily fail to pay attention, animals die pointlessly.

So we live with this burden, day in and day out. At its worst, it can make you feel like quitting. Sometimes I feel like letting someone else raise my food for me. Some other farmer might make a mistake and some lambs might die, but I wouldn't have to bury them. I could probably more or less forget my responsibility for the creatures I've displaced or consumed. Maybe I could pretend that the rice, broccoli and salmon on my plate are the products of some immaculate conception in which nothing had to suffer.

But of course that would be sentimental nonsense. The salmon were captured and killed. Cultivation of the rice paddies and vegetable fields destroyed some animal's habitat. Human beings were–and are–subjected to inhumane conditions to provide our cheap food. There is no free lunch.

When we don't consume, some other creature quickly takes advantage of the extra resources. Some campers drove across one of our empty pastures one late summer day. It was a big summer for grass and too wet to cut hay, so the grass had been left alone all summer. In one round trip their car mashed three prairie voles. One car circled through a 10-acre pasture once and managed to cross paths, fatally, with three voles. The implications for how many rodents had made their home in that pasture during that summer are staggering. If we plowed that pasture, most of them would disappear along with all the creatures who depend on rodents for food–coyotes, bobcats, hawks, owls etc.

Every creature that draws a breath or burns a single calorie has, to some degree or another, displaced another living thing. If you live, then something else loses the opportunity. That's one level of responsibility.

When we engage in the active management of our environment as farmers or loggers, gardeners or city managers, citizens of modern society, we exercise another level of responsibility.

And if we acknowledge that responsibility, if we commit ourselves to truly accepting the obligation, if we choose to be true stew-

ards of the land, we demonstrate our full humanity. We cannot afford sentimentality.

To be good stewards of nature, we have to respect and acknowledge nature's laws. If we love nature we will care for it more successfully. But only if we love nature for what it is. Undoubtedly a thousand small tragedies are acted out in our pastures each year. The prairie voles are monogamous. They take only 30 days to grow from birth to adulthood. Across our fields little mommies and daddies can raise several populous litters in a long summer. When a coyote or a raccoon digs up a vole nest, well, you can imagine the drama. It is never accurately depicted in what we would call a "family" movie. It's not a Hollywood scenario. In nature's grand saga there are no innocent victims or diabolical villains. Every life ends in death. Every life depends on death. If it weren't for the coyotes and raccoons, the fields would soon be ankle-deep in starving rodents.

To love nature, we have to accept its ruthlessness. To care for our habitat correctly, we have to appreciate its intricate, pragmatic machinery.

So nature challenges us: Can we love the world around us unsentimentally? Our enormous achievements have brought most of the planet more or less under our control. Now that we have this potent role in the world, are we capable of truly accepting our responsibility?

Are we courageous enough to love our planet?

CHAPTER THREE

Defining Criteria: The Queries

The Chinese philosopher Lao-tzu said, "A journey of a thousand miles begins with a single step." Mark Twain said, "The secret of getting ahead is getting started. The secret of getting started is breaking your complex overwhelming tasks into small manageable tasks, and then starting on the first one."

It's time to get started. But we need to determine the direction in which we want to travel. Then we can begin defining our tasks.

Individuals can make a contribution to the species' sustainable future on the planet at almost any time. This morning I'm writing on a laptop computer whose power settings are adjusted to conserve electricity, in a house where only one or two necessary lights are on. I have not solved any planetary problems today, but I've made a few small adjustments that help. The coffee I'm drinking was grown organically in the shade of a forest where the big, mature trees were left standing. It was harvested and processed by people earning a living wage, and the farmer made a little extra money because the crop was certified organic, shade-grown and fair-trade.

In a little while I'm going to deliver some sheep to another farmer. Then I'll try to incorporate my day's errands into the trip so I don't have to start a vehicle again today.

These little measures don't make me feel deprived. My awareness that I'm consuming resources and generating waste doesn't make me feel guilty. My consumption is an inevitable and natural condition of living. The small steps I take to reduce that consumption give me proportionately small satisfactions. But over the course of the day, the week, the months and the years those satisfactions stack up into a life that is more fulfilling than it would have been if I hadn't been paying attention.

Thirty years ago I did not feel those satisfactions. I remember feeling a sense of guilt each time I started an automobile or turned on a light bulb. I was neurotically hypersensitive to my own consumptive habits, my own living and breathing. It occurred to me slowly, over the years, that if I continued to feel disappointed in myself each time I embarked on a trip or cooked a pancake on my electric griddle that I would, eventually, grow tired of my own conscience. A persistent sense of disapproval–even when it is self-disapproval–fosters resentment.

The antidote for this negativity growing in me was not easy to find. For a while I just stopped thinking about the future. If every meal I ate, every mile I drove and every breath I drew consumed our precious resources, then maybe I would be better off ignoring the implications. I defined my life by where I lived and the things that interested me at the moment. My life had clear boundaries. I could live in a relatively clean, unpolluted place. I could eat healthy food. I could seal myself off from many of the world's most troubling realities.

Then I had kids and I was thinking about the future all the time.

Once the kids arrived I was suddenly connected with everything going on in the entire world, present and future. My children might grow up to live through famine or war. This felt like a personal, immediate threat. The future of the planet was a daily personal concern again.

But I was already fed up with feeling guilty.

That left me with one clear alternative.

Do something. And do it with a happy heart.

Like most young families we didn't have any extra money. We would have cherished a sleek, fuel-efficient car but we couldn't afford to turn down my grandmother's leviathan, hand-me-down station wagon. Our rented house was not well insulated but it needed to stay warm, especially while we had babies, so the furnace ran all the time. There were lots of trips to the market and the pediatrician. I wanted to minimize my negative impact on the planet but I needed to care for my family.

If I stopped holding myself to an unrealistic standard, I found I could take great satisfaction in small achievements. The landlord was happy to pay for the materials and helped me install new insulation in the attic. It made the house a lot cozier and cheaper to heat. We found an inexpensive, fuel-efficient used car. I kept the leviathan for my short commute to work, but the daily family errands and longer trips could be taken in the smaller car. We bought a living Christmas tree and planted it in the backyard after the holidays. When spring came, we planted a big vegetable garden. Gradually our life became more sustainable and more satisfying.

We're still working on it.

In recent years I've come to believe that most people share some of my goals. Most people want our species to have a great place to live healthy lives. Most people want to contribute to a positive future. But their intention is often obstructed by the things they perceive that they cannot do. They can't afford to install a solar system or buy a new car. They can't effectively insulate an old house or acquire a new one. They are conscious that our environmental problems may be serious, but the solutions feel out of reach. A sense of frustration sets in.

In frustration, they stop thinking about it. They feel a sense of relief. That sense of relief is, perhaps, the biggest threat to the human habitat today.

Human beings need ways of thinking about our responsibilities that don't lead us to frustration. That relief we feel when we stop thinking about the environment can be replaced by the satisfaction of doing something about it. Our achievements are going to be small most of the time. We've been in the habit of comparing those small achievements to the big problems reported in the media. I think that's a mistake.

A good life is made up of small achievements. Human relationships are formed by thousands of short, often trivial communications and shared experience. We build trust that way. Careers materialize from millions of small tasks.

I've developed a habit of testing my ideas and actions, however small and trivial, against a set of questions. At work many of the questions are specialized. "Does this build audience efficiently?" "Does it make money?" "Will it make money?" "Does this contribute to building a positive culture?" "Does this represent our shared values?"

More important, though, are some of the big, general questions: "Is this fair?" "Is it contagious? Will it engage the enthusiasm of our colleagues?"

The exercise is therapeutic. Rather than asking, "Can we eliminate our business' dependence on fossil fuels," we ask, "Is our energy usage fair? Does it contribute to a beautiful, abundant future?"

The answer is almost never a simple "no." Generally speaking, the answer is partly yes and partly no. Where the answer is positive, we can feel some sense of satisfaction and leave things alone. Where the answer is negative we generally find ways of changing our practices for the better and, again, getting some satisfaction from the improvements.

The building where we run our business gives us a relevant example. It is a typical, 20,000 square-foot, flat-roofed commercial building in an industrial park on the edge of a small city. We want it to be as energy-efficient as possible, of course.

Lighting provided one big challenge. Because the building is square, only a few workspaces can be illuminated by windows. The middle of the office is 40 yards from the nearest exterior wall. We installed more efficient bulbs and lighting fixtures, but still our lights burned throughout the workday. Removing any fixtures or turning them off left people without sufficient light to work.

One of our advertisers led us to a partial solution. For a reasonable cost, we installed Solatubes, basically small, round, prefabricated skylights in the roof. Because the building has a typical ceiling of acoustic tiles in frames hung from the roof joists, conventional skylights would not have been feasible. The Solatube skylights in the roof connect to a simple, flexible tube lined with a reflective material like aluminum foil. The foil maximizes the amount of light carried from the roof to a translucent lens in the ceiling. *Voila*, about a third of our lights were replaced by sunlight! Many of our meetings occur in conference rooms lit by sunlight coming down from the roof through a Solatube.

Insulation presented similar challenges. There was a nominal amount sprayed between the roof joists. Adding more was problematic above the hanging ceiling where we run all the wires for our computer networks. We took advantage of a roof replacement to add new insulation to the exterior of the roof between the decking and the weatherproof roofing material. We programmed digital thermostats to turn off the heating and cooling when the building is not occupied.

Have we done enough? Of course not. That's akin to the question of whether we're profitable enough. No business is profitable "enough," or efficient "enough" or big "enough." As we improve, we set higher goals. Along the way we ask ourselves, "How can we be more profitable? How can we be more efficient? How can we grow faster?"

Queries like those break up any goal–however big and intimidating–into manageable pieces. Ambitious people keep track of their progress in thousands of ways and follow their evolution in details. Industrialist Jack Welch (no relation to me) is often quoted as saying, "The devil is in the detail," but 40 years ago the architect Mies van der Rohe is quoted as saying more less the same thing, "God is in the details."[18] One hundred years before that it is attributed to the French writer Gustave Flaubert.[19] The notion is probably a lot older. We can track big processes by observing small changes.

When things go well, managers take satisfaction in the progress. When they go poorly, they take satisfaction from the process of reorganizing their efforts in new directions.

To any knowledgeable businessperson this approach is axiomatic. The businessperson builds a vision of the business at its most successful and then articulates a set of questions to guide us toward that vision. The financial statements and forecasts are obvious illustrations of the technique. The annual corporate report is another.

If it works more or less universally in business then why couldn't it be applied to other large, complex undertakings?

These queries are in no sense any kind of ultimate formula. They are, after all, the work of only one mind. The task at hand–true long-term sustainability for the human habitat - requires billions of minds working together for a long time. I propose these queries only as a way of starting a conversation that might lead to better queries and better conversations. These are my best questions, for what that is worth. I apply them to all my efforts at home, at work and elsewhere, as devices that help me break up my aspirations into manageable pieces and help me feel satisfaction that I am at least making some progress towards my ambitions for my work, my planet and my species.

Is it Beautiful?

If our species is going to develop a vision of a sustainable future, the task will require that a lot of people contribute their own ideas and energy to forming and realizing that vision. If the project is to attract the energy of millions of people, then beauty needs to be in the criteria.

I was on a journalist's junket in Germany during the spring of 1994, about five years after capitalist West Germany and communist East Germany were unified. We drove back and forth from one side of Berlin to the other numerous times. Traffic flowed freely, but the two halves of Berlin were still two strikingly different cities.

West Berlin was an affluent, creative European city whose skyscrapers, shops and museums were comparable to those of New York, Los Angeles or Paris. East Berlin was decrepit and plain–depressing in its institutional practicality. The streets around the core of East Berlin were like the halls of a run-down public hospital.

Fairness and contagiousness were at the core of the Eastern Bloc's communist and socialist policies through the first two-thirds of the 20th Century. If a single concept characterized socialist values, it would be fairness across all the strata of society.

The great thinkers who first conceived of socialism in the late 18th and early 19th centuries–Robert Owen, Henri de Saint-Simon, Friedrich Engels and Karl Marx–put forth fairness and contagiousness as imperative standards on which their new socialist societies would be built. And to some extent or another those societies were built–in the USSR, China, Southeast Asia and Latin America.

The arguments over why those societies didn't last will persist for centuries. The wealth and power of capitalist nations united against the socialists. That didn't make it any easier for them to succeed. And fairness proved difficult to achieve in societies where authoritarian socialist power structures reacted to criticism by brutally restraining their own citizens.

But just as significantly, I think, socialist and communist societies lacked beauty. Their architecture was institutional. Their art was largely thematic, rather than aesthetic. And their lack of beauty, creativity and grace historically made it hard to propagate their ideals.

In the first half of the 20th century lots of Americans were drawn to socialist ideas. By the second half of the century the world had seen the societies built on those ideas and most of us weren't inspired by them.

Without explicit support for beauty, lacking a philosophical commitment, the socialists didn't find the resources to create it. The ornate rooflines and handsome wooden dachas of traditional Russia were replaced by public housing blocks–concrete eyesores. The awe-inspiring architectural tradition of Beijing's Forbidden City was abandoned in favor of Soviet-style monoliths in China's biggest cities as well. Meanwhile in capitalist countries people who prospered were commissioning beauty–and paying for it. West Berlin's classy old mansions were renovated and populated by bankers and entrepreneurs. The same sorts of homes a few meters away in the Eastern Bloc gradually dissolved in the rain, their stoops crumbling and their stucco molding.

Without wealthy patrons to pay for it or an explicit public mission to support it, the beauty of Eastern Europe and ancient China gradually deteriorated.

Did socialism fail because it wasn't as pretty as capitalism? I'd say that was part of the reason.

Even when it was comparatively fair, socialism was not beautiful.

Of course the socialists didn't corner the market on ugliness. America's sprawling industrial parks and tract homes leave something to be desired. But perpetually, in free and prosperous societies, people are inspired to create beauty.

I used to be skeptical about the value of a corporate headquarters. I considered the expensive architects, the fancy materials and the art collections monuments to the corporate ego and a big waste of money.

Then I visited John Deere & Co.

That's right, the tractor company.

Deere's Moline, Illinois, headquarters is nestled into the side of a bluff in a ravine on 1400 acres of wildlife preserve. In 1956 Deere president William Hewitt picked the famous Finnish-American architect Eero Saarinen to build the new headquarters in the Midwestern countryside.[20] Saarinen was among the most influential architects and designers of his day. He designed the Gateway Arch in St. Louis; the IBM and CBS headquarters; John F. Kennedy and Dulles International Airports; and the famous "tulip chairs" that inspired the seating on the set of the first Star Trek television series.

Deere & Company's headquarters are based in three connected buildings, angular, modern constructions in steel and glass. Saarinen chose a special metal for their exteriors, a steel designed to form its own protective coating of iron oxide–rust–as it weathers. The result is a flat, earth-colored finish that blends in with the surroundings while making a striking artistic statement. The building embodies Deere & Company's identity. It evokes soil and rusty plows, as well as a utilitarian and modern sensibility.

I met several Deere veterans who enjoyed telling stories of their first visits to the headquarters, the walls lined with famous art, the executive lunchroom looking out over the reflecting pool and its swans. They were proud of their building and proud of their company. I believe their pride infused Deere's products over the decades and helped create the most loyal customer base of any farm-equipment manufacturer in the world. Deere customers are fanatical in their loyalty.

The pride and loyalty of Deere employees infects the company's customers. I believe the company's headquarters–designed as a monument to architectural beauty that evokes the company's earthy, practical mission–helps create that pride and loyalty.

In the 1970s when the U.S. government subsidized solar energy, thousands of American homes installed awkward, hideous solar collectors on their roofs. Most of the Utopian communes built in those days were ramshackle settlements constructed by amateurs without a graceful or beautiful thing in sight. Sandals and tattered jeans were the uniform of the ecologically sensitive subculture.

Just lately beauty and sustainability have begun a relationship. Fashion designers have begun paying attention to where their materials come from and who manufactures them. A product's provenance and its beauty are both part of its marketing strategy. Where they come together we get the electric sports cars, earth-friendly corporate headquarters and luxury homes that generate all their own power–the kinds of things that inspire real change.

And when efficiency and productivity are added to the mix, world-changing innovation can happen.

Does it Create Abundance?

"Abundance" is a very old word. It came to English speakers virtually intact from Middle English about a thousand years ago. The Anglo-Saxons got it from Old French, who picked it up nearly intact from the Romans who had a goddess, *Abundantia*, who reigned over the concept and guarded the mythical *cornucopia*, the horn of plenty. At some point she passed a torch to St. Abundantia, an Italian girl from Spoleto who made a pilgrimage to Jerusalem and spent five contemplative years in a cave in the Egyptian desert. St. Abundantia was known for her generosity, the spontaneous ringing of bells and the tendency of flowers to bloom in her presence, even in the middle of winter.[21]

People desire abundance. It is a feature of every Utopian vision. But nature reminds us that the symbols of abundance–flowers blooming in winter or a goat's horn that delivers unlimited amounts of excellent food and drink–are mythological. In the real world resources are limited.

The only practical means of creating abundance in our world requires examining the ratio between our capacities and our aspirations. Our capacities can be measured. Our aspirations can be adjusted to fit within our capacities. And if our aspirations are fit within our capacities with some room left over, then abundance is possible.

A few years ago *Natural Home* magazine featured Michael Funk's California foothills home on the Yuba River. Funk made some money in the natural-food business and chose to build his dream home among the waterfalls, gorges and pine-scented forests of the Sierra Nevada. He built the home off the grid to generate all its own photovoltaic electricity. He designed the house with passive-solar energy for heat and efficient natural ventilation. He used reclaimed wood, recycled lumber and timber certified by the Forestry Stewardship Council from renewable sources. He used local granite for walls and foundations, insulation made from recycled denim and wool clothing, natural wool carpets, permanent natural slate for the roofs, natural waxes, and solar hot water. He cultivated extensive orchards and gardens that provide a lot of food for the Funk family and his guests.

With guest rooms and conference rooms for business events and an extensive root cellar, the home was a little bigger than he had originally planned–about 6,000 square feet in all.

Some of the magazine's readers criticized the home's size. The very idea of a big house offends some people.

Those criticisms are not rational, and they reek of dogma. Michael Funk's home is off the grid. No matter how big it is, it isn't burning any fossil fuels. It consumes almost nothing. Perched on its rocky hillside, it's covered a few thousand square feet of marginal natural landscape–maybe enough to feed one goat for a month, in the rainy season. The materials he put into the house were produced as conscientiously as possible. If he had used a little less, well, that would have made some small difference. But the example he provides–of luxury with a conscience–sets a standard for hundreds of thousands of new homes now being planned across the globe.

Presuming that some people–probably a lot of people - will continue to want big houses, isn't it great that more and more homeowners are building their dream homes in conscientious ways?

In fact, isn't it great that people like Michael Funk are not only building houses that provide an example for other big-house projects, but also are risking a little money on experimental technologies that all of us may eventually use in houses big or small?

Funk's example is valuable precisely because it is a big, expensive home. He had the choice of virtually any amenity–multicar garages, swimming pools, indoor tennis courts, heated horse arenas–but he chose to build off the grid with a conscience.

The aggregated positive effect of his good example far outweighs the impact of using a few extra recycled boards.

Put another way, two frugal Americans who live modestly but choose to have four children have, in purely environmental terms, made the choice to build a house bigger than Michael Funk's by bringing more human beings into the world.

Neither Michael Funk nor the prolific parents have done anything evil. Both simply demonstrate the definition of abundance: A surplus of resources over necessity. If we aspire to have big families humanity's resources will be more and more constrained. Or human beings can stabilize their own population and decide for ourselves how much we should consume of the planet's resources. If people want big houses, so be it. If they prefer to build small houses to preserve more of the planet's resources for more people or other living things, then that is the human prerogative.

Every living thing must consume resources. The rate at which human beings consume those resources is a management issue with moral implications. It is not an intrinsically moral issue, however, because as humans consume resources we also create them. Humanity is part of a living system that recycles waste–even our corpses–into new life. We cannot live without consuming.

To judge other human beings based on their rates of consumption implies that we've worked out all the pluses and minuses of one lifestyle or another. We haven't. And the task is so complex that it may be futile.

Who is more at fault for environmental damage, the Southern California commuter burning gasoline in his Chevrolet or the Brazilian farmer burning the rain forest? What about the rich, childless entrepreneur with a vacation home in Oregon compared with the modest Arkansas family with seven children? Or the Kansas farmer with a heavy-duty pickup (me) compared with the sub-Saharan nomad pushing his camels and goats across the overgrazed savannah?

In a world without abundance these troublesome questions become critical. The conservation ethic forces us into a debate over the morality of our lifestyles. If we consume our surplus then societies will need to manage lifestyles with increasing rigor. That will mean weighing the impact of individual choices on more and more sensitive scales. The implications are bleak: a world full of people counting their rations of rice and toilet paper.

In a world of managed abundance, on the other hand, humanity could make room to explore and experiment with technology and lifestyles. Some houses may be bigger than others. Individuals can make wise choices and manage the planet for prosperity. Just as some of the pastures on my farm go ungrazed each year, we could leave part of the Earth unexploited to preserve its resilience and potential. On an abundant Earth there's room for life to flourish and for beauty to blossom. On an abundant Earth there is time and space in which to negotiate fairness.

Without abundance it's difficult to imagine how beauty or fairness might be created. Without abundance it's difficult to imagine a sustainable human future, much less a desirable one.

Is it Fair?

Because fairness is a subjective judgment, it cannot be nailed down. Take any human activity or condition and ask the question, "Is this fair?" and there will be disagreement. Ultimately, fairness can be decided, but not determined.

Fairness is a measurement of consensus, judged by participants. When a group of people comes together in a voluntary activity–a company, a game or a social group–the participants are consenting to the fairness of that activity and its rules. Fairness is determined in real time as the participants interact with each other within the rules of the game. If we consider the rules unfair, we either argue our way to a new set of rules or we don't play. That's why fairness is so important, even if it can't be pinned down.

Justice is sometimes hard to visualize. If a race of people has been enslaved for generations, how do we determine just compensation? If an entire culture lost its homeland in a war, where can justice be found for the individual members of that community? Often, it can't.

Even when justice can't be determined we can seek a sense of fairness. Fairness is available where justice is out of reach.

Fairness can be visualized when justice cannot.

Julius Caesar, Attila, Genghis Khan, Napoleon Bonaparte and Adolph Hitler do not appear, through the lens of history, to have been particularly concerned with fairness. Certainly their enemies didn't always perceive them as "fair." But to influence the world in which they lived, even the dictators and despots had to negotiate a sense of fairness within their constituencies. The Romans could not raise their armies unless they treated their soldiers, in some sense, fairly. Then as now, the army provided opportunities for boys (and now girls as well, because as a society we've decided it's more fair to include both genders in the military) from underprivileged communities to gain some education, to travel and to achieve some economic and social success.[22] Military service, past and present, offers opportunities more based more on merit than on background and provides for some people, therefore, a fair alternative to a career in business or government. Caesar and Hitler also found it necessary to levy taxes to establish and maintain their empires and a tax system is more effective if it is considered, if not fair, at least *fair enough* by the popular opinion. The Babylonians invented the census about 6,000 years ago,[23] which allowed them to tax their empire proportionately, and they established a system *fair enough* to keep their diverse subjects cooperative. It may not have been fair, but it was *fair enough.*

Napoleon Bonaparte founded the Bank of France, reformed the French tax system and improved France's schools to help sell the idea of a fair monarchy to the French people.

The Magna Carta was essentially an effort to bring elements of fairness into 13th-century British society, by limiting some of the powers of the British monarchy.

The unfairness of British tax law was a big motivator for the establishment of the United States of America. King George III might have averted the revolution if he had only possessed a keener sense of fairness, as the Americans perceived it.

The United States were "united" by their aspirations toward fairness. Fairness was the primary theme of the fledgling nation's Declaration of Independence and the guiding principle and main bone of contention at the Constitutional Convention. Patriots still defend the American system of democracy and free enterprise based on how it provides equal access to the machinery of government and the fruits of economic development. In a word, its fairness.

The so-called Boston Tea Party, viewed as a seminal event at the founding of the United States was, in fact, an illegal act of vandalism perpetrated against innocent merchants to protest what was perceived as an unfair tax. My country's founding fathers were protesters, subversives, some vandals and insurgents–call them what you will. They rebelled against unfairness.

And many American would agree that the darkest chapters in U.S. history–the Indian wars, slavery, the Civil War and segregation–were characterized by our failure to apply our standards for fairness.

When perceived from the outside, it's hard to see any great world power as governing fairly. Rome conquered much of the world by military force and subjected foreign nations to taxation without providing any access to the decision-making machinery of its government. The insurgents battling U.S. soldiers today in the Middle East believe that the American presence in Muslim countries and the establishment of Israel in the geographic center of Islam are unfair to Muslim peoples. Buddhists in Tibet and Muslims in central Asia rebel against Chinese authority. Pakistan resists the influence of its powerful neighbor, India. A sense of fairness–or the lack thereof–is at the very heart of every major conflict in the world today.

Yet every successful nation must be perceived as fair by some percentage of its own citizens in order to survive. So behind every example of conquest and colonization across history, there existed a group of people who considered their leaders fair and their government reasonable–the Roman citizenry, the Mongol hordes, the French aristocracy. Those were the people inside the consensus process that forms the backbone of every society. And every society I can think of, past or present, includes a percentage of people who don't feel the social contract is fair. Those people–alienated from the society in which they live–commit crimes, foment rebellions, subvert government and short-circuit the economy. Because they feel the rules are not fair, they naturally feel less moral obligation to obey the rules.

The highest goal of politics might be to instill a sense of fairness in society, since that sense of fairness promotes tranquility, productivity and prosperity. The cooperation that undergirds a healthy society–the social contract–is based on a sense of fairness. Without it, a society is unhealthy and unproductive and, ultimately, ceases to exist.

Naturally the most powerful groups in any society seek to consolidate and protect their resources. In the process they constrain the free flow of resources to the most deserving institutions and projects. A healthy sense of fairness keeps resources flowing so that our society remains dynamic and innovative. Efficiency is a function of fairness.

The big challenges facing our species today are global. The efficiency of our communication and transportation combined with the growing size and density of our population is knitting us together, forming a single global interest group that needs natural resources, clean air and clean water. If Mexico's air is polluted, so is the air of the United States, Guatemala, Belize, Nicaragua and El Salvador. If the water in the Congo River is contaminated it taints the water of the Central African Republic, Angola, Republic of the Congo, Tanzania, Cameroon, Zambia, Burundi and Rwanda. When toxins are released into the oceans, they eventually touch every shoreline in the world.

When societies encounter a threatening phenomenon that does not respect political boundaries alliances are necessary. In World War II the "Allies"–England, Russia, China, the U.S., Australia, Belgium, Brazil, Canada, etc.–faced the "Axis powers"–Germany, Japan and Italy. Eventually, nearly every nation in the world joined one group or the other. Both sides wrote treaties that delineated the rights and responsibilities of the participating nations. They determined a shared code of fairness that would govern their behavior as long as they needed each other.

At the time, the governments and societies of Japan, Italy

and Germany may have been as different as any three nations on earth. Japan was governed as a monarchy. Germany was a socialist democracy. Italy was a fascist dictatorship. Under pressure, they agreed upon a set of rights and responsibilities.

Likewise it's hard to conceive of a single political entity encompassing the United Kingdom, the United States, the Union of Soviet Socialist Republics and the Republic of China. Yet that union took shape comparatively quickly when the need arose and it has lasted, in some form right up to the present day. It formed the basis of the United Nations.

The United Nations today is the principal agency attempting to address global environmental issues. In 1992 the organization published the United Nations Framework Convention on Climate Change (UNFCCC). The goal of the treaty is to protect the global climate by stabilizing human production of greenhouse gases, but it sets no specific limits and describes no mechanisms. Essentially, it is a document concerned with fairness, and it provides for "protocols" to be approved along the way that set limits and define mechanisms. Predictably these protocols–including the definitive Kyoto Protocol–are controversial. At least the Kyoto Protocol is controversial in the United States. As I write this, the United States is the only significant emitter of greenhouse gases that has not ratified the protocol. Unfortunately it is also the biggest emitter per capita, and second only to China in total emissions. Americans face the largest changes in lifestyle if our nation is to reduce emissions significantly. Some politicians argue that mandatory curbs on American emissions would unfairly inhibit the U.S. economy. Leaders in other nations respond that the unwillingness of the world's richest people to do their part is more unfair.

Debates over whether human activity is causing climate change are distractions. Human population growth has profound implications for our habitat, both now and in the future, regardless of the conclusions drawn from our climate-change debate. The real argument today is over what is fair. A lot of Americans, myself included, believe we are perpetuating the squabble over whether climate change is occurring mostly because we don't have a rhetorical leg to stand on in the debate over the fairness of international standards. We're the richest people in the world and its biggest polluters, yet we don't wish to change our lifestyles.

The only practical approach to solving environmental problems is based on a sense of fairness shared by those affected. We are all in this together. There will always be argument over the subtleties. That's how consensus is maintained. But we can't ignore the issue of international fairness, the central issue of the discussion.

It's simplest to begin imposing a sense of fairness on our personal affairs before expanding our efforts to the global scale. All the major world religions advocate charity for the poor. Charity represents fairness in its most elegant form. Those who have something extra share with those who lack the basic resources. The fundamental virtue of the concept is difficult to criticize.

In a world of limited resources, the wealthy person can contribute in two ways–by sharing resources or by refraining from consuming resources–food, air, water, energy that are, therefore, available to others.

Our vegetable garden and fruit trees produce maybe 20 percent of the produce my family and I consume over the course of the year. Maybe less. It varies dramatically with our level of dedication to weeding, canning and freezing. My efforts are inconsistent, but I love watching the sun and soil create all those diverse and delicious foods: okra, asparagus, plums, pumpkins, blackberries and dozens of others. My enjoyment is enhanced by the recognition that my organic garden, teeming with biological diversity, might otherwise be a comparatively homogenous and unproductive patch of grass. My food otherwise might come from some monocultural field where nothing but the crop could live. By converting a patch of lawn to garden we provide new habitat and sustenance for millions of other living things - both in the garden and around the world where other creatures including other human beings can enjoy the small surplus created by our backyard project.

The coffee in my cup this morning is triple-certified: Fair Trade, organic and shade-grown. Its Fair Trade certification indicates that the coffee farmers and their workers were paid more for their beans because their labor practices and economic contributions were conscientious. The certification provides us with a fairer choice. Organic farming protects the soil air and water. It's fairer to the living things that share those resources. And because coffee plants can thrive in the shade, it's possible to leave the forest intact on a shade-grown coffee plantation. The plants are marginally less productive in the shade of the big trees, but the forest, overall, is helping produce a healthier planet.

I suppose my triple-certified brew costs about 20 percent more than comparable conventional coffee but I enjoy it twice as much, so I could drink half as much and still be ahead.

The benefits of my choice are not abstract. My coffee provides a conscientious farmer in Sumatra or Nicaragua with a better living. Trees that otherwise would be bulldozed and burned are left standing. Maybe I preserve nesting places for a few tropical birds.

There are millions of ways of incorporating a sense of fairness in our daily lives. Do we courteously let others merge on the freeway? Are we honest in our business dealings? Do we share the household chores? Cynics may laugh at these humble notions, but taken as a whole our awareness of the value of fairness creates one of the most valuable of our institutions, a civil human society.

In business the opportunities are more compelling. Do we compensate our suppliers and colleagues fairly? Do we return a fair day's work for our wages? Do we refrain from exploiting cheap resources if they are destructive to the environment and human society? Are we a source of productive energy in the economy?

Fairness is both practical and inspirational. It is a fundamental value that undergirds all cooperative human endeavor, as well as society itself. It provides an ideal to which we can aspire, a source of standards that elevate our efforts and our achievements. How can we do without it?

Is It Contagious?

Contagiousness is to sustainability what fairness is to justice. When we ask, "Is this contagious?" we expect a conditional answer. We are asking, "How contagious is it? How repeatable is it? Will this catch on?"

Sustainability is an important ideal. The concept forms the basis for all our efforts to protect our habitat. It is also a perfectly impossible standard. If nature teaches us anything, it is that nothing is sustainable indefinitely. In the course of time, everything changes.

Contagiousness can be visualized when sustainability cannot.

Contagiousness is both practical and flexible. There are two qualities of contagion that represent success. We immediately recognize the value of contagiousness across time into the future. Solar power and wind power are superior choices because the sun and the wind will continue producing energy perpetually. We are not capable of exhausting them. That is their great practical virtue. But they are also valuable for their immediate contagiousness around the world, today. Everywhere in the world, the sun shines and the wind blows. Free power is popular. There are places where sunshine is more persistent and where the wind blows harder and more consistently, but they are essentially available to everyone. Once you have the right technology, they are free. For that reason, they are enormously versatile sources of energy capable of running mechanical pumps to bring groundwater to livestock in India or to send a Tesla sports car hurtling down the freeway in southern California.

What passes for sustainable in the current vernacular is usually only repeatable. Repeatability is the discipline through which we pursue the worthy but ultimately unattainable goal of sustainability.

Let's look at local food production as an example. When you buy food grown by local farmers, you can reduce the amount of energy required to transport that food. We know local agriculture is repeatable, because for thousands of years it was the only kind of agriculture in existence. And the idea of knowing your farmer is more and more popular. You have a better opportunity to learn about the farmer's land-use practices and to make sure the long-term productivity of the land is protected. It's proving to be a contagious idea.

If local foods are valuable in the marketplace, then the farmer and the community have economic reasons for preserving farmland, which can enhance the local culture and the local landscape. Local agriculture encourages the cultivation of more diverse crops. Local food can be delivered in a thousand different ways–car, truck, bicycle, oxcart or on foot anywhere there is arable land. It is entrepreneurial: Anyone who can borrow a couple of acres of fertile land can get into the business and enhance the local economy. It is not dependent on big, energy-intensive transportation networks or heavy farm machinery.

The diversity of local agriculture across the continents makes food production more reliable, overall, since the diversity of local products makes food production more resilient. A spring storm in the huge apple orchards of the northwestern United States might destroy millions of apples and devastate the economies of hundreds of small towns. But if enough people are growing apples in small orchards across the country in Massachusetts and Minnesota and New Mexico, then there will be apples to eat. And if the farmers in Washington and Oregon are growing hops, kale and hazelnuts alongside their orchards, the storm won't wipe out their livelihood.

So local food production is *contagious*, thanks to its economic and environmental advantages, plus it contributes to the consistency–the inherent repeatability–of our food system. We can individually contribute to the long-term stability of our food source by buying locally grown foods.

As we build local food networks, we provide models for farmers around the world. Local agriculture is contagious across time and across geography.

The consideration of fairness and contagiousness provide us with tools to measure the relative value of our options.

The Hologram

I'm fascinated by holograms. We see them all the time these days on our credit cards. A three dimensional image appears on a two-dimensional surface. As you turn the credit card in your hand, the little dove on the silvery stamp in the corner turns as though it were a real object in your hand, rather than a picture of the bird. Some credit-card holograms are tiny depictions of the earth.

The image is not a photograph. It is not, properly, even a picture. It is a reproduction of the way light from two different perspectives is "scattered" by the presence of the object, diffracted when the two light beams interact, and then perceived from a third perspec-

tive. If we change the third perspective by turning the hologram in our hand, our eye perceives the image changing as though the object was turning.

Weird, huh?

Scientists worked for decades to create useful holograms. First they studied how we perceive all images–both real objects and pictures –based on light entering the lens of the eye. Light is, of course, radiation, and when we started studying radiation in the late 1940s, our knowledge of how light affects the eye and the optic nerve. Lasers–the most focused and controllable form of radiation–gave us new tools for study and invention. Our knowledge of the physics continued to improve and lasers got cheaper and more controllable over the next decades.

Our eyes, it seems, record the three-dimensional world by interpreting a mosaic of perspectives on that world from different parts of the eyes, and by moving the eyes to create tiny differences in our point of view. The difference in two images from two locations on our face a few millimeters apart give our brains enough information to understand size, depth and movement. To replicate that complexity in an image, the hologram artificially replaces the differences in the real image from two perspectives with two small, separate images that are subtly different, surrogates for the inherent complexity of a real, three-dimensional object.

In March 1984, National Geographic Magazine ran a hologram of an eagle on its cover, "embossed" on the same sort of reflective surface used on credit-card holograms, much larger and in very high resolution. Hundreds of thousands of people were suddenly holding in their hands the first hologram they had ever seen, turning it this way and that, watching the eagle turn as though it were an object rather than an image.

It was poetic that the magazine that first carried modern photographic technology into some of the world's most remote regions would also bring holographic technology—a brand new sort of image - into the mainstream for the first time.

My conviction that we need a collective vision for our future led me to consider the way we form images, which led me to holograms. Humanity's perception of its present world and its vision for the future are formed from billions of individual perspectives. Each individual human possesses a unique vision, a single point in the light field. Each perspective records the person's place in space and time. Each point of light forms a complete image, a complete vision for the future. When we reproduce the light field projected by those billions of unique visions, we get a three-dimensional picture of humanity's combined vision. Effectively, we can't perceive the future in three dimensions without taking into account the entire light field.

So if we are to create a new vision for our future, we need to illuminate it from more than one perspective. Our vision needs to exist in an infinitely complex field of perspectives.

The scale of this challenge could be discouraging.

But maybe if we approach the problem as a physicist would, it will prove more soluble than we expect.

A photograph reproduces an image from a single perspective, the camera's lens. The camera records the light bouncing off the scene. A hologram records the light field surrounding an object. When we look at a holographic reproduction our eyes are exploring that light field.

Every minute point in the light field contains as much information about the object as a photograph. The scene could be reproduced from each minute point of light, like a tiny photo. Each tiny photo is subtly different because it was recorded at a different point in the light field.

When our eyes look at a scene, they perceive the light bouncing off each minute detail of the objects in that scene. As we move, or the objects move, our eyes catch tiny variations in each minute detail. Those variations give us our three-dimensional perception of objects and motion. We can admire a beautiful mountain range, ski through a grove of aspen or drive a car.

The light field recorded in a hologram provides our eyes with the same kind of information. It presents the scene from thousands or millions of minutely different perspectives. Our eyes read those myriad perspectives and perceive three-dimensional objects. As we look at the hologram from different angles, our eyes perceive the same changes in the light field they would perceive if we were moving around the original scene.

No one could build a hologram by hand, recording each minute point with its tiny variations across the whole light field. But by shining the right kind of light on the scene from a couple of different perspectives and then perceiving it from precisely the right position, we may be able to form an image that appears sharp and real from any of the infinite number of perspectives from which it might be viewed.

For the purposes of illuminating a vision, statements of fact are unreliable. Facts change with perspective. A dollar is worth a dollar, yet that dollar is much more valuable in the hand of a child in a Tijuana slum than it is in the shops along Rodeo Drive in Beverly Hills. The ten-pound barbell that's trivial to us when we're 25 years old presents a formidable physical challenge at 85. If the value of a dollar or the burden of 10 pounds of steel vary dramatically with perspective, then less substantial more subjective facts must be even less reliable. Our estimations of deforestation, desertification, climate change and acid rain vary wildly with our perspective.

So if we are to help billions of people illuminate a new vision, facts are not necessarily the most useful sources of light.

CHAPTER FOUR

Take the First Steps: Where to Place Our Feet

Intelligence is sometimes measured by the number of cortical neurons in the brain, a more precise measurement than simple brain volume.[24] Human beings have about 11.5 billion cortical neurons, more than any other species. Chimpanzees are in second place with about 6.2 billion, and bottlenose dolphins are in third with about 5.8 billion.

An alien biologist visiting from a distant planet might look at the remarkable similarities in our physiology and conclude that chimpanzees would live pretty much as humans do, only more simply.

But there's something definitively, well, *human* about us.

Chimpanzees and dolphins live pretty much as they did 100,000 years ago, so far as we can tell. Not so *Homo sapiens*. Until just 20,000 or 30,000 years ago, the evidence suggests, humans lived as the animals live, browsing for fruit, nuts, small prey and carrion. But we were different. We had technology.

The earliest stone tools belonging to the ancestors of Homo sapiens appear to be about 3.4 million years old.[25] They were simple: rocks chipped to create sharp edges. For a long time that was the limit of human technology.[26] Somewhere along the line we learned to attach stone points to wooden shafts, inventing the spear and the arrow. It appears that technology progressed very, very slowly for a very, very long time. Humanity didn't make any big lifestyle changes, so far as we can tell from the archaeological record, until about 40,000 years ago when we started wearing jewelry, painting on cave walls and playing little flutes made of bone.

There is, of course, no way of knowing what the first flute-playing, necklace-wearing cave-dweller was thinking, but based on our knowledge of human nature an informed person can guess at the sequence of thought that led to the acceleration of human technological development.

We first migrated out of Africa about 10,000 years before we had flutes, necklaces or, as far as we can tell, clothes. We discovered that most of the world was relatively cold. Or very cold. You can't wander very far north of the Mediterranean Sea naked, on foot, before winter makes its frigid potential known. Europe is more enjoyable in December if you grow a nice coat of fur, or make one. For us, technology was the answer. No trace of the first human clothing has been found, but we can guess that the earliest *Homo sapiens* immigrants to move north invented the first suit.

The next thing you know we needed matching belts and handbags.

It seems there were already humans living in Europe when we, *Homo sapiens*, arrived from the south. *Homo neanderthalensis*, Neanderthals, had lived in Europe for about 100,000 years before we arrived and were, evidently, comfortable and successful in the cold, dark forests of the northern continents. Neanderthal brains were just as large, possibly larger, than ours. For a long time anthropologists thought the Neanderthals were our ancestors but recent DNA studies indicate that they were probably a completely separate species very like us[27] but adapted to life in the north. It seems probable, based on the DNA evidence, that the two species of human rarely interbred. Africans carry no Neanderthal DNA. In northern races, between 1 percent and 4 percent of a person's genes might have come from Neanderthals[28]. Neanderthals were about our height, but much stronger. Based on their heavy bone structure, scientists think they might have been twice as strong as today's professional football players. They were almost exclusively carnivorous, while we Homo sapiens were more omnivorous.[29]

The Neanderthals disappeared about 30,000 years ago. Scientists debate the cause of their extinction but it seems pretty likely that we either out-competed them for resources or wiped them out in interspecies conflict. This is a controversial topic. However, our technological superiority to the Neanderthals is not so controversial. Not long before the disappearance of the Neanderthals archaeologists have documented our species' "Great Leap Forward[30]," in which we replaced our old tools with a bunch of new and improved models. Neanderthal technology did not change over the same time period, so far as the scientists can tell. Where we can separate contemporaneous *Homo sapiens* artifacts from Neanderthal artifacts, we find that *Homo sapiens* had more varied, highly developed and destructive technology at their disposal.

Needless to say human beings have killed each other by the millions since the disappearance of the Neanderthals. With each generation we wage war in more inventive and devastating ways. The destructive power of our technology advances in step with its redemptive power.

The archaeological evidence combined with the more recent historical record indicates that technology was *Homo sapiens'* ticket out of Africa and that, when we encountered a strong, competitive human species in Europe and western Asia we characteristically went about protecting our expanding interests using superior technology.

Our expansion has always been supported by technology and pragmatic violence. North America saw mass extinctions of most of its large mammals soon after *Homo sapiens* populated the continent 12,000 to 15,000 years ago.[31] The continent lost five species of horse (no native American horse species survived); camels (no species survived); several elephant-like creatures including mastodons and mammoths (no species survived); North American llamas (ditto), lions and cheetahs (ditto and ditto); two types of deer; three types of antelope; a giant moose; two species of oxen similar to the Arctic musk ox; a giant beaver; all four species of ground sloth; a large condor-like bird called a teratorn; giant armadillos as large as automobiles called glyptodonts and a smaller relative called pampatheres; two types of giant bear; both types of saber-toothed cats; and several large pig-like species including giant peccaries and North American tapirs[32]. What all these creatures had in common is that they were either good to eat and vulnerable to our weapons, or they were competitive and/or dangerous to humans. The Clovis People who populated North America at the time were hunters. They are known to us mainly through their stone arrowheads and spear points left behind for archaeologists to find[33].

Most of our inventions are more benign than the spear and the arrow. The wheel provides a popular example of our ingenuity. Since we learned to walk upright, our hands had been available to carry things. Since we could carry objects for long distances, we could use technology more effectively. A chimpanzee dependent on all four limbs for mobility cannot effectively carry much stuff, and so technology is less valuable to the chimp. We can use technology effectively because we can move with it.

The wheel allowed us to carry much more.

The earliest depictions of people using wheels date to about 3,500 years BC, from some Polish pottery picturing a wagon[34]. It was probably invented a thousand years earlier. Wheeled vehicles spread rapidly across the civilized parts of Europe and Africa, judging by the archaeological record.

Among the Romans' technological advantages that helped them conquer other countries were water wheels, improved wagons and speedy, nimble chariots. The people of Australia and the Americas didn't get the wheel until Europeans brought it to their continents. Without the wheel or the associated technologies related to horsepower, the Native Americans and aboriginal Australians were at a distinct technological disadvantage to the interlopers. And the interlopers more or less took over.

Technological change does not progress evenly across history. We've witnessed the sudden, rapid improvement of information technology during our own lifetimes. Today's cell phone harnesses capabilities that would have exceeded the powers of world-class supercomputers 30 years ago. But ours is not the first period of rapid technological advancement. Similar spurts of ingenious creativity have occurred throughout history. The chain-driven "safety bicycle" was invented around 1885[35]. The modern automobile appeared at almost the same time.[36] The Wright Brothers took flight over the dunes at Kitty Hawk less than 20 years later and the first airline flew with passengers aboard within a dozen years or so[37].

In 30 years mobile humanity went from the invention of the modern bicycle to airline travel.

Across our panoramic past human beings have used technology to expand around the globe and exploit its resources with growing ingenuity. We've also killed each other more or less continuously in battles over territory, resources and ideas.

If humanity continued that pattern of expansion and conflict, tomorrow's crowded planet might be a very unpleasant place. Human history gives us plenty of evidence to support a pessimistic outlook.

But history also gives us plenty of reason for optimism. On the humble foundation of skin clothing and bone jewelry we have built a wondrous technological superstructure to support ongoing innovation.

The human intellect is capable of fostering rapid technological change, and human beings are also capable of rapid changes of heart. Until 1920 American women were not allowed to vote in U.S. elections, nor could they participate in most democracies around the world before the 20th century. Fifty years ago African Americans were relegated to separate water fountains, restrooms and schools across the southeastern United States. Just a few decades later, the citizens of the United States elected an African American president.

Human cultural norms and our consensus definitions of fairness can, apparently, turn on the proverbial dime. And we don't always wait for crisis to change our minds. The abolition of slavery and the endorsement of equal rights for women and minorities were introduced to our society as mere ideas. And those ideas changed our society.

The Bishnois, a Hindu sect residing in the deserts of northwestern India, have lived for 500 years according to a strict set of principles designed to protect their environment and the living things that share it.[38] "Bishnoi" means "29" in the local dialect. The sect follows a set of 29 specific rules and they adopt "Bishnoi" as their surname. Their rules are both specific, as in, "Do Not Cut Green Trees," and general, "Be Compassionate to All Living Things." Ingeniously, they have designed a lifestyle around environmental protection. The 600,000 Bishnois build their homes of mud and thatch their roofs with a plant that no local animals eat. They avoid using electricity, automobiles or plastic. They farm and sell simple arts and crafts. They've maintained their simple lifestyle in modern India's booming economy with remarkable ingenuity; ingenuity employed in the pursuit of an ideal.

So far, as a species, humanity has mainly worked on its expansion. That's been our big project. Our innovations have made possible a rapid expansion in the quantity of human life on earth. But the same technological foundation is used, with equal facility, to improve and sustain the quality of human life. Just as the wheel, the internal-combustion engine and the computer have carried us across every continent and into outer space; our knowledge and imagination provide us with health, comfort and myriad sources of joy. For our quality of life, contemporary society owes a lot to modern sewage treatment, aspirin, indoor plumbing and, arguably, the Internet.

Today humanity tends to focus on its traditional agenda, creating more energy and more food. We've demonstrated our talent for those projects and we enjoy exercising our ingenuity in familiar ways. The evidence suggests, though, that supporting human expansion won't be our main project in the future. Our ingenuity will be required on some new projects.

The Earthship

*In his 1989 book, "*A Coming of Wizards,*" Michael Reynolds says four mystical beings, which he called "wizards," appeared to him in psychedelic visions and have guided his work. He writes that the wizards taught him to "denormalize" his thinking and tap into his own, personal "energy band."*[39]

The source of his vision was unconventional. The results of his mystical inspiration, however, are practical successes in the real world.

Mike is the inventor of the Earthship, a home design that uses recycled materials and nature's own solar machinery to create snug, self-sufficient houses. When I met him in 1982 he'd already been building Earthships for the better part of a decade. They were scattered across northern New Mexico and southern Colorado.

They weren't like any other houses in the world. Mike had spontaneously, maybe instinctively, set out to solve several different puzzles at the same time. He wanted his houses to be energy self-sufficient, comfortable, beautiful and to re-utilize waste materials in their construction.

Mike half-buried his houses in south-facing hillsides and created their south walls entirely from high-quality insulated glass so they would capture the heating energy of the sun. He built durable, moisture-proof roofs, buried them in insulating soil and planted native plants there so the roof could grow its own summer shade, which naturally thinned and let the sun warm the roof in winter. He invented a unique ventilation system that pulls cool air from outside and pushes overheated air out through skylights during warm weather.

The Earthships needed to store solar energy to be used overnight and during cold, dark weather. Mike designed massive interior walls four feet thick and positioned them in the sunlight streaming in from the south-facing windows. He constructed thick floors of concrete and adobe that soaked up the sunshine all day then radiated warmth at night.

Old tires, bottles and tin cans overflow our landfills, so Mike decided to use them as building materials. The massive interior walls of his Earthships are made from old tires. Other walls use cans and glass bottles like bricks, mortared with concrete or adobe. The "bottle walls" are left exposed so that sunlight shines into some of his whimsical rooms through a mosaic of multicolored bottles and jars he salvages from the dump.

To stay off costly, inefficient utility grids Mike outfitted his houses with photovoltaic solar electricity, wind turbines and water-collection systems. He filtered and reused the water from the sinks and bathtubs in the toilets.

Because creating an Earthship is a labor-intensive process, Mike kept the mechanics simple. He figured very few contractors would sign up to build Earthships. They are effectively handmade. They take a lot of hours. So he developed building techniques for amateurs. Anyone can quickly learn to build a wall from concrete and tin cans or bottles. He invented a method of packing sand inside stacks of used tires that creates massive, stable interior walls. You can master the process in a few hours. Once they're stuccoed they have a beautiful natural shape and they store a lot of thermal energy. In the winter, they exude warmth through the cold night. In summer, they stay cool in the heat of the day.

Built-in planters grow food year-round inside the Earthships. One owner picks bananas in the middle of winter from a tree that sits in the window of an Earthship situated at 7,000 feet elevation in the Rocky Mountains. Some of the Earthships include indoor goldfish ponds.[40]

Mike built several Earthships himself, but soon he was coaching an army of Earthship builders, most of them do-it-yourselfers who wanted to play a personal role in the creation of their own homes. Earthships have been built in every shape and size imaginable from little one-room beer-can bungalows to the late actor Dennis Weaver's multimillion-dollar Earthship estate in Ridgeway, Colorado. Construction of the 8,500-square-foot home reportedly repurposed 3,000 old tires and more than 350,000 discarded aluminum cans.

There are Earthship subdivisions and complexes of Earthship condominiums. Earthships now stand in Jamaica, Mexico, Nicaragua, India, Japan, South America, Europe and Africa. Mike is the subject of a documentary film, "Garbage Warrior," and has been interviewed on every major television network.

Not every Earthship is beautiful, at least not to passers-by. But look in the eyes of the Earthship owner and you'll see an unmistakable glow of enthusiastic affection when they talk about their homes, especially if they built the house themselves. To their owners, even the funkiest Earthships are lovable. And some of them are architectural wonders.

The early prototypes were experimental. Some of them seemed to soak up the cold right out of the earth, and no woodstove would heat them. Others broiled their occupants, summer and winter. Sometimes Mike went back and fixed them with a new idea or two. Sometimes the homeowners sorted the solutions out for themselves.

Still today, nearly 40 years after their invention, they are the cutting edge of residential architecture.

I've ridden up and down dirt roads with Mike, looking at Earthships and listening to him talk about them. Although he was a licensed architect, the history of architecture wasn't interesting to him. Obviously, he didn't operate in any established tradition. He didn't even seem to be very interested in the history of the Earthship, his own creation. Mike talked mostly about the future, a future in which the Earthship philosophy of beauty and efficiency would be a major force in the world. The Earthship was, after all, invented for the future. Mike incubated the contemporary philosophy of "humanitarian design" whose practitioners include people like Nathaniel Corum, designer of hurricane-resistant housing in Haiti, solar homes on the Navajo reservation and the cabin for Plastiki, the yacht made from discarded plastic bottles that sailed across the Pacific ocean. Whether they realize it or not, a whole generation of architects owes its identity, in part, to Mike Reynolds.

You don't see many references to Mike's visiting wizards on any of the thousands of web pages about Earthships these days. Alien visitations obviously don't get a lot of credit for the achievements of today's humanitarian designers or architects. But I keep my copy of A Coming of Wizards *as a reminder that sometimes a visionary needs to "denormalize" how we think about things.*

CHAPTER FIVE

The Power of Invention

The Prius Effect

Executives at the Toyota Motor Company were wrong about the Prius. They seriously underestimated how popular it would be.

When it appeared in 1997 the world's first mass-produced gas-electric hybrid was not recognized as a serious challenge to the conventional internal-combustion engine. Its potential wasn't clear, even to the people in charge of selling it.

About 18,000 sold to Japanese drivers in 1997. A few more hit the Japanese streets in 1998 and 1999. On Earth Day 2000, Toyota announced that the car was on its way to the United States for the first time and the first American drivers stepped into their new hybrid cars in August that year.

In the United States, the Prius was a sensation.

Over the next five years, the only way to get a new Prius in North America was by ordering one in advance from a dealer. The waiting time for a new Prius extended to more than six months. Its popularity was not based on economic necessity. Gas was cheap. In 2000 regular gasoline sold for about $1.30 a gallon and inefficient sport-utility vehicles were in their heyday. Toyota called the first website for Prius buyers the "Pioneer Purchase" site. About 6,000 Americans signed up and got their hands on a Prius that first year, and about 20,000 sold worldwide, most of them in Japan. The next year, 2001, about 29,000 Priuses sold worldwide. By 2007 Toyota was selling 10 times that, 181,000 cars in the United States alone. And people kept putting their names on the waiting lists.

The sales numbers would have been much higher if production had kept pace with demand.

No other fuel-efficient car was nearly as successful. The Toyota Yaris, which gets 80 percent of the Prius fuel mileage and costs about half as much, sold half as many units in 2008. At 2008 fuel prices, you would have to drive your Prius at least 50,000 miles before fuel savings recovered the price difference.

The Honda Civic Hybrid was a dud in comparison to the Prius. Although its price and fuel efficiency were comparable, the Civic Hybrid sold about 20 percent as many units. While Toyota sold 159,000 Priuses in the United States during 2008, Honda sold about 31,000 Civic Hybrids.[41]

The Civic's fuel mileage, price, technology, reliability and overall quality were all comparable to the Prius'. The big difference between the two vehicles was their appearance. The Civic Hybrid looks like any other Civic, except that it has a little "Hybrid" emblem on its trunk lid. The Prius looks like, well, a Prius. It's distinctive. Some call it funny-looking. It's perfectly recognizable from half a mile away.

So why would the Prius outsell the Civic Hybrid by a factor of five to one? Because the Prius is cool. Its wonky design instantaneously became a symbol for environmental awareness and frugality. Driving a Prius projects the driver's identity as a person who cares about the planet and enjoys new technology. The same could be said of the buyers of any hybrid, but the

Prius design projects the driver's identity more effectively. The Prius is conscientious and fun at the same time. So the Prius is cool. The Prius driver is, by association, both conscientious and fun. So the Prius driver is, by association, cool.

The Prius also emphasized the fun of new technology. It featured a large computer screen where the driver, when backing up, could see a wide-angle view from the car's rear bumper. The rest of the time Prius owners could use the same screen to watch elaborate animations illustrating the hybrid technology and reporting fuel efficiency.

Watching Prius drivers you can get the sense that they are enjoying their cars in ways most of us don't. I used to share my commuting schedule with a Prius owner whose driving style mystified me. He never drove the posted speed limit. Generally, he was slower than the traffic and his speed was erratic. One day, I would pass him driving 65 or 70. The next day he'd be dawdling along at 55. One day as I passed him I noticed he wasn't looking at the road. He had his eyes trained on the center of his dashboard, at the Prius information screen. Then I thought I understood why he drove at varying, unusual speeds: He was tracking the car's fuel efficiency and adjusting his pace to see if he could improve his fuel mileage. He was playing the Prius equivalent of a video game.

My friend Fred drives a Prius. Fred is a retired school principal in his seventies. He's politically conservative. He loves BMW motorcycles and he and his wife, Gladys, spend several weeks every year traveling on his immaculate touring bike. When they're not traveling by motorcycle, they drive a Prius. When I was in the car with him, Fred demonstrated how the video camera automatically turned on when he put the Prius in reverse. He pointed out the car's complete silence as it backed out of a parking space and maneuvered around the parking lot on electric power. We got out and he had me touch the cold exhaust pipe.

Fred loves good technology. From his perspective, his car–like his motorcycle–was making a statement about great technology, not environmentalism or politics. Like million of other people from all walks of life, Fred thinks the Prius is cool.

The history of the Prius illustrates an exciting phenomenon we might call the Prius Effect.[42] When a new idea or a piece of technology ignites the human imagination it can spread rapidly. At the dawn of the new millennium when 12-miles-per-gallon sport-utility vehicles ruled the American road, a funny-looking little car with 14-inch wheels (they've increased wheel sizes since then) and a video screen in its dashboard suddenly became one of the most popular automobiles in the United States. Movie stars drove them. Soccer moms wanted them.

Pundits up and down the political spectrum doubt society's capacity to change. It makes us sound wise, I guess, to express skepticism. The Prius Effect suggests that consumers, in general, are more flexible and inventive than most pundits imagine.

The Prius, and the Prius effect, demonstrate how a product can be more successful and have more impact if it answers our queries positively.

It's Beautiful. A bunch of consumers, 2 million or so worldwide, have found the Prius sufficiently beautiful to plunk down their hard-earned cash.

It Creates Abundance. If the Prius uses, on average, two-thirds the gasoline of an average car worldwide, then Priuses are preserving about 303 million gallons of gasoline each year.[43]

It's Fair. Shoppers exercising their power of choice in a very competitive automotive industry have created the Prius Effect and made the Prius a resounding success.

It's Contagious. The Prius is to cars what the Chuck Taylor is to footwear. For a decade it has embodied a wonky sense of cool. As long as we're interested in transportation, efficient, innovative automobiles will demonstrate their value. As long as we're interested in a healthy world, technology that preserves our habitat will change lives and markets.

Conscious Capitalism

In his 2009 book, *Be the Solution: How Entrepreneurs and Conscious Capitalists Can Solve All the World's Problems*, Michael Strong makes two points no human being should ignore.

1. **The entrepreneurial spirit is one of the most powerful forces, maybe THE most powerful force, for creativity and innovation in human society. Free enterprise liberates that spirit.**
2. **Human endeavors gain energy from a consciousness that incorporates the good of humanity and the health of the planet. Conscious capitalists have an advantage over their competitors.**

The book offers compelling evidence for entrepreneurism's ability to solve problems and change society. Two chapters are written by John Mackey, founder of Whole Foods Market and, with Strong, cofounder of C3, a nonprofit dedicated to "cultivating conscious capitalists." Mackey's energy and consciousness were instrumental in developing a little Texas health-foods store into an $8 billion Fortune 500 company in just a couple of decades[44].

Another chapter is contributed by Muhammad Yunus, the Nobel laureate economist who started the Grameen Bank when he loaned $27 to 42 poor Bangladeshis in 1976, effectively inventing "microfinance." Based on the model he invented, it's estimated that more than 110 million entrepreneurs worldwide build their bootstrap businesses each year with "microloans".[45]

A former educator, Strong uses his experience of starting a charter school in New Mexico as an example. Rural New Mexico is not known for high-quality public education. (Only about 20 percent of the students in the New Mexico district I attended until eighth grade achieve "proficiency" in science, math and social studies.)[46] An administrator from the University of New Mexico told Strong that students in his region were "not capable of passing AP (Advanced Placement) courses."

The second year Strong's Moreno Valley High School was open, it ranked in the top 150 schools in the nation for the proportion of its students enrolled in AP courses. In its third year it was 36th on that list, and its passing rate for standardized AP tests was double the national average[47].

Mackey, Yunus and Strong all tell the story of how human energy expands in an environment where people visualize successful outcomes and engage personally in creating those outcomes:

Mackey and his colleagues, thousands of whom are also shareholders in Whole Foods Market, created a dominant grocery chain based on the idea that people wanted healthy food and other conscientious products available in a refined retail environment.

Yunus dramatically changed the lives of hundreds of millions of the world's poorest people, simply by trusting them to use his loans constructively and pay them back on time. At his own bank alone, he's lent about 8 million[48] very poor people almost $9 billion. The default rate has been around 1 percent.[49] As a comparison, the default rate for business loans guaranteed by the U.S. Small Business Administration was 2.4 percent in

2004 and increased every year after until 2008, when it was about 12 percent.[50] In February 2010, the default rate on all office properties, retail properties, hotels and industrial properties in the United States was almost 4 percent.[51] According to Moody's Investor Service, the cumulative default rates for all rated companies between 1983 and 1998, a relatively prosperous period, was 8.64 percent, and even the best "investment-grade" loans to corporations defaulted at a rate of 1.47 percent.[52]

In other words, it might be safer to lend $20 to each of a million small-scale entrepreneurs living in poverty than it is to lend $20 million to a big public company in a wealthy nation.

Of course we don't need to go to Bangladesh to see the transforming power of entrepreneurialism.

THE PICKENS PLAN

T. Boone Pickens is the embodiment of the Texas oil tycoon. Worth about $3 billion, according to *Forbes* magazine, he's militantly conservative Republican with a big house in Dallas' prestigious Preston Hollow neighborhood and an enormous ranch in the Texas panhandle, to which he commutes on weekends in a private jet.

He's also, arguably, the world's leading advocate for wind energy.

In 2008, just a couple of months after his 80th birthday, Pickens published "The Pickens Plan" and committed $58 million of his own money to promote it.[53] The plan proposes the rapid development of giant wind farms across the central plains of North America specifically to replace the electricity we are currently generating with natural gas. The natural gas would then be used, in the Pickens vision, to fuel clean, efficient transportation. The then-80-year-old Texan billionaire made dozens of public appearances in 2008 across the United States and was interviewed by reporters in every major news medium. His website for the plan, *www.pickensplan.com*, is a masterful demonstration of the power of the digital media with a cute little animated Boone preaching about our dependence on foreign oil. Cute little animated wind turbines spin in the background. The blog is called "The Daily Pickens." The site distributes software widgets that help users reduce their own energy consumption and influence their lawmakers.

With a click, visitors can join local Pickens Plan groups, take a pledge supporting the plan, join a "virtual march" in support of the plan, contact lawmakers through email and social networks and–wow–chart their own contributions as plan supporters by establishing a "push.pickensplan.com" account, effectively grading their own commitment.

The "Boone Cam" has recorded hundreds of *cinema verite* encounters between Pickens and his famous supporters, including Sarah Palin and Arnold Schwarzenegger. Pickens shows himself traveling to an appearance on the talk show, *The View*, with Barbara Walters and Whoopi Goldberg. Pickens seems excited about sharing the stage with Barbara and Whoopi. "I think we reach every audience. And the reason we do is because, one, that they see me as a guy who's sincere about what he's doing… They have confidence in what I'm talking about. If I'm seen as an honest, sincere guy and I'm pushing something that's good for America, then I'm going to get those women with me."

To push his plan, Pickens is conspicuously reaching out to people who hadn't previously appeared on his dance card. The revolving quotes at the top of the Pickens Plan homepage are from people such as President Barack Obama and Senator

Harry Reid, a Democrat who called Pickens his "mortal enemy" when Pickens played an instrumental role in defeating Democratic presidential candidate John Kerry.

In *Bloomberg Markets* magazine's coverage of the National Clean Energy Summit in October 2009 Reid says, "I started taking missionary lessons from the group supporting T. Boone Pickens... I now belong to the Pickens church. He's been a good friend and a real visionary..."[54]

Why are Harry Reid and Whoopi Goldberg publicly giving their love to a swaggering, swashbuckling energy tycoon? Pickens is, after all, protecting his own investments in wind power. His new role as an environmental visionary is an outgrowth of his new business as a wind-farm developer. The governmental support he is drumming up may eventually provide tax dollars to build the energy grids that are critical to his success. He is raising awareness so he can use tax dollars to support his own ventures.

The Pickens Plan is a self-serving marketing effort to support the Pickens businesses. But in the process of building his public-relations machine T. Boone Pickens has given new legitimacy to wind power. By giving renewable energy a Texas drawl and a patriotic tattoo, Pickens has brought wind energy's practical benefits to light for tens of millions of skeptical Americans.

Like the Toyota Prius, T. Boone Pickens is pragmatic and technologically adept. He describes environmental benefits in practical terms that the average person can understand. Most remarkably, he's short-circuited the tribal politics that tend to separate "tree-hugging environmentalists" from the citizens of the "conservative heartland." In the Pickens Plan, and in the real world, wind power is good for the earth, promotes national security and enhances the U.S. economy. Millions of acres of prairie could be converted from marginally profitable farmland to highly productive power generators. Farmers and ranchers can still grow food around the bases of the turbine towers. We haven't finished measuring every environmental impact of large-scale wind power (there's some legitimate concern about the effects on bird populations), but so far it looks like an environmental and economic winner. Worldwide humanity doubled its wind power capacity to about 121,000 megawatts between 2005 and 2008, and about 1.5 percent of electricity consumed worldwide is generated by wind power, including 19 percent of Denmark's power, 11 percent of Spain and Portugal's and 7 percent of Germany's.[55] In Italy, more than 800 small towns have turned wind power into an economic-development opportunity, generating their own power and selling their surpluses to utility companies.[56] Texas, all by itself, has more wind-power capacity than all but five countries worldwide. Think about the added potential of New Mexico, Colorado, Kansas, Nebraska, Wyoming, Montana and the Dakotas and you begin to get a sense of proportion. If Americans had electric transportation, it's conceivable that the Great Plains could supply all North America's energy through giant wind-power plantations.

"This is a global game-changer," as Boone has said.[57] "It's a no-brainer."

It's Beautiful. Not everyone thinks Pickens or his windmills are beautiful, but in comparison with the strip mines and smokestacks they will replace wind farms are scenic enhancements.

It Creates Abundance. Energy from the wind, harnessed by the right technology will be there as long as it's needed. As engineers learn more about transmission, turbines and blades, our technology will only get more efficient.

It's Fair. Pickens was a middle-class kid who has made, and lost, several fortunes over the course of a flamboyant entrepreneurial career by working hard and gambling his winnings on new business ventures. His latest efforts are meant to benefit his business, but the whole planet could benefit as a result.

It's Contagious. The Pickens organization has plugged in all the available "viral" marketing machines, and activists from all over the political spectrum are publicly supportive. Renewable energy, produced in the country where it is used, is a catchy idea. And the Pickens Plan could provide opportunities for hundreds of thousands of enterprising businesspersons up and down North America's Great Plains for centuries into the future, not to mention new opportunities around the world if it is copied in other countries.

Active Passive

If wind-power is a no-brainer, what about passive solar power? Sunlight is ubiquitous, clean, renewable and free. Residential heating requirements could be cut dramatically simply by capturing the solar energy that lands naturally on our houses. Imagine if all new homes in temperate and cold climates had a row of tall, insulated windows on their solar exposure (the south side, if the home is north of the equator) alongside a heat-absorbing concrete floor in the room with the windows. All day long the sunlight warms the house and heats up the concrete. At night the concrete radiates warmth.

The basics of passive solar architecture are simple.[58] First, the building needs what the engineers call an "aperture" through which the sun can shine–in other words, a window. If the sun shines into a window in your home or office, then you have a passive solar collector.

Second, to store some of that solar energy you need an "absorber," some "thermal mass" that can be heated by the sun. Dense substances like stone, concrete or adobe store thermal energy. Sometimes a water tank is used as a storage device with the added benefit of being able to distribute warmth through the plumbing to where it's needed.

Less dense materials like wood or carpet can't store heat effectively.

For a building to be warmed by passive solar energy there needs to be some way of distributing the heat through the house. In renegade architect Mike Reynolds' Earthships, nearly every room has its own solar exposure and thermal mass, so there's no distribution problem. In more complex structures, fans, ducts and blowers may be used to circulate warm air.

And passive solar buildings need some control mechanism to regulate their temperature, open windows, broad eaves that block the summer sun and insulated window shades.

It's fun to think about homes heated entirely by the sun, but the larger benefit today could come from a tiny alteration in the way developers think about site design and construction so millions of new houses could derive a small part of their energy directly from the sun. Very minor changes can orient buildings more efficiently and place some thermal mass in the sunlight. Every calorie of solar energy captured on a cool day preserves a calorie of some other fuel. If all our new construction were designed with solar energy in mind, imagine the global benefit. The reduction in energy consumption and carbon emissions are incalculable, but they would be enormous.

One intriguing thing about passive solar energy is that it's not an industrial energy source. There's no opportunity for Boone Pickens to build giant passive-solar generators. Passive solar energy is universally available but can only be harvested one building at a time. It's embarrassingly underutilized today, not for lack of financing, technology or infrastructure, but for lack of recognition. It only needs a little human awareness to make it one of the world's most important sources of household heat.

Today most new homes are sited without any reference to solar energy at all. A few builders are catching on, however, and making the simple adjustments that turn new houses into solar collectors. They are adding big insulated windows, facing them toward the sun and painting their concrete floors in energy-absorbing dark colors. Homeowners are pouring concrete pads under their new sunrooms so they can harvest free heat from nature, in the simplest way possible.

It's Beautiful. Sunshine.

It Defines Abundance.

It's Fair. Nearly every house on the planet has some access to free solar energy.

It's Contagious. Available everywhere! Free today!

PHOTOVOLTAICS

The fastest-growing energy technology in the world is also solar, but it's very unlike passive solar. Photovoltaic solar collectors are high-tech devices that capture solar energy in a supremely adaptable and portable form. Photovoltaic panels and films, made mostly from silicon, convert sunlight into electricity. The photons in sunlight, hitting a collector, create free electrons that can be siphoned off as electrical current. Beginning in the early 2000s, worldwide production of photovoltaics had been doubling every two years until 2008 when the rate of growth suddenly accelerated, more than doubling the global photovoltaic generating capacity in just one year.[59]

At the end of 2008 it was estimated that photovoltaics

were generating about 15,000 megawatts of energy worldwide, enough to provide about 4 million average U.S. homes with all the electricity they need, and photovoltaic expansion continues to accelerate.

Most photovoltaic installations are small, designed mainly to supply a single building, or even a single device, like my electric fences or the little pump on our household solar-hot-water system. But solar power stations are proliferating. A single new photovoltaic power plant, Topaz Solar Farm, is proposed to cover 9.5 square miles in central California near San Luis Obispo. Designed with a 550-megawatt capacity (the total electricity needs of about 150,000 North American homes), is scheduled to begin generating electricity in 2011.[60] Before Topaz Solar Farm, the largest photovoltaic generator in the country, the DeSoto Energy Center in Florida, had a capacity of just 25 megawatts. The largest in the world was the 60-megawatt Olmedilla Photovoltaic Park in Spain,[61] so the Topaz plant will set a new standard 9 times larger.

New technology that concentrates solar energy is likely to inspire construction of solar power plants more productive and more efficient by several orders of magnitude in coming years. Think about the power of a beam of sunlight focused through a magnifying glass. In a few seconds, it can light paper on fire. Concentrated solar energy can be used to multiply the power of a photovoltaic array, or to heat water and create steam to drive generating turbines. Some power stations set up their solar collectors on swivels to track the sun. The German Aerospace Center reported that concentrated solar power should be as cheap as power from coal or natural gas by 2015.[62]

In the autumn of 2010 two giant new California solar power plants were approved for construction. The 6,000-acre, 709-megawatt "Tessera" project in the Imperial Valley uses large reflective dishes to concentrate solar energy to heat hydrogen gas that drives a generator. [63][64] Chevron Energy Solutions' project is a photovoltaic installation on 422 acres in the Lucerne Valley near San Bernardino. Together, the two plants are expected to generate enough electricity to power more than 560,000 homes.

The manufacturing of photovoltaics is already a big business, getting bigger rapidly. Industry sources estimated the size of the industry at about $30 billion in 2009, expected to be $70 billion by 2013.[65] Shi Zhengrong, one of the richest new billionaires in China, made his fortune manufacturing photovoltaics.[66]

Some property owners get free photovoltaic systems thanks to "power-purchase agreements," under which an investor buys the panels and installs them. The property owner pays nothing up front, but continues paying for the electricity generated by the panels until the equipment is paid off. The investor may acquire low-cost energy from the new installation as part of the deal. Apartment buildings in California are getting solar power through a power-purchase agreement organized by the California Solar Initiative. The city of Berkeley, California, is evaluating a similar program, which offers homeowners solar installations paid for, over 20 years, through a special property tax.[67] The new tax is painless, since the property owners are saving as much on their utility bills as they are paying in new tax. About 75 percent of commercial photovoltaics are installed with the help of some kind of power-purchase agreement.[68]

And the technology is getting better. So-called "thin-film" photovoltaics are manufactured on a flexible surface that adheres directly to a metal roof. The electronics fit neatly under a cap that runs along the peak of the roof and the whole apparatus looks integrated and natural.

Among the most intriguing new developments in photovoltaics are transparent collectors that can be integrated into windows. This technology could turn everyday objects into solar power plants. Japanese engineers have developed transparent collectors that generate electricity from ultraviolet light, allowing light in the visible spectrum to pass right through. The implications are astonishing. Imagine transparent solar films in the sunroofs of cars or the windows of skyscrapers. Every outdoor surface is a potential source of electricity. Glass buildings could power their own air conditioners themselves. Electric vehicles, parked outside, could charge their own batteries.[69]

A U.S. company called Covalent Solar makes glass that contains subtle, nearly invisible dyes that concentrate and deflect solar energy to photovoltaics in the frame of a window. Windows and skylights can become solar collectors, seamlessly integrated into a building or vehicle.[70]

And because the dyes in the glass concentrate the energy, less surface area is necessary to generate a given amount of electricity.

When cars and buildings are coated with collectors, there's less need of heavy, inefficient and toxic batteries. Electricity can be generated where and when we need it.

The sun is the fundamental source of nearly all our energy: the fuel human beings burn and the food we eat. Life exists here thanks largely to our precise proximity to the sun, neither too close nor too far away. The existence of life on earth is product of either divine predestination or an eloquent accident. Our planet orbits just close enough to an energy source of exactly the right size to support carbon-based life forms like us. The sun's energy is consistent, predictable and abundant, more than adequate to provide all our energy needs.

It's Beautiful. At least the sunlight is. And large-scale photovoltaic developments like to be sited on flat, barren deserts. Copacetic.

It Creates Abundance. That old sun just keeps on shining!

It is a little inconvenient, of course, that the sun doesn't shine at night, when one's particular location is on the far side of the planet. Like wind energy, the solar energy source would have to be described as "intermittent."

It's Fair. Photovoltaics take a minimum of natural resources to produce energy quietly and unobtrusively. Solar panels have very long lifespans, so once they are installed they are cheap to maintain.

It's Contagious. Since most of the expenses associated with construction are related to labor costs, developing nations actually have an economic edge in photovoltaic development. It is spreading around the world.

Geothermal

Ironically, our pursuit of fossil fuels has brought us closer to a much larger, more sustainable source of energy. The solid rock and soil on which we humans live our lives is essentially a thin skin of cool solids on top of a big ball of extremely hot molten rock. On the continents, the earth's solid "crust" is less than 20 miles deep.[71] At the bottom edge of the crust the temperature of the rock is at least 1,000 degrees Fahrenheit.[72] Deeper, it just gets hotter. As we drill for oil and gas, we come closer and closer to an energy source that makes our tiny reservoir of fossil fuels look pathetic in comparison.

Most of that heat is retained from when the planet was born as a glob of molten rock. Heat is also generated by the decay of radioactive minerals spread throughout the planet's interior and friction generated by the natural movement of liquid rock.[73] It appears these phenomena will keep on generating heat for billions of years.

Twenty miles is not far to drive in a car, but it's a long way to drill through solid rock. That's the main reason geothermal energy isn't a primary source of fuel, yet.

The crust of the earth is not so thick everywhere, however. The floors of our deepest oceans may be only a couple of miles from the outer mantle of 1,000-degree rock. Oil and gas wells are often that deep, although the energy companies can't yet drill them in the extreme pressure at the bottom of the deep ocean under 12,000 feet of water[74]. Geothermal energy is more accessible in places along the edges of tectonic plates where the earth's crust is much thinner. Sometimes the plates separate and allow molten rock to flow out on the surface from volcanoes. Scalding steam shoots from geysers where cool surface water makes contact with the planet's hot interior at Old Faithful in Yellowstone National Park, for instance or *El Tatio* ("Old Granddad") in Chile. (When we humanize geothermal energy we tend to give it identities that are venerable and reliable.) The Valley of Geysers on Russia's Kamchatka Peninsula offers abundant evidence of the scale and power of geothermal energy resources.

The total heat stored in the earth's interior is hundreds of thousands of times greater than our most aggressive projections of our power needs. The energy under our feet dwarfs our wildest ambitions for power consumption. If technology could efficiently harness geothermal energy to produce steam and drive turbines, every building, vehicle and machine on earth could be powered forever by geothermally generated electricity.

Modest applications of geothermal power are already in use in millions of buildings around the world. A few of them draw hot air or steam directly from the earth. Where very hot geothermal energy is near the surface–in Iceland, for instance–hot groundwater can be piped into radiators and swimming pools. Reykjavik is warmed by hot groundwater pumped through radiators and circulated below the streets to keep them free of ice and snow.[75]

Of course that sort of obvious geothermal resource isn't available in most locales. Ground-source geothermal pumps, on the other hand, are useful almost everywhere. They push air or liquids through underground grids or coils to warm or cool a building from season to season. Because the underground temperature is stable year-round, generally warmer than the external temperature in winter and cooler in summer, ground-source heat pumps save some of the energy that furnaces and air conditioners use in heating or cooling. Effectively, they use underground temperatures to cool a building in summer and to heat it in winter.

Ground-source geothermal works anywhere you might want the inside of your home to be warmer or cooler than the outside. In other words, anywhere people heat or cool buildings ground-source geothermal can reduce the cost. In the best locations, it can reduce the consumption of energy for heating and cooling by 75 percent. Chances are there's someone in your neighborhood already reducing the energy bill with a ground-source system. As of 2010, there were probably about 2 million systems installed worldwide.[76] The U.S. Department of Energy estimates that at least 50,000 new ground-source systems are installed in the country each year.[77]

The biggest immediate opportunities in large-scale geothermal energy development involve tapping high-energy geothermal sources to produce steam that drives electric turbines. Iceland, El Salvador, Kenya, the Philippines and Costa Rica, all nations with active volcanoes, already get more than 15 percent of their electricity from geothermal generating stations.[78] The largest geothermal power plant in the world is in North America and is also one of the oldest. Pacific Gas and Electric built

The Geysers power field in Northern California in 1960. The network of 18 active generators has a total capacity of about 1,500 megawatts[79] and supplies electricity to five surrounding counties, providing about 60 percent of the power needed in the coastal region between the Golden Gate Bridge and the Oregon border.[80]

The development of geothermal electric generation–or the lack of development–illustrates our lack of vision when it comes to energy policy. Geothermal energy is virtually limitless. The generation machinery may need to be replaced but the planetary furnace just keeps on burning. Massive amounts of power can be generated from a central plant with minimal disruption to the surrounding environment and it efficiently converts to electricity, the most portable, clean and convenient of our energy sources.

Geothermal power plants are, however, in the vernacular of today's energy policy, "capital intensive." That means they require a larger initial investment than coal-fired power plants. The geothermal plant takes longer to pay off its construction costs.

The two elements in any financial equation are time and money. If the calculation changes the way time is valued, the solutions are different. We want our investments to pay off quickly, hopefully in a few years, certainly during our own lifetimes. But if the financial equation puts more value on permanence, then geothermal looks more attractive. If permanence is given its proper value the geothermal power plant may prove itself to be a much better investment than its coal-fired competitors.

Historically we've done a poor job of evaluating the environmental costs of burning fossil fuels. Those costs are usually "external" to the economic evaluations that direct new investments. In other words, the economic models that drive new investment don't acknowledge the environmental costs of burning fossil fuels because they don't have to be paid until long after current investments return their dividends. As society contemplates the costs of reclaiming old strip mines or cleaning up toxic spills economists generally don't go back and apply those costs to the fossil-fuel economy of ages past, so our calculations also fail to apply those costs accurately when we contemplate new decisions about what kind of power plant to build next.

If, by burning fossil fuels, humanity is altering the climate in ways that will reduce agricultural productivity or displace large numbers of human beings 20 years from now, then the costs of those consequences should be added into the financial equations that direct decision-making today. If a new coal-fired power plant or a new fleet of SUVs will contribute, materially, to the reduction in worldwide agricultural productivity a decade later then the costs of that damage should be added to the cost of the plant or the cost of the car.

If the United States needs a strong military in part to protect our supply lines of energy from foreign countries shouldn't a portion of our military spending be incorporated into the cost of our fuel?

Imagine the implications.

Yes, it costs a lot more to build a geothermal electric plant than it does to build one that burns coal. But have the costs and benefits been accurately measured? A hundred years from now when coal will, presumably, be more scarce and more expensive the geothermal furnace will be burning as hot and bright as ever.

Even if the science on climate change is incomplete, shouldn't the potential costs of burning more fossil fuels be taken into account? Even if there's only, let's say, a 50/50 chance that burning fossil fuels is causing climate change, shouldn't there be an economic equation that takes that possibility into account? How much is it worth to take that risk?

It's time to recalculate the value of geothermal power, and a lot of other things.

It's Beautiful. As long as we're careful about where and how we build. As long as we're careful about where and how we build geothermal power plants they can help preserve the environment and the landscape.

It Creates Abundance. The earth's energy is absurdly plentiful and, for all intents and purposes, permanently so.

It's Fair. Geothermal development doesn't diminish the power source, and it doesn't impose the environmental damage caused by one nation's power needs on another nation.

It's Contagious. Once technology taps into the planet's big, permanent fireplace, it will keep providing energy virtually forever. It's accessible from every continent. We're accustomed to being dependent on fossil fuel, a dependency that has acted as sort of an inoculation against new sources of industrial-scale power. But we're more susceptible to new alternatives every day.

The Smart Grid

Our current power grids are dumb.

They are great examples of 20th-century technology, but they should get much better.

We have the technology today to make our power grid more sustainable, cleaner, more robust and more reliable just by replacing old-fashioned metering with "smart-metering"[81] and agreeing to pay enterprising power consumers for generating some of their own electricity.

Today, almost all our electricity is distributed from power plants through the power grid to customers. The electricity only flows one way. The utility generates the power, which flows through wires to homes and businesses. The homes and businesses use the power. The utility measures how much power its customers use, and sends us the bills.

The new, smarter grid allows every power customer to become a power generator as well as a power consumer. The customer and the utility are interconnected. "Smart meters" measure the power flowing both directions and the utility compensates the customers for their contributions to the power supply.

Where "net metering" is available, utilities measure the customer's "net" power usage, that is, the amount the customer uses minus the amount the customer produces. If you can generate some of your own electricity with photovoltaics, wind or any other power source, the utility buys it from you and sells it to other customers nearby.

When electricity is distributed across long distances, some of the power is lost in the process. About 6 percent of the power generated in the United States is lost to transmission inefficiencies.[82] If utilities empower individuals to produce their own power and pay them for it, the electricity is distributed more efficiently because it doesn't have to travel as far.

The utility customer gets compensated for the power, the utility gets a new, inexpensive power source and the grid becomes more reliable and efficient.

Our old-fashioned grid is unnecessarily vulnerable to weather and incompetence. When things go wrong, homes and businesses can go without power for days or weeks. On a hot afternoon in August 2003, a technician in Ohio forgot to restart a computer program after a routine procedure. Then maintenance problems shut down a nearby power plant and some power lines sagged into trees nearby in Walton Hills and Parma, Ohio. Within hours, 55 million people in the United States and Canada were without power.[83] Every year hundreds of thousands of North Americans experience temporary power outages due to weather. Scientists in 2005 estimated that power outages cost the United States about $80 billion a year, on average.[84]

The principal method for preventing outages is to produce surplus electricity so that peak demand doesn't stress the system. That's costly, both for the utility customers and for the environment, unless that electricity is being generated by utilities, individuals and businesses using clean, renewable energy sources. The utility can acquire that power at an attractive price, and it doesn't have to plow billions of dollars into new generation facilities.

Our power grids are getting smarter. Most U.S. states now have laws that authorize net metering. Part of the grid used net metering in at least 35 states at the time of this writing[85]. Unfortunately, implementation of net metering and smart meters has been relatively slow. Consumer demand may accelerate the process in the near future, and consumers will probably open new pricing negotiations with the utilities as well.

Imagine a power grid that includes millions of individual generators, photovoltaic panels, wind turbines, big coal plants, natural gas cogenerators, etc. interconnected with smart meters, paying on a net-metered basis and supporting each other. On the long days of midsummer when North American demand for electricity peaks, the photovoltaics are also generating more electricity. When overgrown trees interrupt the power supply from a coal plant in Ohio, wind power from Pennsylvania takes up some of the slack.

Photovoltaics and wind energy were pioneered by independent spirits who wanted to live "off the grid." The most negative aspect of an off-the-grid system is the necessity of storing electricity in batteries, an expensive, toxic and inefficient technology. Interconnection with a smart grid allows individuals and businesses to benefit from generating their own power without the necessity of storing it in batteries.

And our supply of electricity becomes more reliable and secure when the big industrial generators are supplemented by thousands-or millions-of small independent producers. In other words, we reduce risks when we don't put all our eggs in one basket.

David Gelbaum is one of the country's most influential advocates for smarter grids. He's a successful investor and generous philanthropist whose attention has lately been trained on green technology and wilderness preservation.[86] Since 2002 he's invested about $500 million in about 40 different clean-technology companies, including renewable energy and smart-grid-technology companies. At the same time he's given almost as much money to environmental charities, including $250 million to the Wildlands Conservancy, a land trust he co-founded to preserve wilderness in California and to promote "distributed generation," that is, decentralized small generators spread widely across the smart grid. He's betting a lot of money on the success of the smart grid.

Unfortunately, utilities have hampered efforts to implement net metering on a large scale. Most states limit the amount of power an independent generator can sell to the grid, even where net metering is available. In most places, consumers are pushing their utilities and governments to liberate the utility grid, so it can get smarter.

It's Beautiful. Or it can be so long as we pay attention. Fewer high-voltage transmission lines will be necessary. And fewer smokestacks.

It Creates Abundance. Obviously. A billion generators is better than one.

It's Fair. On the Smart Grid, utilities and customers are partners. Everyone is a buyer. Everyone is a seller. The utilities control the economics, of course, and fair policies obviously have to be renegotiated.

It's Contagious. Every utility grid in the world can be a smart grid. Presumably, with new technology, grids will only get smarter over time. Pretty soon, power customers just won't put up with stupid grids.

Roots Agriculture

At first glance George Siemon and Doc Hatfield don't appear to have a whole lot in common. Siemon has the look of a Berkeley anthropologist. He wears wire-rimmed glasses and grows his hair long. Hatfield is an Oregon rancher straight from central casting: tall, lean and dressed for the part, complete with hat. A white Stetson.

But George and Doc and a bunch of conspirators are revolutionizing North American agriculture in the most traditional way possible. They are putting consumers back in touch with the people who grow their food.

Siemon runs the Organic Valley Family of Farms, a network of about 1,700 farmers in 29 states who own the food company as a cooperative. He was one of the cooperative's original seven farmer-members. He likes to call himself the C-E-I-E-I-O.

Doc and Connie Hatfield spearhead Country Natural Beef, a network of over 100 far-flung beef ranchers organized according to the same principles: When ranchers and their customers get together they pretty much agree on how our food should be produced, with health and humanity the top priorities. Farmers and ranchers are eager to protect their property and their way of life. Educated consumers have proved they are happy to pay for the improvements.

Food producers and food consumers want a food industry that respects human health, nature and animal welfare. People may disagree on the relative value of these virtues but everyone acknowledges that they have some intrinsic worth. When you bring the producers and the consumers together they support agriculture that is more environmentally responsible and more compassionate. That business model is more sustainable, economically, than the conventional industry in which food processors, distributors and other middlemen take most of the profit.

As George Siemon told me, in the process of running Organic Valley, "there's quite a bit of doing what you think is right. Farmers apply common sense and fairness to business–no side deals. What's fair is fair."

Perhaps the quality that most characterizes the new generation of agricultural cooperatives–organizations like Organic Valley and Country Natural Beef–is their *transparency*. No side deals. What's fair is fair.

Organic Valley started as a group of Wisconsin dairy farmers backed by a network of small distributors. Over time they expanded into eggs, meat, orange juice and soy products. The 1,700 farm families in the Organic Valley cooperative in 2010 accounted for about 10 percent of all the organic farmers in the country.[87]

The company's leadership is obsessive about its standards for food and its standards for fairness. George Siemon invented his own version of the "food pyramid" in which the best food is grown with your own hands on your own property. Second best comes from local farmers you know personally. Then, third in line, is Organic Valley's own product, organic foods from conscientious national or regional organizations.

Organic Valley is equally strict about the distribution of its profits. Forty-five percent goes to the cooperative's member-farmers. Forty-five percent goes to employees. And the remaining 10 percent is donated to community causes the cooperative members support.

In contrast, the average U.S. corporation donates about 1.2 percent of its profits.[88]

The secret to Organic Valley's success has been recognizing the true values and real priorities of food consumers and matching those up with the values and priorities of family farmers. Both groups, it turns out, want clean air and water. Both want to keep our farmland beautiful and abundant. Both recognize that food produced in a fair and conscientious way is worth more money.

Organic Valley's founders were inspired by the Mondragon Cooperatives of northern Spain organized in the 1950s to improve the Basque economy. Now there are almost 300 Mondragon Cooperatives with 93,000 employee owners generating 17 billion Euros a year in revenue.[89] They are twice as profitable as the average Spanish business, pay salaries more than 10 percent higher than the Spanish average and their productivity, per employee, is at the very top of Spanish corporations.

In the past five years Organic Valley's total sales have increased 250 percent to more than $600 million.[90] About 400 people work at its headquarters in tiny La Farge, Wisconsin (population 788[91]) and the cooperative is adding about 50 new employees each year. The job growth helped the village of La Farge earn about $1 million in federal aid in 2010 to provide streets and utilities for the cooperative's expansion.[92]

In several ways Country Natural Beef looks like a younger cousin to the Organic Valley Cooperative (which might look like a younger cousin to the Mondragon Cooperatives, in a certain light). Doc and Connie Hatfield, the founders of the rancher cooperative, were out to solve two problems when they started the organization in 1986. The first, most pressing problem was economic. Raising beef on the open range in the arid North American West wasn't paying off. They would lose their ranch, and their lifestyle, if something didn't change.

Their second problem was, well, philosophical. In the market where they did business, beef was a commodity. Success was achieved by delivering cattle at the lowest possible price per pound. The Hatfields say that system was ruining their land and victimizing their animals. "We just didn't feel like we could do it that way any more," Connie says.

So, mostly out of economic necessity and a passionate desire to preserve their land and their lifestyle for the next generation of Hatfields, they reinvented their business.[93]

Joining forces with 13 other ranching families, the Hatfields formed Country Natural Beef and reached out to consumers. Through natural-food stores and local food cooperatives they offered consumers meat that was humanely raised and healthier. They certified their humane agricultural practices and environmental stewardship through the Food Alliance, a nonprofit that screens farmers, processors and distributors for environmental responsibility, social responsibility, safe and fair working conditions and humane treatment of animals.[94] Country Natural Beef has even created its own "Raise Well" set of standards for animal welfare and set up a standardized method of raising beef cattle, specifying the animals' diets and lifestyles.

When they were starting out, Connie Hatfield personally visited health-food stores in her region to pitch their new product. They learned, firsthand, what conscientious consumers were looking for and they set out to provide it. They developed new methods and found new allies who could feed, transport and slaughter their animals in more conscientious ways.

The Mondragon Cooperatives, Organic Valley and Country

Natural Beef were not invented by social scientists. All three were created in the crucible of free enterprise. First and foremost they had to make money. But all three were developed in the secure knowledge that consumers care where products come from. And all three discovered that cooperative ventures are often more productive because their personnel are stakeholders, and conscientious companies are more productive than average because their personnel reflect that spirit of productive conscientiousness.

All three have prospered by doing good–and doing it well.

And they are the tip of the iceberg.

The Local Harvest website[95] lists more than 20,000 local farms reaching out directly to their consumers and adds about 20 new farms every day. They also list more than 600 places consumers can sign up for food "subscriptions" from local farms, or CSAs (Community-Supported Agricultural operations) and almost 5,000 farmer's markets across the country.

Local Harvest's founder, Guillermo Payet, gives all the credit to the consumer. "People love knowing exactly where their food comes from," he says.

It's Beautiful. Organic Valley and Country Natural Beef both advertise their products with photos of their producers and their farms and ranches. When Doc Hatfield speaks at an event he sometimes recites a poem he wrote with his daughter, Becky. The poem appears on their organization's homepage under the headline, "Our Product is More Than Beef: …

…It's a trout in a beaver built pond, haystacks on an Aspen-framed meadow.
It's the hardy quail running to join the cattle for a meal,
The welcome ring of a dinner bell at dusk."[96]

The perpetuation of beauty is part of the product.

It Creates Abundance. The purest distillation of our concept of abundance is reflected in this planet's miraculous capacity for supporting life. Responsible agriculture institutionalizes nature's abundance, promotes it and preserves it.

It's Fair. That's one of the principal value propositions in roots agriculture. The cooperative and the local CSA tell the stories of specifically where the food comes from and how it is created so the customer can be confident that the process is economically fair, and as fair as possible to the creatures involved.

It's Contagious. Organic Valley is demonstrating how to spread a farmer-owned food corporation across the landscape. It continues to grow significantly even through economic downturns. Mondragon Corporation exemplifies how contagious the philosophies of the cooperative can be across other industries, with 256 companies in finance, heavy industry, research, training and retailing. The Mondragon example inspires Organic Valley. And Organic Valley's example leads Country Natural Beef as well as tens of thousands of groundbreaking agricultural enterprises across the world. Contagiousness is inherent to the idea of roots agriculture. Its benign effects on society and nature are its primary marketing concepts.

Wad Blake

My grandfather's name was Wad Blake. Wad was a nickname, of course, but no one ever called him anything else. He signed his checks John W. Blake but his birth certificate said "Wylie Rose Blake." His parents must have thought better of the "Rose" later. The nickname made it a moot point.

Raised in Oklahoma by Okies and Texans, he was a storyteller. In the tradition of that part of the country, his stories were loud, entertaining and occasionally factual. His father was a little blue-eyed cowboy who never weighed more than 130 pounds. His mother was dark-skinned and big, topping 300 pounds. Physically, he took more after his mother. Among his towheaded siblings he said he "looked like a rat turd in a bowl of rice." He greeted everyone with a booming, "Well, howdy!" or a "Que hubo?" *depending on their native language, and an enthusiastic* abrazo. *He taught me how to say, "Kiss my ass," in Choctaw. To entertain kids, he would pretend to take off his finger, or take out his dentures and tell jokes with them in his hand.*

Most of the stories he told were about the animals, people and scenes of his youth. They took place on or around the small subsistence farms of the Ozark Mountains. He chased stray mules through the brush and camped out with his family's cattle on "borrowed" land in the mountains.

His horse, Twenty Grand, was the fastest and meanest horse in the country. Twenty Grand once bucked so high that he and the horse landed in the bed of a wagon. His Uncle Will was so strong he could lift a 500-pound cotton bale on his back. His dad rode the trail drives between Texas and Kansas, and once was deposited unconscious in the top of a tree by a herd of stampeding cattle.

I could go on and on. From the time I was about 3 years old, he took me along to his hangout at the cafe in El Paso's Southern Pacific train depot. He spoke Spanish and taught me the rudiments. I thought he was brilliantly fluent and articulate. I can still hear his confident Mexican slang delivered in an Okie drawl. It makes me smile.

I gradually stopped believing in the accuracy of his stories but I never stopped believing in their integrity.

Grandpa surrounded his yard on a sand dune at the Mexican border with wagon wheels he scavenged and brought back from the Ozarks. He called his place "Blake's Belly Acres," but on the sign he'd misspelled belly as "Belley." He loved pointing that out to visitors, just so he could share a laugh at his own expense.

He built his home from three defunct wooden boxcars mounted on a cinderblock foundation and nailed together. He was a signal maintainer for the Southern Pacific Railway. He got a tip that the railroad was selling worn out boxcars for cheap. Because they had been refrigerator cars, they were already insulated with sawdust and newspapers a foot thick inside the wood-frame walls. He had them hauled to a two-acre plot of land on a sand hill near the foot of Mount Cristo Rey in Anapra, New Mexico. Gradually over the course of a couple of decades he enclosed the crawl space and put up siding. It didn't look half bad. By local standards, it was pretty nice. I was 6 when I "helped" him build the carport. When I was 18 he was still showing guests the ragged notches I sawed in the rafters when he wasn't looking.

A small gas space heater in the center room warmed the whole house. It was "air-conditioned" by a single swamp cooler. We would sit in front of the grate and let the cool, moist air condense on our faces.

Grandpa took me everywhere. He took me to Mexico and California, the feed store and the barber. He put me on horses. He tried to put me on a unicycle. He helped me raise a flock of pigeons. He taught me how to kill the squabs with a knife, humanely suggesting that I push a little harder to end their lives more quickly. He intentionally got us kicked out of a remote Oklahoma diner for speaking Spanish, evidently mistaken for Mexicans, since the sign in the window explained that such foreign personages were not welcome there. He helped me spell it out–"No Mexicans Allowed"–after we were ushered out to the sidewalk.

He despised racism, even before that word was widely used. He admired frugality and invention. He spray-painted the tubs of old washing machines and turned them into outdoor planters. He revered recycling, another word not in use at the time. The house, the sheds, the fences and the yard-art were all created from junk.

He showed acquaintances his gas bill to prove how well insulated his boxcar-house was. He thought I should learn how to make lye soap and skin opossums. I was barely out of diapers when he started telling people I could read. I figured out how to read just to live up to my billing. He told people I was strong, and I started carrying big rocks around the yard.

He was a big man with enormous hands who made his way among rough people in rough places. I was a skinny, fearful kid and I believed I was the apple of his eye. I guess I still believe it.

My grandpa was keenly interested in sustainability, but he certainly wouldn't have called it that. He loved cheap, beautiful things. He loved inventing things from junk then showing them off. He loved the kinship he felt with the poor people he lived around. He was willing to live a little more simply than necessary in order to celebrate that kinship. He loved the feeling that, with a little ingenuity, a person could create a fine life from almost nothing. He loved working his theories out in the real world.

His stories were populated by horses, goats, chickens, cattle and mules, inventors and visionaries, crackpots, goofball ideas and technological miracles. And now, of course, my stories are too.

CHAPTER SIX

How Did We Get Here?

Until fairly recently, the people we depended on lived nearby. Most human beings never traveled more than a few miles from their homes. People lived and died in the same small clan, typically, with a venerable set of traditions and a deep-seated suspicion of anyone who didn't speak the same language.

Among aboriginal societies it's very common for the name of a tribe to be the equivalent of "the human beings" or "the people" in that tribe's language. Out of about 100 Native American tribes listed on the *native-languages.org* website,[97] more than 30 define the name of their tribe in more or less that way–"the people," "the original people," the "true people," or "the best people." The "best people," the Illiniwek from which the state of Illinois takes its name, now call themselves the Peoria, which evidently means "backpack people."

Most traditional societies could afford the luxury of seeing their personal tribes as God's chosen people. The Judeo-Christian Bible is, of course, full of these assertions by the Israelites. Historically, people consistently and systematically considered their local, tribal interests superior to the needs and interests of other people who spoke a different language and wore a different style of footwear.

And a lot of people persist in believing this way. To a surprising degree, our modern wars, including both World Wars, have been tribal wars. The First World War's catalyzing event was the assassination of the Archduke Ferdinand, monarch of the Austro-Hungarian Empire, by Gavrilo Princip, a Serbian student. Princip evidently believed he was defending his ethnic group. The Nazi movement, which initiated World War II, was explicitly a tribal movement designed to distinguish the Aryan race from other Europeans. Predictably, the people trying to distinguish themselves as "Aryans" defined themselves as the original speakers of Indo-European languages and therefore, in their opinion, the "original people" of Europe.[98]

The ancient ethnic and geographic divisions of the Balkan States, including Serbia, are cultural fault lines along which violence has often erupted since the 19th century, in both World Wars and right up through the end of the 20th Century. That's why, when groups of people are locked in irreconcilable conflict, we say they are "balkanized."

A strong tribal identity must have been important to a society's historic survival. Durable ethnic divisions characterize human history in every part of the world. Human beings would obviously have a poor survival rate without the support of a unified community. Cooperative hunting and gathering is a lot more efficient than fending for oneself. And when the world is divided into territories belonging to armed factions, the basic pattern of early human history, a tribal defense system is critical to an individual's survival.

Ethnic conflict among human tribes is visible as a continuous feature of the archaeological record. The first evidence of human civilization, as archaeologists define it today with organized agriculture and settlement in towns and cities[99], is visible in 8,000-year-old evidence from in the Middle East in the region encompassing the Tigris and Euphrates river valleys, the "fertile crescent" that scientists call Sumer, which is now known as Iraq. The Sumerians produced our earliest examples of written language, literature, natural history and mathematics. They invented civilization.

Some people called the Akkadians drove out the Sumerians about 4,000 years ago, but the Sumerians staged a comeback about 200 years later. Then they were invaded by the Elamites who eventually were conquered by the Babylonians and the Assyrians until Cyrus the Great of Persia scooped them all up into the Achaemenid Empire. Then came the Parthians, the Sassanid Persians, the Rashidun Caliphate, the Umayyad Caliphate, the Caliphate of Cordoba, the Abbasid Caliphate, the Mongols led by Hulagu Khan, the warlord Tamerlane, the Black Sheep Turkmen, the White Sheep Turkmen, the Ottoman Empire, the Safavid Dynasty and the British, who chose eventually to give Sunni Arabs most of the authority in the country.

At the time of this writing, Iraq is occupied by the United States and claimed by various factions of Sunni Islam, Shiite Islam, Kurds and others.

The history of human civilization is, clearly, a history of tribal conflict.

When one telescopes a reading of thousands of years of history, as I did above, it makes it sound as if ancient history was peculiarly antagonistic. But many of Iraq's historic dynasties lasted hundreds of years–much longer than the United States of America has existed–and the world today is, apparently, vivisected by evolving human conflict to much the same degree as it has been for millennia. Our statesmen and philosophers describe an ideal world in which we have outgrown humanity's destructive tribal antagonisms, but we have never seen a sustained general peace among nations in all of recorded history.

The so-called "Axial Age" started around 600 BC and led up to the times of Christ, Buddha and Mohammed. During that age religious reformers and philosophers instigated a wave of unprecedented global social change. The historian William H. McNeill has theorized that our modern religions are, in part, a response to what he called the "closure of the ecumene."[100] Ecumene is a term geographers use to describe the empty space between human communities. McNeill argues that few truly isolated human communities have existed since four centuries before Jesus of Nazareth was born, when human territorial claims filled in the last of the available land in Europe and Africa. He suggests that most of contemporary religion and philosophy was shaped by the need for new ways of cooperating with neighbors; schools of thought that helped us mediate the natural conflicts between communities.

McNeill also argues persuasively that communication between human communities led to faster proliferation of human knowledge, technological advancements and general prosperity. So people who had religions and philosophies that facilitated communication were more successful. Those religions spread across the globe. They helped us mediate tribal conflict. Of course, they didn't eliminate it, and its destructive consequences are still visible almost everywhere today.

Mesopotamia's "fertile crescent" is not so fertile any more. According to a study funded in 2001 by the United Nations Environment Program, the cradle of civilization and birthplace of agriculture has almost completely dried up over the past four decades and is now mainly a wasteland of desert and saltpans.[101] The region has gone through periods of decline throughout history when war and social upheaval have led to bad stewardship. Most recently, the governments of Iraq, Iran, Syria and Turkey have dammed the rivers that feed the Tigris and Euphrates. Because populations are growing in the region and because both international conflict and internal insurgencies make cooperation difficult, the dams were built without regard for the neighbors. The lush irrigated landscape that previously covered about 7,000 square miles now is less than a third of its previous size.

Both population and weather have contributed to the damage, but the root cause of the destruction has been a failure to cooperate. The nations of the region fail to recognize their mutual interests and make destructive choices based on short-term goals.

The pattern is repeated all over the world. Development in California damages Mexican fisheries. Pollution from German factories acidifies Scandinavian lakes. Extravagant Westerners argue to limit China's national carbon output. China demands per-capita guidelines to curb wastefulness in the West. In the meantime, the buildup of greenhouse gases accelerates.

Human population growth and transportation technology closed the physical ecumene 2,500 years ago. Humanity is today closing a different ecumene, a different sort of space that used to divide us. Human societies are closing the distance between our national best interests. Our interests are converging in the way our communities once did.

From our luxury box here in North America it's relatively easy to look down at the world's environmental problems–and especially overpopulation–as though those problems belong to other people. Our continent is comparatively clean and uncrowded. North Americans make environmental messes, to be sure, but we usually have the money and technology to clean them up, or at least pretty them up. Our own birthrate is a sedate, relatively steady 14 births per 1,000 population, per year. The United States adds about four new immigrants to our population for every 1,000 people already here, each year. Our population grows about 1 percent per year–enough to keep housing prices up but not enough to overwhelm public services.

Even so, our annual 1-percent growth rate will produce an additional 36 million people in the United States over the next 10 years. That's about one new Seattle/Tacoma metropolitan area each year.

We Americans think of ourselves as independent and innovative. We like to ascribe our wealth and influence to our system of free enterprise and the personal liberties promised in the U.S. Constitution. And it's true that our systems and philosophies have been conducive to economic success. That's undeniable. However, it's equally undeniable that we had an enormous head start in the race to dominate the industrial revolution. We inherited a sparsely populated continent packed with natural resources. When it comes to natural resources–especially fertile agricultural land–our nation was born with a silver spoon in its mouth.

Most geographers today seem to agree that at least 40 million people lived in the Americas when Columbus landed in 1492.[102] One century later 90 percent of those native people were gone mainly due to diseases introduced by Europeans. Africans, Europeans and Asians had been traveling, trading and procreating together since humanity evolved. When a new cold virus emerged in northern Europe in 1200 A.D., people were probably sneezing in Beijing within a few years. The populations of Old World nations developed natural resistance to each other's diseases. Disease was always present, of course, and sometimes its effects were catastrophic. The "black death," an epidemic outbreak of bubonic plague, is estimated to have killed about half of Europe's population around the beginning of the 15th Century.[103] But the scale of population loss in the Western hemisphere is unique in recorded history.

With the native population devastated, European immigrants found here a fertile land mostly free for the taking. American culture has mythologized the settlers and dramatized their conflicts with Native Americans. But imagine what the conquest of the Americas would have been like if there had been 10 times as many native inhabitants.

Our country's history would have been very different, to say the least, and European settlement as we understand it today might not have occurred at all. If there were still 40 million or 50 million native people in the Americas in 1776, competing with the 25 million Europeans who lived here then[104], how different would our history be? And what about our present?

We are taught in the public schools and in the media of the United States that our free-enterprise system is the primary cause for our prosperity. It's common knowledge. Americans extrapolate, popularly, that free enterprise is the key to our future success. But what if our historic prosperity is mainly due to the fact that Europeans brought the Industrial Revolution to a depopulated continent where they could make maximum use of their new tools to develop its resources? Free-enterprise philosophies did a great job of facilitating the development of the North American continent and many, many people benefited. It worked great in the development of all that natural abundance. But how well will it work in a world of severely constrained resources? The fact is, we can't be sure.

People naturally look to their histories of achievements for guidance in dealing with today's problems. But what if our ancient belief in fecundity ("Go forth and multiply..."), our industrial tools and our economic reliance on unending growth are each, in their own way, depleting basic natural resources that cannot be easily replaced? Then where does humanity turn, tomorrow, for a guiding philosophy? If our post-industrial belief systems were specially tuned to facilitate our species' rapid expansion, how do we adapt them to a new, sustainable model?

Perhaps our species will need new insights. Perhaps we need a new set of shared values. Undoubtedly, it will require a new way of seeing the world.

Max, et al.

We met Max Gonzales in the mountains of northern New Mexico about 25 years ago. He lived in the Cruces Basin Wilderness five months a year in a canvas tent. Most of the time, he had only his two horses, a dog and 1,500 sheep for company. His supplies were packed in on horses, every two weeks or so. He could listen to a Juarez radio station when he had fresh batteries.

The Cruces Basin is a remote wilderness area about 35 miles northwest of the tiny village of Tres Piedras, which is about 30 miles west of Taos. To reach it requires driving dozens of miles on primitive seasonal roads that close after a hard rain, sometimes for days at a time. The

U.S. Forest Service recommends that you keep extra food and water in your car when you visit since you might be trapped if the roads flood while you are there. Max's employer had a summer grazing permit for a big flock of sheep. Motorized vehicles aren't allowed in established wilderness areas, so Max's supplies were brought in on pack animals.

Max was a gregarious person without any romantic attachment to the sheepherder's lonely vocation. He learned his trade on his uncle's rancho *in the central highlands of Mexico. The work paid a lot better in the United States. Max said he missed his wife and his three daughters–he called them his "chamacas"–back home in Guanajuato. He missed his friends. Once or twice each summer he made it to Taos for a few beers and some conversation at a local bar called Los Compadres where most of the clientele spoke Spanish. The rest of the time he was up there in the mountains by himself.*

Sometimes backpackers like us showed up for a few days to hike the trails and fish in the streams, but Max didn't speak English and the campers generally didn't speak Spanish. Still, Max did his best to communicate. Sometimes he made friends by fishing. He could lie on his stomach next to the stream, dangle his hands in the freezing water and toss trout out on the bank with a quick scooping motion. We worked for hours with our fly rods to accomplish what Max could do in a few minutes.

He developed his fishing technique to entertain visitors. He said he didn't like fish, and didn't eat them. His staple food, he said, was macaroni and cheese.

He was there for the money. He was making about $4,500 a year. Even if you adjust for inflation, that's not much of a wage in the United States, but it was OK for a farm kid from Mexico without a green card, and his boss covered his meager expenses so the whole paycheck could be mailed home to Guanajuato.

Without Max, or someone like him, the rancher who owned those sheep would have been out of business. A legal employee would have cost the rancher at least twice what he was paying Max, if you could find a competent person willing to live in the mountains alone for half a year. And if the rancher had been paying legal U.S. wages, he probably couldn't have competed against the wool and meat being imported from Australia and Chile.

Immigrant sheepherders have been an important part of New Mexico's economy since the 19th century. Likewise the economies of Colorado, Wyoming, Montana, Idaho and Nevada.

My childhood home on the Mexican border was in an immigration corridor. If the weather was not too hot, we could sit in the back yard and watch dozens of people cross the border carrying water and cheap bags full of their possessions, every day. Often they stopped and asked if they could drink from our hose. The women wore pantsuits. The men favored cowboy outfits. They were, generally, polite and grateful. My grandmother's well house was an 8-foot by 8-foot shack infested with black widow spiders. My father once discovered three men living in there, apparently waiting for a friend to show up and drive them al norte, *up north, where they could get jobs. From the accumulation of food containers, it appeared that they had been living there for days, if not weeks.*

Across the United States, you can't travel very far without meeting an immigrant. Nearly every small town has a few Chinese cooks and dishwashers. Your cabdriver in Minneapolis might be from Somalia or Laos. The woman who cleans the lobby of your Chicago apartment building may have grown up in Ecuador or Bulgaria. I once had a lively conversation with three young guys working in a restaurant where I ate in Washington, DC. They were from Sierra Leone. I was only vaguely aware that there existed a placed called Sierra Leone, the "Lion Mountains," named by a Portuguese explorer. I told them it sounded like a wonderful place. They said Washington was much better.

My wife and Max hit it off. Her Spanish is better than mine and she'd visited Guanajuato. I suppose most sheepherders would generally rather chat with a 23-year-old woman than with her college-kid boyfriend. Anyway, once Max struck up a conversation with Carolyn he pretty much neglected the sheep. They talked about his home and his family. He wondered if we ever went to Los Compadres. They talked about his life in the mountains. We had only been married a few months at the time but our friends Jon and Barbara, with whom we were camping, had been married a couple of years.

"Married two years and no chamacos*?" Max wanted to know. "Why not?"*

It's possible that Max just wanted to talk about sex, but Carolyn thinks he was genuinely curious about families in los Estados Unidos. *Max had been married four years. He had three daughters. He expected this pattern to continue for some time to come. Carolyn told him our friends didn't want children yet. Max looked confused. Carolyn mentioned the possibility that they used birth control.*

Max seemed never to have heard of such a thing and listened intently as Carolyn attempted to explain the general concepts.

I still think it's possible Max was simply enjoying the line of inquiry and if Carolyn was willing to educate, he was willing to be educated. But it's equally possible that he had not encountered the concept of birth control before in his life. Carolyn had lived in central Mexico and believed that in rural areas of Guanajuato province young people might never have heard of condoms or birth-control pills.

We never saw Max again. The next time we camped in the Cruces Basin there were no sheep there. I wonder about him occasionally. I wonder how many chamacos *blessed his home, finally. I wonder if he has grandchildren by now. On a summer morning, when I'm out checking my own sheep, I sometimes wonder if he's up there this year, in the Cruces Basin or some other isolated mountain valley, listening to the radio broadcast from Juarez and dreaming of home.*

CHAPTER SEVEN

The Big Ponzi

In Italy, the human population is officially stable. According to the U.S. Census Bureau[105], which keeps track of populations around the world, Italy gained about a million people between 1995 and 2005, but has now stabilized around 58 million legal residents.

Likewise Spain. Spain's official population is projected to be stable around 40 million people for the foreseeable future. Germany is steady at 82 million. And Finland. Stable at about 5 million people.

Numerous economic studies show that the most prosperous countries generally have slower rates of population growth. Economists have even given the phenomenon a name. They call it the "demographic-economic paradox.[106]" It's a paradox because a lot of wise people, including Thomas Robert Malthus, have theorized that prosperous societies will have more children because they can afford them. Not so, apparently.

As developing nations achieve a certain level of prosperity, the health and education level of their citizens improves. When a society improves health and education–for women, specifically–the birth rate falls. Prosperous people recognize the incentives for raising small families. In more prosperous countries, the quality of life is determined more by the family's overall level of education than by the number of laborers in the household. And affluent people in the world today are reasonably confident that all their children will survive to adulthood. In poor countries with high childhood-mortality rates it makes sense to hedge your bet on your offspring by having more of them.

In much of the world, a large family is a genetic–and social–insurance policy.

Poor people, if they want to be cared for in their old age, can improve their chances by having more children. If you're very poor, your children are your employees, your economic safety net and, eventually, they provide your nursing home in their own houses.

Also, of course, the world's poorest people often don't have access to health education or birth control, for that matter.

Birth rates in Spain, Germany, Finland, France and Italy are even with or below mortality rates.

The governments of those nations and most other relatively wealthy nations around the world have chosen to buttress their sagging populations by admitting immigrants. It is a widespread strategy. Sometimes it appears to be an altruistic strategy. Immigrants find economic opportunity in their new, more affluent surroundings. Most Americans can tell an inspiring story of some immigrant ancestor who came to the Western hemisphere and found prosperity here.

In fact, however, immigration provides a pragmatic solution for the nation as well as the immigrant. Countries with stable populations have serious economic problems that are solved by immigrants. Policymakers know this, and open or close their nations' gates to foreigners in response to economic conditions.

Japan's population is expected to decline slightly over the next few years. Japan doesn't admit many immigrants. Historically, Japan has been proud of its ethnic homogeneity and Japanese leaders have openly attributed the country's low crime rate and relatively peaceful society to its lack of diversity. However, Japan is quietly reconsidering its historic anti-immigration policies now that its aging population faces looming labor shortages. As life expectancy has increased and birth rates have decreased, Japan has created a nation in which there are not enough young, productive people to provide for the needs of the elderly. Japanese industry is finding it difficult to maintain its productivity and support its retirees at the same time. Journalists and social scientists describe Japan's "population crisis," as a "demographic time bomb[107]," so in spite of a history of isolation in a country whose residents are almost 99 percent pure Japanese[108] (and whose foreign residents are mostly descendants of Chinese and Korean laborers who were born in Japan and speak only Japanese), Japan's government is considering opening the island nation up to new foreign immigrants.

According to Lester Brown's 2008 book, *Plan B 3.0: Mobilizing to Save Civilization*, about 43 countries around the world have populations that are essentially stable[109]. All 43 of those nations are prosperous. All of them except, so far, Japan, control their populations and their labor forces by opening their doors to immigrants.

A lot of people, including Lester Brown (who updates his *Mobilizing to Save Civilization* book series every year), find reason for optimism in the relative economic health of developed nations with stable populations. Those nations seem to provide a model for sustainable prosperity around the world. Our optimism is supported by trends in China, where population growth is beginning to equalize while the standard of living is rising.

On the other hand, the populations of some of the world's poorest countries, including Ethiopia, the Democratic Republic of Congo, and Uganda, are on track to double within 40 years. India is adding about 80 million people a year. Countries like those are providing valuable immigrant labor across the globe, without which many of the rich nations with stable populations would founder, economically.

The growing global population fills in labor gaps where needed, and provides growing markets for international manufacturers. Japanese automakers sold about 9.5 million new cars across Asia in 2008, mostly in countries other than Japan. In fact, auto sales in Japan are falling steadily while they grow in countries with expanding populations. As I write this, Ford Motor Company is publicizing the introduction of its new subcompact car called the Figo in India. The company's executives say they see very little growth in the U.S. or European markets. So they are going where the customers are, that is, to a nation with a growing population and a growing economy.

India, China and dozens of other nations are becoming prosperous by providing inexpensive goods and services to the rest of the world. Their large populations provide inexpensive labor. When I call to question a charge on my Visa card, I generally talk to a customer-service representative in India. My bathrobe was made in Turkey. The dress shirts in my closet came from China, Brazil, the Philippines and Honduras.

Indian consumers, in turn, buy Japanese Toyotas, Fords from the United States and Italian shoes. The aging populations of Europe and Japan are not promising markets. Their populations are not expanding and their standards of living are not improving. Growth in the U.S. consumer market, in isolation, would be mediocre. In the U.S., it's particularly difficult to visualize our economy absent the 38 million documented immigrants[110] and at least 8 million to 12 million undocumented foreign workers who both supply inexpensive labor and bolster consumer spending.[111]

Over the past three years, Japan has exported, in goods and services, about 7 trillion yen more, on average, than it has imported, a number equal to more than half the country's gross domestic product over the same time frame.[112] Germany exported 178 billion Euros worth more than it imported. The Netherlands' positive balance of trade was about 32 billion Euros. Wealthy nations with stable populations are dependent on exports to support their prosperity.

Economic expansion depends on population expansion. At least it has for as long as we've been keeping track.

So humanity faces a dilemma. On one hand, the habitat won't allow the human population to expand forever. That just won't work. But if the global population stabilizes, we face an unprecedented economic problem. Prosperity depends on an expanding human population to support our expanding global economy.

A Ponzi scheme, also known as a "pyramid scheme," is a scam in which an unethical financial entrepreneur promises investors big returns, which he fraudulently generates from the contributions of later investors. Bernard Madoff is the most notorious recent perpetrator. He raised tens of billions of dollars from thousands of investors before he went to jail in 2009.[113] New investors heard about the big returns earned by earlier contributors to the scheme and eagerly put their money in, which allowed the con artist to fool several successive new generations of victims over the course of two decades. Every Ponzi artist faces a day of reckoning. Eventually, he runs out of new investors. His actual returns have never been equal to the dividends he paid out, but he made up the difference by draining new accounts. Eventually, he can't pay dividends any more. He doesn't even have the money to return to late investors because he's spent their money paying off earlier contributors, building his reputation as a genius.

Our economic dependence on population growth bears a disturbing similarity to a global Ponzi scheme. It's relatively easy to create "economic growth" so long as there are more consumers every year. Directly or indirectly, we are all dependent on population growth for our livelihoods. But eventually, resources run short. Every pyramid scheme eventually collapses when the supply of new investors dries up. If we accept the obvious fact that this planet's resources are not unlimited, then eventually the global supply of new consumers will be constrained.

The connection between population growth and economic prosperity was clearly recognizable 600 years ago. One of the earliest recorded treatises on economic expansion was written by an Arabian philosopher, Ibn Khaldun, in 1377:

> *"When civilization [population] increases, the available labor again increases. In turn, luxury again increases in correspondence with the increasing profit, and the customs and needs of luxury increase. Crafts are created to obtain luxury products. The value realized from them increases, and, as a result, profits are again multiplied in the town. Production there is thriving even more than before. And so it goes with the second and third increase. All the additional labor serves luxury and wealth, in contrast to the original labor that served the necessity of life.*[114]"

Six centuries ago an Arabian philosopher understood the basic machinery pretty clearly. Economic growth is generated by population growth, augmented by technology and motivated by improving lifestyles.

Fundamentally, every additional human being in the world

is one additional customer. When the total number of potential customers for the world's businesses declines, then the total potential volume of business declines. Our traditional model for economic growth is sabotaged by a stable or declining human population. We can, probably, create new systems for distributing value and maintaining prosperity for a stable population. But we've never had to do that before. Maintaining prosperity in a stable population will require new tools.

Until now most economic study has been preoccupied with the reasons one country's economy is healthier than another's. The comparisons help us discover the best practices. Over the years, we've improved economies by learning from each other and adopting the models that are most successful. On the whole, the evidence has demonstrated that nations with market-directed economies are more successful than those with centrally planned economies.[115] The big centrally planned economies of China and the former Soviet Republics have, over the last few decades, converted to more market-driven systems. And they have found new prosperity.

Economists have paid a lot more attention to the relative success or failure of national economies than to the larger dynamics of the world's economy. Students of economics understand the reasons why one nation outperforms another better than they understand the fundamental forces that direct the human economy as a single entity or the symbiotic relationships that support groups of national economies. Likewise we find it hard to track economics across long periods of time. What events occurred in the 19th century that made some nations prosperous in the 20th century? Are events occurring today that might undermine our economic health 30 years from now? We're pretty comfortable looking at one national economy and its condition today. When we aggregate more than one national economy and then try to track economic trends over time, the equation's complexity increases by orders of magnitude. It's difficult for the economist to get his or her arms around the global economy as it evolves across the decades.

Economists are aware of this gap in understanding. They recognize the complexity of their subject matter. They make allowances for what they call "externality." In economics, "externality" refers to the effects of an economic event on parties not directly involved–people in faraway places, in the past or in the future. The most vivid illustrations of externality, these days, come from the environmental realm. The carbon we've added to the atmosphere by burning fossil fuels has had relatively little effect on the people who pumped the oil, sold the oil or burned the oil. Most economic studies quantify our reliance on fossil fuels as a logical reliance on a relatively abundant natural resource. Viewed in this way, fossil fuels have been a precious resource fueling prosperity and innovation for more than 100 years with almost no bad effects. If negative environmental consequences are not felt within the economy where the petroleum is produced or where it is burned, then those consequences are "externalities." It is increasingly evident, however, that burning fossil fuels has a generalized effect on the health of the planet overall and that it will have an effect on the health and welfare of future generations.

Those effects are external to most economic models, and it's hard to quantify them.

Economists are attempting to measure the effects of externalities like long-term environmental consequences. Economies that accurately evaluate the costs of their products are more efficient. If oil were taxed to pay reparations for the long-term environmental consequences of its extraction and consumption, then governments could use the additional revenues to mitigate the damage. Consumers might use less oil because it would be more expensive.

Either way, the "externality" of environmental damage would be a measured factor in the economic equation. We would at least be aware of the true economic effects of our behavior.

Nigeria's birthrate would be external to most equations measuring economic growth in the United States even though Nigerian labor provides a lot of affordable oil to Western industrialized nations, and lots of Nigerians emigrate to wealthy countries where they provide high-quality, low-cost labor. Africa's population increase is not routinely measured as a factor in the economics of England, France or the United States. But effects are felt nonetheless in both negative and positive ways.

Some economists conclude that stable populations are good for national economies because the most prosperous nations record the lowest birth rates–the demographic-economic paradox again. Though we can speculate on the effects of stable population on economies, the fact is we don't have any real-world knowledge to draw on. A few nations have stabilized their populations, but they depend on population growth in other parts of the world to supply cheap labor and new consumers.

Every nation in Western Europe is supplementing its population with immigrants.[116] In 2005, the most recent year for which I could find a firm number, 1.8 million new people moved to Europe from elsewhere. Somewhere between 45 million and 60 million people living in the United States today are in first-generation immigrant households.[117] About 17 percent of people living in the United States are immigrants.[118]

Bluntly, we have no examples of economic growth occurring in the absence of human population growth. The expansion of our species has always supported the expansion of our economies for as long as we've been keeping track, yet wealthy nations generally ignore the growth in foreign populations when they measure their own prosperity. It appears that the United States is an economic success story standing on its own two feet, but to what extent does our prosperity depend on a steady stream of ambitious immigrants? On the other hand, how prosperous will we be when North America's population reaches a billion people?

Population growth is a Ponzi scheme and we're setting up future generations as its victims. We are paying into the base of the pyramid with our natural resources.

The spectacular collapse of the $100 billion energy company Enron at the beginning of the 21st century offers a chilling illustration of our capacity for ignoring evidence in favor of comfortable self-delusion. The smartest financial analysts in the world's most successful economy believed Enron's managers' wildly inflated valuations because they profited from that belief. In spite of abundant evidence to the contrary, Wall Street believed Enron represented $68 billion in assets because that belief temporarily benefited everyone–management, bankers and investors. For a time, skepticism profited no one. When those assets were finally called upon to generate cash, however, $68 billion in market value evaporated in just a few weeks.

It is not popular to suggest that our planetary assets are not sufficient to cover our long-term needs. No one is making a profit from skepticism. For that very reason, the value of those assets is likely being exaggerated. In fact, you can bet on it.

In his 2009 book, *Plan B 4.0: Mobilizing to Save Civilization*, Lester Brown asserts that humanity is already consuming its "asset base," and setting the stage for our global pyramid scheme to collapse around us.[119] He points, in particular, to agriculture's dependence on groundwater supplies. Our current levels of agricultural production are dependent on water pulled from aquifers that recharge very slowly, like the Ogallala aquifer under North America's central plains. It's economical–even cheap–to pump groundwater and create food until the aquifer is drained and our asset base is consumed. Then our fertile farms are suddenly barren. The pyramid collapses.

Comparisons between our exploitation of natural resources and Bernie Madoff's Ponzi scheme are popping everywhere these days.[120]

So far, technology has accommodated and augmented population growth. We've seen our "green revolution" spread across the globe and feed the multitudes. The globe remains, however, a finite resource.

If we could create a planetary biological machine that would support an unlimited human population, eternal growth, then our current economic theories would equip us to create permanent human prosperity. But that mythical machine–effectively a perpetual-motion machine–is an impossible fantasy.

In the imagination, space travel offers a longer-term solution. One attraction of science fiction is its ability to extend the human frontier to the limits of the human imagination. Star Trek's famed mission statement declaimed our potential to "explore strange new worlds and boldly go where no one has gone before." If that were possible then our current economic theories and philosophies might carry us on, uninterrupted, to flourish across the universe. Unfortunately, right now our manned spacecraft can fly no farther than our own small, sterile moon.

At this point it looks as if our economic tools may become obsolete before we perfect intergalactic space travel. For the time being, good stewardship and economic invention are probably higher priorities than building a better spaceship.

Mahmoud, Stone, Abraham and Isaac

The Africans showed up at our door on a sunny, chilly November afternoon. Two men introduced themselves as "Stone" and "Abraham." In the background stood a young woman with a gregarious little boy, Henry, about 2 years old. They were looking for goats.

Goats are relatively rare in our area. Beef cattle and pampered horses are the most common animals in the local pastures. So Stone and Abraham had been driving around the countryside asking farmers if they knew someone with goats. They were directed to our house. We had goats.

The Africans wanted to throw a party. In Ghana, their home country, goats provide the meat for celebratory events. I walked the visitors out to the pasture to look at two bucks we didn't intend to keep over the winter. They agreed to buy both.

We arranged for them to come back Thursday morning–Thanksgiving by coincidence–and I would haul the goats, the men and their equipment out to an isolated pasture where the Ghanaians would take the first, mortal steps toward preparing their celebration.

Most of our young goats and sheep are sold in the fall before we start feeding hay. We deliver them to farms or slaughterhouses. For our own meat, we take them to a small, family-operated slaughterhouse where they are handled humanely and killed instantly by a blow to the head.

Either for tradition or to save money, the Ghanaians wanted to dispatch the animals themselves.

I consider my dependence on the slaughterhouse a little bit of an indulgence. The emotions I feel when our animals must be killed and eaten are a sort of penance I pay. I see these creatures born. I care for them through their brief lives, name them and count them. They eat from my hand. They grow and thrive. They make me smile and sometimes laugh. This emotional penance I pay is a penance all of us owe for having lived, for having displaced and consumed other living things. When I drop a group of goats, lambs or cattle off at the abattoir I always feel that I'm shirking some of my responsibility. I feel sad, but I would feel the wound more deeply if I spilled their blood myself.

The Ghanaians took on that responsibility. I watched as they killed the two goats with a long knife, slicing through the veins of the neck. It's a cliché to mention that the blood was red, but it was so very red, against the green grass, it seemed almost theatrical. Our eyes are probably tuned to see it that way. When one sees a splash of blood against the ground it marks the occurrence of something very, very important. Danger. Food. Birth. Death.

In a few seconds our animals were gone. What remained was food.

Stone and Abraham were city boys and Christians, but they said they had grown up with Muslim friends who had shown them how to butcher goats and sheep with simple tools at home. The Muslims in Ghana, they said, butchered animals both for religious rituals and parties. Since they were Christian, Stone said, they just did it for parties.

A few days later, in early December I got a call from Mahmoud. Mahmoud came to Kansas from Libya years ago. Mahmoud is a math professor and the leader of a local Muslim community. He wanted to buy some sheep. He saw my ad on Craigslist.

Dec. 8, 2008, marked the Muslim holiday Eid al-Adha, when families worldwide commemorate Ibrahim's willingness to sacrifice his son, Ishmael, in obedience to Allah. In Christian Sunday School we called Ibrahim Abraham and Ishmael Isaac, but the story is the same and the queasy feeling we get when we consider a father putting the knife to the throat of his tiny son must be shared among Christians, Jews and Muslims worldwide. It's one of the Bible's–and the Koran's–most disturbing images.

Eid al-Adha is timed according to the Islamic calendar, so it moves around on our own Gregorian timeline. In 2009 it landed in late November, the day after Thanksgiving.

Why would God ask Abraham to sacrifice his little boy? The story's usually told as if He was just testing Abraham's faith. As soon as it was obvious that Abraham was going through with it, God said something like, "Never mind. I was just testing you. Go get that young ram that's tangled up in those bushes over there. Sacrifice him instead."

I've never been completely satisfied with that interpretation. If God, our creator, were omniscient, why would he need to test Abraham? God knew what was going to happen. Like all sacred stories, this one is supposed to teach us something. What are we supposed to learn from Abraham's gruesome trial? Is it as simple as, "Obey God, no matter what you are told to do," or is it something more compli-

cated? I don't believe I could follow Abraham's example of obedience. My faith, if you call it that, is nowhere near that strong.

Mahmoud's faith directs him to kill his Eid al-Adha sacrifice with his own hands, to separate the meat into three shares and to give away a third of it to the poor, the other third to members of his community. Only one third is retained for his own feast with family and friends.

But he's the guy who has to place the knife against the animal's throat and spill its blood.

When I tell friends about Mahmoud and the Ghanaians they are, quite often, repelled. Many people in 21st-century America seem to feel that the act of killing one's own food is barbaric. Instinctively, they recoil from the whole idea. To the contemporary American, it seems more civilized to pick up pork chops or boneless chicken breasts at the supermarket.

I respect the vegetarian's fundamental preference to cause as little pain and suffering to sentient beings as possible. I don't agree, necessarily, that veganism or vegetarianism accomplishes this, but I respect that belief system and sense of commitment.

A few acres of grain and vegetable fields displace millions of living organisms that would naturally live there. Natural pastures preserve the habitat and accommodate many more species in a much healthier environment than plowed ground. None of us lives, except through the sacrifices of other living things.

Mahmoud and my Ghanaian customers have chosen, for very different reasons, to maintain contact with the natural order of things–the bloody, painful and profound natural order of things.

In past winters I've sold animals to other devout Muslims, like Mahmoud, and watched them complete their ritual sacrifice. When Abraham lifted Isaac onto the altar he would have remembered placing goats and sheep there before. He must have visualized the life draining from Isaac's eyes just as the light flickers and fades in the eyes of a lamb when the blood drains from its brain.

As Americans we conflate the idea of ritual sacrifice with gifts to charity or tithing at church. But the charitable distribution of the sacrificial meat or the loss of a little income are minor sacrifices, I think, in comparison with the emotional blow you receive when you take a life with your own hands. Of course home butchering is routine in many cultures. Of course it's natural. Of course other people may not feel the wound as acutely as I do. But the care taken by my Muslim customers indicates that they are fully aware of the importance of the act of killing. Their elaborate rituals are designed to reinforce that awareness. They feel the muscles of the goat's neck–so like the neck of a child–bunch and resist the stroke of the knife. They hold the animal as it struggles. Then they feel its struggles end. With this experience, I may or may not understand the lesson of the story of Abraham and Isaac any better. But I much better understand its power.

A couple of days after Thanksgiving, our Ghanaian customer Abraham phoned and invited us to a party. In his suburban Kansas home we chatted with his friends from West Africa. We ate spicy goat stew and cassava. We watched recordings of a variety show from Ghana. The room vibrated with laughter and the smells of chilies and billy goat.

The party was full of life, in the shadow of death.

The little boy Henry, Abraham's son, who had stopped by the farm with them on that first day, crawled from one lap to another, smiling at us and hugging our necks.

CHAPTER EIGHT

Austerity is a Drag

Over the past four decades we've watched the "environmental movement" grow from an ideological, tie-dyed clique into a mainstream global consensus. The world's biologists, physical scientists and economists are growing closer to general agreement that the environmentalists have been right all along. The world's resources really *are* limited. Humanity really *is* depleting those resources at unsustainable rates. The protection of the planet really must be a cornerstone of our economic and political plans.

I don't think environmentalists can take much credit for this dawning realization, however.

We environmentalists have, for the last 30 years, been among our society's least effective leaders and least pleasurable companions. The explicitly anti-environmental U.S. administrations under Presidents Reagan, Bush and Bush were, to some degree, popular because of their opposition to the "environmental movement." Environmentalists were characterized, not inaccurately, as *naïfs*, proudly holier-than-thou, obstructing progress and prosperity.

In his 2006 essay, "Beyond Hope," Derrick Jensen claimed that the most common words he heard spoken by environmentalists, everywhere, were "We're f****d."[121]

He exaggerates, but he has a point. "The End is Near!" is not an inspiring message. Pessimism seldom motivates change.

Go around to any large gathering of dedicated environmentalists and I think you'll soon begin absorbing a lack of optimism and a general sense that human nature is too deeply flawed to respond appropriately to the environmental crisis.

I sometimes ask people to name the most humorous environmentalist they know. I generally get a blank stare.

The attitudes of many environmental activists reek of Puritanism. As conservationists, we savor our superior wisdom. We're judgmental. Behind many of life's pleasures–good food, fine drink, nice cars, electric lights, flushing toilets–we see unnecessary consumption, which we condemn. This is, in fact, a quasi-religious point of view with its own rituals and taboos. Because humanity is responsible for environmental problems we are, ipso facto, all sinners. We have characterized ourselves, universally, as the guilty parties and we often indulge ourselves in self-flagellation, going about in our hemp sackcloth and ashes, predicting the end of the world.

Environmentalism, like other faiths, identifies all human beings as sinners. But environmentalism offers no forgiveness and no salvation.

If the environmental crisis has a spiritual dimension, then its leaders need to offer a path to redemption. Otherwise we may succumb to what professionals in the budding discipline of "ecopsychology" identify as a form of paralyzing grief for our declining habitat, grief with its usual accompanying symptoms: anxiety, despair and emotional numbness.[122] Grief could be preventing us from addressing our challenges in a meaningful way.

People interested in a beautiful and abundant human future need to acknowledge the potential of technology. Part of the reason why environmentalists have not developed a bigger audience over the decades since Rachel Carson published "Silent Spring[123]" in 1962 is our reflexive demonization of machinery. If we are "competing for hearts and minds" as the cliché goes, then we need to endorse technological solutions that our audience will find as compelling as the automatic transmission and the Jacuzzi bathtub.

Machines make us more powerful, mobile and comfortable. Their speed and momentum can also aggravate the damage done by our mistakes. Most of us have marveled at one time or another at the shocking results of a minor automobile accident. The fender-bender that was barely felt in the driver's seat distorted sheet metal and shattered glass. Those of us who drive tractors and bulldozers usually have a story of when we turned the machine a little too quickly and tore a hole in the dam of our pond or destroyed a barn door. We travel 550 miles per hour in airliners that weigh almost a million pounds. There's bound to be some collateral damage. With great power comes great potential–for good or ill.

The destructive potential of our technology doesn't prevent us from feeling the exhilaration of rapid acceleration. The human manias for speed and mobility have contributed generously to the destructive buildup of carbon dioxide in the atmosphere. Still, it doesn't do us any good to deny the joys of horsepower.

My teenage son and I thrilled to the sound of Audi's R10 racecars rumbling by on my TV screen, dominating the pack at Le Mans, Laguna Seca, and Sebring beginning back in 2006. Audi's diesel-powered cars contributed a new baritone note to the chorus of tenors in sports-car racing. The revolutionary new diesels were about 10 percent more fuel-efficient than the competitors, the equivalent of a 30-lap advantage in endurance races like the 24 Hours of Le Mans. And beginning in 2008 they burned bio-diesel brewed from food waste,[124] a very low-sulfur diesel fuel that is said to reduce carbon-dioxide emissions by as much as 90 percent when compared with traditional diesel fuels. Audi was virtually unbeatable on the racetrack after introducing the diesel power plants and race organizers bent over backwards to try to diminish the Audi advantage by reducing the capacity of fuel tanks and mandating pit stops. In other words, the car was a leader both environmentally and on the racetrack. Best of all, the racecar's reputation has helped make fuel efficient Audis sexy. Teams in a 2008 fuel-efficiency marathon drove the sporty Audi A4 diesel more than 1,000 miles between Basel and Vienna at highway speeds getting over 60 miles per gallon, average! Four teams got better than 68 miles per gallon in conventional Audis off the dealer's lot.[125]

Is automobile racing environmentally responsible? That's a hard question to answer. Worldwide, it probably does a lot less harm than unnecessary trips to the grocery store. Racing technology probably helps make passenger cars more efficient. On the other hand, racing extols speed and deifies horsepower.

In any event, I don't think human beings are going to end our love affair with powerful, nimble transportation machines. We love fine contraptions. That's human nature. Therefore, I think environmentalists should strive to understand the joy experienced by the race fan, the motorcyclist and the snowmobiler, and we should use that understanding to stimulate the human imagination in ways that benefit the planet.

Elon Musk's imagination was stimulated a few years ago to create the Tesla roadster, a groundbreaking all-electric sports car. It's available for sale at dealers across the United States today for a little over $100,000 and about 1,000 people owned one at the time of this writing[126]. It goes from zero to 60 miles per hour in 3.7 seconds. Tesla drivers sit in premium performance seats surrounded by black leather with cream accents. On demonstration rides, dealers like to suggest that their passenger turn on the radio just as they punch the accelerator pedal. Under full acceleration with the g-force bearing down, they can't lean forward far enough to touch the radio buttons.[127]

And the Tesla is far more fuel-efficient than the Toyota Prius, traveling more then 200 miles on a single, $2.00 charge. It's about six times as efficient as any comparable sports car, and generates one-tenth of the pollution even if the electricity is generated by an old-fashioned coal-fired power plant. If the electricity is generated by the wind, well, its carbon footprint is virtually nil. The company's founder said the Tesla enterprise became profitable during the summer of 2009. He had raised $300 million in venture capital and had access to $465 million in low-interest loans from the U.S. Department of Energy.

He was preparing to plow his 2010 efforts into the launch of the Tesla Model S sedan scheduled to go on sale in 2012 for under $60,000.[128] After fuel savings, he estimates the true cost of the sedan at about $35,000. [129]

Elon Musk is no starry-eyed dreamer. Quite the opposite. He was 28 when he sold his first company, the publishing-software startup Zip2, for just over $300 million. (Not including a video game he invented at age 12 and sold for $500.[130]) Then he started the company that would become PayPal, which he sold to eBay in 2002 for about $1.5 billion.

Musk thinks fast, luxurious electric vehicles will revolutionize human transportation. "We're going to see things we'd never dreamed of," he says, like battery-powered cars with a 1,200-mile range and electric-powered supersonic planes.[131]

Engineers and tinkerers have already revolutionized the efficiency of our technology, at least in comparison with a few years ago. The household refrigerators sold in California today use 75 percent less electricity than the models from the 1970s. The National Academy of Sciences reports that, by 2035, fossil-fueled automobiles could get double their 2010 fuel mileage without sacrificing power or capacity.[132] NASA is designing airliners that burn 70 percent less fuel and are 70 percent quieter than today's Boeing 737s.[133]

I've published magazines dedicated to collectible machines—antique tractors, classic motorcycles, that sort of thing. From the first antique tractor show I attended, I noticed how much I enjoyed the company of the people who love old farm machinery. Likewise, the classic motorcycle guys. The people at the antique-tractor shows and classic-motorcycle races are, on the whole, a lot of fun. They wipe their machines off with clean rags, attending to every detail as if the apparatuses were favored children. They wander the show grounds with big smiles on their faces. They tell long, amusing stories about how they found a priceless old tractor in an abandoned barn or how they tracked down their motorcycle's rebuilt carburetor in a mechanic's shop down in Mexico.

On the whole, the machine collectors are as joyful as any group of people I've ever been around. They laugh a lot more than environmentalists.

What I've concluded is this: People who love interesting machines love the human ingenuity that went into them. They love human ingenuity, which helps them love humanity, which helps them love themselves. Their joy is infectious. They're great company.

This is why, I think, people become involved in these peculiar hobbies that, from a distance, look a lot like drudgery. They spend their spare time covered in grease, laboring hard to disassemble and reassemble obsolete machines. If someone tried to coerce us into repairing a decrepit 40-year-old motorcycle, we might be difficult to convince. And yet that kind of challenge engages the imaginations of hundreds of thousands of people who literally can't wait to roll up their sleeves and engage with these rusty, greasy mechanical puzzles.

It's just this kind of passionate ingenuity we need to create a constructive vision of our future on earth.

Environmentalists are better leaders when we can better love human ingenuity. True sustainability will be crafted by human ingenuity with a keen eye for nature. We will need to form partnerships with the natural world, to ingeniously utilize its resources in ways that preserve its natural productivity.

For about 4 million years, human beings were hunter-gatherers. We couldn't put much pressure on our habitat because as soon as the food or water ran a little short, we moved on. If we couldn't find food freely available, our numbers dwindled. Then, just 10,000 years ago, humanity got its agricultural thing going.[134] By some estimates, when agriculture was introduced human population growth rates increased 100-fold. In a geographic area that previously spawned 100 new human inhabitants each year, suddenly there were 10,000 new people every year. The land could accommodate the growth, thanks to agriculture. Studies of population densities from the time indicate that the "carrying capacity" of human habitats also increased by a factor of 100 when agriculture was introduced.

In one way it was a better deal for nature, too. By using a comparatively small space intensively, human beings left more of nature untouched. An agricultural society uses less property, per capita, than a hunting-and-gathering society. A lot less. But as we became attached to particular locales and as our populations, thanks to agriculture, became less vulnerable to variations in the weather, we also invented overgrazing, deforestation, erosion and topsoil depletion.

Desertification is the oldest type of long-term environmental damage we can trace directly to human activities.[135] Biologists and archaeologists read the signs of land abuse and growing deserts in the Middle East dating back to the very earliest years of agriculture 12,000 years ago during the Neolithic Revolution. Almost as soon as humans domesticated their first goats and sheep, it appears we began overgrazing our lands.

Many farms of the 21st Century are, comparatively speaking, biological wastelands. Plowed, fertilized and cultivated from property-line to property-line, much of the world's most productive land has been stripped of its wildlife. Walk through a soybean field anywhere in the Midwest, then take the same sort of stroll through a native prairie in the same region, if you can find one. The contrast is shocking. The prairie, especially the "tallgrass" prairie, is among the world's most fecund environments. Hundreds of species thrive in a thick carpet of plants growing unbelievably fast. In three months I have watched a particularly lush acre of my undisturbed pasture grow five tons of grass. One acre, three months, five tons. No artificial fertilizer or irrigation. And Nature has designed the prairie to accomplish varying versions of this miracle every summer, year in and year out, for as long as the rain falls and the sun shines.

Ecologist David Tilman has been studying the productivity of the prairie at Minnesota's Cedar Creek Natural History Area for more than a decade. He has compared the productivity of the land planted in a natural mixture of several species with the same land planted with only one highly useful species. In the December 2006 issue of *Scientific American* he reported that the diverse natural prairie produced 238 percent more "bioenergy" than the same land planted in one agricultural species. Furthermore, the diverse, natural prairie stores two-thirds of its productivity underground, making a native grassland a naturally carbon-negative no matter what the tops of the plants are used for. Grasslands are designed to pull carbon from the atmosphere and store it in the earth. At the same time they efficiently turn sunshine into plants that can be repurposed as food and fuel. The prairie can feed people and replenish the earth's resources, at the same time.

The visionary scientist Wes Jackson[136] describes modern agricultural economies as "brittle." When an entire region depends on a single product–say corn–and an unusual weather pattern devastates the corn crop one year, the region's economy is also devastated. The system is "brittle" because if you put a little unusual pressure on it, it breaks. Jackson's label could describe the whole global food machine. As population growth forces our agricultural systems to higher and higher levels of productivity, disruptions like unusual weather patterns harm us in ways that are more widespread and long-lasting.

Pesticides, herbicides and industrial fertilizers pollute water supplies and destroy wildlife. Even as the White House and the Ford Foundation were trumpeting industrial agriculture's achievements in the 1960s, Rachel Carson was taking note of the sudden decline of wildlife around the world where pesticides were used.[137] New health problems proliferate in farming communities. According to the U.S. National Cancer Institute within the National Institutes of Health, farm workers today face unusually high incidence of leukemia, non-Hodgkin's lymphoma, multiple myeloma, soft tissue sarcomas, and cancers of the skin, lip, stomach, brain and prostate.[138]

The bare earth between the rows of corn or soybeans erode in the absence of the root structures and plant matter that enrich and stabilize undisturbed soils. Plant varieties are developed to maximize the nutrition derived from every square meter. As that nutrition is pulled from the soil and trucked away to feed human beings and livestock, the soil is depleted and the crops are increasingly dependent on artificial fertilizers. Those fertilizers are specifically designed to benefit the crops immediately, and have little lasting positive impact. The soil is gradually robbed of its natural assets, paying off our present obligations at the expense of future generations. Like a failed investment bank, the farm's assets have eroded slowly without anyone much noticing.

There's good evidence that, as we've increased the productivity of our farmland, we've also made our food less nutritious. Some studies suggest that up to 75 percent of the natural minerals we could expect to find in a piece of fruit or a bowl of spinach may be missing if our fruits and vegetables are grown using aggressive industrial agricultural practices. [139]

At Wes Jackson's Land Institute in Salina, Kansas, scientists have been working since the 1970s to create a new Natural Systems Agricultural Model that protects the environment, productivity and human health, at the same time.[140] Using the natural prairie as a sort of design template, Jackson and his colleagues invented a system they call "perennial polyculture" that plants a variety of agricultural species in a single field, and specifically choosing species that reproduce themselves every year, reducing the need for plowing, planting and other activities that damage prairie soils. They have bred new varieties of wheat, sorghum and sunflowers specifically for their revolutionary system.

The perennial polyculture system is not yet working at a practical level. That doesn't mean it isn't important. The scientists at The Land Institute have given us a blueprint for an agricultural system that could support us perpetually without depleting the soil or pumping carbon into the atmosphere. Even if no single Land Institute invention were ever implemented globally, that blueprint creates a new standard for agriculture that will survive, and will help our species to survive, perpetually.

It's a standard that promotes beauty and abundance.

The Case Studies

Applied to our own endeavors, my wife and I have found that the simple queries introduced in this book have changed our priorities and redirected our efforts. In our home, this line of thinking has changed our goals and aspirations. On our farm, it has reinforced some of our practices and altered others. I experimented with different ways of evaluating our efforts before settling on the four questions. They provided sound guidance in almost every setting I could think of, more effectively than any of the other possibilities I considered.

Of course there are no standard answers to these queries. Their application depends completely on the people involved. The point of the exercise is to initiate change. The queries don't describe our destination, except in very general terms. We aim to create a sustainable, beautiful and abundant future for ourselves and the other creatures dependent on this planet. The queries may help us identify our next few steps. Some individuals and organizations will make bold, pioneering decisions. They will go off in bold, pioneering directions. Others may make only small, incremental changes in the ways they are doing things, laying firm foundations for more dramatic change later on.

The potential for broad impact is greatest among those who approach change tentatively–because that's bound to be the largest group. Innovators are always rare. The sea changes temperature one degree at a time. Most people and organizations change slowly, in small increments.

I offer here three case studies of how the queries might direct change within three very different organizations–our own Rancho Cappuccino; the business I run, Ogden Publications; and (at the extreme other end of the size and influence spectrum) Google, Inc.

Our farm is a small private enterprise with an implicit concern for public benefit. It's our home as well as a small business.

Ogden Publications is a private company that, among other things, attracts audiences interested in sustainability. Even though concern for the future is woven into the business' DNA, we buy a lot of paper, ship a lot of magazines and fly our employees and associates all over the world. It's not easy to be an environmentally responsible business.

And Google is, arguably, the most powerful institution of the digital era, massively prosperous and profoundly influential through the way it distributes access to information on the Internet.

The queries don't give answers. Those have to be provided by the people involved. The idea is to raise interesting issues and provide a framework for great conversations.

CASE STUDY ONE

The Farm, Rancho Cappuccino

Rancho Cappuccino is what we call our farm, 50 acres of tall-grass prairie a few miles outside Lawrence, Kansas. I live there with my wife, Carolyn, two dogs, two cockatiels and our live-stock. At any given time we keep 15-20 head of black angus, Hereford, and cross-bred cattle; 20-60 head of katahdin and katahdin-cross sheep; 15-30 head of mixed-breed goats; about 40 chickens; two or three donkeys and a 14-year-old gray mule named Zero.

The farm provides most of our food and most of our recreation.

Farming is the reflection of our value system. Rancho Cappuccino is the vessel for our lives. Most of the time we can't imagine changing this lifestyle, although on the morning I'm writing this it's about 10 degrees Fahrenheit outside and I need to move hay out to the cattle through snow drifts three feet deep. Today, my feelings are mixed.

Someday we'll have to quit when the physical demands are too much for us. That's probably a ways down the road.

For today, the farm is the center of our lives in many ways and the focus of much of our attention.

Is it Beautiful?

Carolyn and I won't be bringing in a panel of landscape architects and interior designers to judge our efforts around our farm and home. If we did, we probably wouldn't get high marks. The shrubs along the front of the house are overgrown. The sidewalk is crumbling here and there. The arbor I built in front of the chicken house looks ungainly–some might say ugly. But the expert's assessment doesn't matter. The objective evaluation isn't important. It's the aspiration toward beauty that provides motivation and joy.

We'll be replacing the shrubs one of these days and repairing the sidewalk. I'm going to get some vines to grow over my arbor and disguise it.

Suburban lawns on two sides, a strip of woods on the east and a big field of corn or soybeans on the north surround our farm. Our natural pastures probably look unkempt to some people, but a couple of neighbors have commented that it's nice to see the grass growing tall in the spring. Around the house, we leave about half the grass unmown through the summer. Those undisturbed patches of prairie are my favorite features on the property. Indian grass, two species of bluestem, several species of grama, buffalo grass, switchgrass and two dozen other species compete for space out there and grow tall, some of them soaring well above our heads. At the height of summer you can't see our biggest bull in the middle of a pasture in grass six feet tall. In the parts of our yard where we don't mow or graze, the height and density of the plants is a monument to nature's bounty. The grass is taller than our heads and so thick that walking through it is like plunging through deep snow. It moves continuously in the wind and changes color over the course of the season, from an intense green in spring to a prairie kaleidoscope as the grasses mature in late summer, flashing a hundred shades of green, yellow, purple and red in sun. I try to take photos as the year progresses, but they never quite capture the beauty of it.

If you live within sight of Biscayne Bay or Mount Rainier you probably find my passion for 50 acres of manure-strewn Kansas prairie quaint–or maybe pathetic.

It wasn't exactly love at first sight.

I always found the land here fairly attractive. The natural savannah is easy on the eyes. The exposed limestone in the hillsides gives it a Western flair I like. The air smells good here, grassy with a hint of juniper.

But the land, like any true love, becomes more beautiful the more time you spend in intimate contact. I think this is particularly true of the prairie. From a distance the grasses are a green blur. The trees are small and indistinct. The hills are only hills. The flowers are mostly small and grow close to the ground. You have to draw near and stare for a while to pick out the reds, blues and yellows of the different species, like subtle strokes of color in an oil painting. The old prairie juniper on a grassy hillside becomes, on close examination, one of the world's most majestic trees, gnarled, deep green, festooned with little ice-blue berries.

People everywhere probably have this experience of gradual infatuation with their landscapes. The Grand Tetons inspire love at first sight, but the rancher who spends six decades making his living on the grass at their feet can understand their beauty in ways that require familiarity. The land's steward knows the tawny color of the stones under the shallow riffle at a particular bend in the creek. He knows the place in the exposed pasture where the wind is likely to build a series of symmetrical snowdrifts and the particular blue shadow they make. The farmer may grow fond of a little stand of willows that fill up with butterflies in May. The angler remembers a mossy log that glows like an emerald in the water under a stream bank when the raking light strikes it 20 minutes before sunset. A deer hunter reminisces about a patch of forest not only because he found a big buck there, but more because he watched dawn make its gradual way through those woods a hundred times before he claimed his trophy.

Is Rancho Cappuccino beautiful? Yes. Are we making it more beautiful? Of course I believe we are. I think we are creating beauty with our care and stewardship, by paying attention to the farm's appearance and doing the work necessary to improve its health. But we're creating beauty more fundamentally, internally, by learning about the place, loving it and treating it with care. Year by year, its beauty is more compelling to us as we know it better. Beauty is, indeed, in the eye of the beholder.

Our recognition of beauty is the definition of beauty–in a person, a farm, a landscape or a planet. And as the individual aspires to make a place or an enterprise more beautiful, he or she cares for them more deeply, and better.

My wife and I will attend to the farm's maintenance. We will paint and prune. We want friends, passers-by and future owners to appreciate it. But they'll have to pay close attention if they want to learn to love it the way we do.

Does it Create Abundance?

When my wife and I consider whether Rancho Cappuccino helps create abundance, we need to look at all three underlying questions: Does it enhance natural resources, improving supply? Does it help reduce demand? And, does it help us embrace simplicity?

The mere fact that we raise food on our 50 acres makes a contribution to the supply of resources. If we were not farming the property, it might support horses or llamas, it might be subdivided for suburban housing or it might simply be neglected through the growing season and then burned off each spring to control weeds and wildfires. By rotating cattle, sheep and goats on the pastures we try to maximize the efficient conversion of grass into meat, while protecting the health of the land. We have to balance the overall productivity of the property against the need to protect the soil and water–and our desire to make it beautiful. We're confident that our property is far more productive than it was before we owned it, and that we make a sizable and material contribution to the conservation and supply of natural resources–healthy food, clean water and a diversity of living things.

Of course we also consume some resources that we wouldn't if we lived in a townhome. We drive a little farther to work. We own a heavy-duty pickup, a stock trailer and a compact tractor. We need diesel fuel for the truck and tractor. We haul animals here and there. We use electricity to thaw water for the livestock. To balance the extra consumption we buy more efficient automobiles when we can, we continue to maximize the efficiency of our energy usage and we try not to drive unnecessarily.

In the sum of things, we're pretty sure we're making a positive contribution to efficient food production. There's more food, produced more efficiently, and a healthier environment than would exist in a world without Rancho Cappuccino.

But does it reduce the net demand for resources?

The life of part-time farmers who also pursue demanding careers is neither the simplest nor the most frugal of human lifestyles. We drive back and forth to jobs every day–and we often feel compelled to exceed the speed limit, slightly. We travel for business by car and airplane. My wife and I work in separate offices, when we work at home, burning separate lights and, obviously, running separate computers.

Of course human productivity is a natural resource, also. I believe my wife's dedication to teaching creates benefits in the future for people and the planet. If she left teaching to stay home and can vegetables on a wood stove, would the world be better off? Probably not.

It is my privilege through my work to engage people in conversations about a healthy, sustainable human future. Would my contribution be more positive if I stopped publishing and retreated to the frugal simplicity of a farm? I don't believe it would.

Also, Carolyn and I travel for pleasure. We love South America and Hawaii. When I'm in New York or Los Angeles for business my wife sometimes comes along. We enjoy the museums, the music and the food. We particularly enjoy exploring the natural environment–deserts, mountains, islands and oceans. Travel is a luxury, but it also enhances our appreciation for human beings and the natural world. It is one of the products of abundance that I would rather not do without.

Furthermore, it's not logical to think that we can visualize an abundant future if we don't understand and appreciate abundance in our own lives. I believe we need to explore and appreciate the world–both intellectually and physically–in order to make a positive contribution to the collective human vision. In this respect, travel may be among the most important and constructive of our activities.

So we balance and manage our consumption of resources against our responsibilities to contribute to the world and our opportunities to explore and appreciate the planet.

The question of whether my lifestyle helps promote simplicity is not easy to answer. My wife and I raise most of our own food. That certainly sounds like it promotes simplicity. Of course it also requires that we manage equipment, vehicles, animals and land. We have demanding careers and something like two additional full-time jobs running the farm. It might promote simplicity, but it doesn't always feel simple.

On the other hand, if peace of mind is part of simplicity's definition, then our lifestyle supports simplicity in a profound way. We love to travel, but our favorite place is Rancho Cappuccino. On most holidays, this is where you'll find us. The farm inspires us to pour our love and attention into the land and when that land returns to us our food and health our appreciation is compounded. In a sense, that's human existence at its simplest and most elemental. Rancho Cappuccino helps us understand on a visceral level the basic realities. The sun shines. The grass grows. We live in a miraculous pantry stocked with solar energy. Our gardens mix sunshine with minerals and make tomatoes, blackberries, pumpkins and okra. We bring it together in our kitchen and freezers. Finally, it is all united at the dinner table with our friends and family.

The process clears my mind.

Is it Fair?

There's an insoluble issue at the center of any consideration of fairness. No matter where you live in the world, chances are that place was previously occupied by a culture different from your own. Chances are almost equally good that your homeland, wherever it is, was taken from its previous occupants by force. The evidence indicates that there are very, very few locations on the planet that have been occupied by only one culture, and there are relatively few convincing stories of peaceful assimilation.

Is the forcible conquest of another culture fair? I think most people would say it is not. However, it is so consistent a theme in human history that attempting to weigh the territorial rights of one culture against another generally leads us into a dialectic quagmire from which the societies cannot extract themselves in less than a couple of centuries, if ever.

For the sake of this discussion, I'm going to limit the question of fairness to one generation. Let's confine our discussion to the means by which we acquired our property from its previous owner, whose name is Bill. We paid him for it. He believes he received a fair price. We agree. We're friends today.

Because I can't meaningfully address the claims of the several different cultures who lived here before us, the seller and I will call it "fairly acquired" and move on to other areas of concern.

In the background of any discussion of land ownership is, of course, the question of economic disparity. Not everyone can afford to buy a farm like ours. It is not luxurious or glamorous, but it cost more than an average home in Kansas. (It cost a lot less than an average home in Seattle, San Francisco or New York, however.) Is it fair that some people have more money than others? Should we, in the name of fairness, refrain from owning things that an average family might not be able to afford?

Our North American culture's belief in free enterprise implies a belief in economic mobility. We believe in the potential for economic self-improvement. We see ourselves as industrious people pulling ourselves up by their own bootstraps. Our society still delivers on the promise of that vision. Right now many of the world's wealthiest individuals–people like Bill Gates, Warren Buffett and Larry Ellison–have accumulated their wealth and power during their own lifetimes. Those three individuals are among the four wealthiest people in the world at the time of this writing.[141] Three out of four of the richest people in the world are Americans who built their fortunes through intelligence, enterprise and hard work during their own lifetimes. Seven out of the world's 10 richest people are self-made billionaires from four different nations:

1. Bill Gates' father was a Seattle lawyer. His family was affluent, but not wealthy, at least not by American standards. Gates founded Microsoft and helped invent the first widely distributed operating system for personal computers.
2. Investor Warren Buffett grew up in Omaha, Nebraska's, middle class. His grandfather owned a grocery store. His father was a stockbroker who was elected to the U.S. Congress.
3. Larry Ellison was born to an unwed mother and raised by an aunt and uncle in a two-bedroom apartment in Chicago. He dropped out of college to move to California and write software. He founded the database behemoth Oracle.
4. Ingvar Kamprad grew up on a farm in southern Sweden and used his childhood savings to start IKEA, the international furniture retailer.
5. Karl Albrecht's father was a miner and then a baker's assistant in Essen, Germany. Karl and his brother, Theo, founded the international discount grocery chain, Aldi.
6. Theo Albrecht is Karl Albrecht's brother and partner.
7. Amancio Ortega began his career as a boy doing odd jobs in shirt stores around La Coruna, Galicia, Spain. He built his fortune in the fashion industry with dozens of international brands. His father was a railway worker.

The other three people in the top 10 inherited their money– only 30 percent of the group. Economic mobility is a visible reality in many places around the world.

When people talk about economic disparity they call forth two contrasting images of fairness. On one side is the question of whether any system can be called fair if it rewards some human beings with mansions and private jets while others do without adequate food. Conversely, would our economic system be fair if it didn't offer compensation to those who work harder and invent more? And without economic incentives, wouldn't human beings be less innovative? Aren't economic disparity–and economic mobility–important sources of energy for human endeavor?

Tacitly, most nations have codified their economic theories based on a compromise incorporating both concepts, while perfecting neither. There are hungry and homeless people in most countries. Nearly every country taxes its wealthiest residents to provide social programs to its neediest, while allowing the wealthy to remain wealthy. No one, it seems, is satisfied with his own country's system. We are generally even less satisfied with the systems of other countries.

As always, our sense of fairness evolves and changes.

So, is it fair that Carolyn and I should have a farm of our very own? By American standards we are far from wealthy, but we are better off than most. Perhaps the answer to this question from a personal perspective is that, yes, we think we've achieved what we've achieved in a relatively fair system and we do not feel guilty for living at Rancho Cappuccino. We feel fortunate. We are conscious that many have less. We share a little through charities, including the Heifer Project that distributes food and livestock to poor people around the world. It's a way of recognizing our good fortune. In the future, we hope to share more.

We sell our animals for meat at prices most people can afford–a little more than the price for supermarket meat. When possible, we donate meat through charities that can turn it into meals for the needy.

We don't hire illegal aliens. In fact, we don't need any employees except a friend who stays at the farm to keep an eye on things when we're out of town. Another friend, a fellow farmer, shares labor with us on the rare occasions when an extra body is needed, and we return the favor.

That's how we work on being fair to people less fortunate. Fairness–like contagiousness, beauty and abundance–is not so much a standard to be achieved as it is a criterion to be interpreted and applied. We strive for fairness, even though it can't be clearly defined much less perfected. In the striving, I think we create a better world. We don't exploit workers. We produce meat in ways that protect the environment for every living thing that shares our habitat.

But is the whole system fair to the livestock?

After a recent talk I gave in San Francisco, a man raised his hand and asked me how I could distinguish between "human slavery and animal slavery."

Now there's a provocative question.

I think we're as humane as any livestock farmer can be. Our animals live natural lives in a clean place. They are well fed. We handle them as gently as possible, and as seldom as possible. We allow all our calves to stay with their mothers until they wean naturally, rather than separating them young so the cows will breed again sooner. We keep a bull so our animals don't need to be trucked around or confined in a squeeze chute to be artificially inseminated. In fact, our cattle go their whole lives without being roped, run through a squeeze chute or hauled, at least until they are sold or slaughtered. We choose our slaughterhouses in part based on their humane treatment of the animals they kill. We look for facilities that handle the animals gently and take care not to traumatize them unnecessarily. There's a surprisingly wide variety in the habits of people who handle livestock in close quarters all day. Some people are rough with them. Others take a lot of care with the animal's feelings.

We don't brand our animals or tag their ears. Because they have ample room, clean water and because we don't haul in replacement stock very often, we virtually never require a veterinarian, so the animals don't have to go through the disturbing experience of being confined and handled. Most livestock hates to be confined in small spaces or handled by human beings. I believe a lot of farmers cause problems during their birthing seasons by watching their animals too closely and upsetting the mothers' sense of security. Imagine a human mother trying to give birth while being monitored, much less handled, by a predatory species.

Most importantly, our animals are never alone. Cattle, sheep, goats, mules, donkeys, chickens, turkeys and dogs are all social creatures that crave, most of all, the companionship of their own kind. In particular, they are happiest in the herd, flock or pack where they live in a stable social order. So we do our best never to keep any of these animals alone.

The cat's another story, of course. He seems to like his luxurious solitude.

We aim to give our animals natural, healthy lives.

In the end, of course, they are killed for their meat.

Is this fair? That's a fascinating question. All life ends in death, including yours and mine. Nearly every animal in the natural world–particularly the herbivore–ends its life in the jaws of a predator. In the natural world, they are either taken by a predator early in life before they become strong enough and fast enough to escape, or they are taken when old age begins to slow them down. It is natural, but is it fair?

So far as I can tell, human beings are the only predator that shows any concern for the comfort of its prey. Other predators commonly begin to devour their victims before they are dead. Some swallow their prey alive. In times of plenty it's not uncommon to see predators toying with prey, seemingly for sport. I'm convinced that the prey's feelings are not a consideration for most predators.

So in a sense, to be killed by human beings is a lucky break for an herbivore if we achieve our goal of killing them quickly and humanely. Otherwise, they are inevitably dragged down and mauled by something less considerate.

Most of our livestock would not survive long without our care. The sheep and goats depend on the protection of our donkeys and mules, who naturally become members of the flocks and instinctively protect their friends from roving predators. Without that protection, the sheep and goats don't last long. They are not fast, strong or shrewd enough for the wild.

All the livestock depends on hay in the depths of winter. Even if they could roam freely across the landscape, they are not well equipped to feed on the dormant grass beneath a foot of crusty snow. Survival rates would go way down without the hay we cut, bale, and deliver.

I think our mules and donkeys might do OK without our help. Horses and donkeys thrive in the wild elsewhere. Domesticated sheep, goats and cattle don't typically survive very long in the wild, though, unless they have their own predator-free island in a warm climate.

Without intentional breeding and human care, the sorts of animals we raise wouldn't exist. There would be bison here where we live, elk and whitetail deer in place of cattle, sheep and goats. In the absence of human beings, there would be mountain lions, wolves, bears and coyotes to prey on them. If human beings hadn't come to North America, there might be saber-toothed cats, dire wolves and cave bears, too. Mastodons and camels. Giant porcupines and ground sloths.

But we do live here and I can't figure out any reason that we have any less right to live here than any other species. I don't think our existence, in and of itself, can be defined as "unfair."

Neither could I define it as unfair to eat meat. If it were, then the very existence of predators would be an offense. The whitetail deer is not morally superior to the coyote. Without predators, the ecosystem would be grotesquely overpopulated, a zero-sum environment where every creature was jostling with every other creature for a few plant-based or carrion-based calories. Predators are a necessary and beautiful part of our elegant system. A world without them would not be a less painful, less traumatic place. The pain and trauma of mortality would merely take slightly different shapes. There would be more disease. Death, on the whole, would take longer.

There is, of course, the argument that a vegan diet uses less of the planet's resources. That's fundamentally true, and if our goal is to maximize the human population while minimizing our consumption then the vegan discipline certainly makes sense. Eventually, though, human population growth consumes the entire surplus, anyway. All the grasslands and forests get plowed up to grow carrots, corn and soybeans.

And if one accepts the ethic that requires us to consume as little as possible, as individuals, then aren't we stuck in that tiresome old austerity paradigm? Don't we all end up in sackcloth eventually?

On the other hand, since human beings can feel empathy for the animals we consume, do we have a moral responsibility not to consume them?

That is, I think the best argument for vegetarianism. Since humans can conceptualize the pain felt by our prey, should we nurture our empathy and refrain from eating meat?

I think about this question a lot. In a few days I'll load five of my young rams into a trailer and take them to be killed. A few days after that they will be in our freezers. I held them when they were babies. Over the past nine months I've watched them grow from two-pound, curly-headed sprites into 80-pound monuments of ovine masculinity, created from grass. They are out there in the snow this morning, sparring and bucking, sharing a big bale of hay.

Each of them has a personality and I care about each of them as individuals. When I take them to be killed, I'll feel that familiar twinge. It is a specific sort of pain I would not feel if I were a vegan, or if I purchased my meat at the store.

So which is the more genuine demonstration of empathy: To refrain from predation altogether or to consume meat feelingly, with genuine sadness and appreciation for the creatures we consume?

The plowed acre where the crop farmer grows grain and vegetables displaces millions of living things. There are all kinds of studies and estimates of insect populations, but the most conservative of them indicate that tens of millions of individual insects live on an acre of prairie or forest, significantly fewer if that land is cultivated and only a fraction survive if it is plowed, fertilized and sprayed with pesticides and herbicides.

A lot of people would like to believe in a myth of innocence, a myth in which human beings, if they are sufficiently enlightened, do not contribute to the painful deaths of other creatures. That is a wholly unrealistic vision, of course and indulges a cartoonish understanding of the natural world. If a hunter hadn't eaten Bambi's mom, something else surely would have.

I respect the discipline imposed by a vegan lifestyle. Like any rigorous exercise it demonstrates a commitment to an ideal, and that's admirable.

But I've chosen to exercise my own compassion through active engagement with the natural world as a gardener and a farmer. I don't feel my lifestyle is any less fair to our fellow creatures than the lifestyles of my vegan friends in town.

If it is slavery to be consumed by other creatures then we are all slaves to that aspect of nature. Predators, bacteria and viruses victimize us all and, eventually, we are all consumed.

Questions of fairness–toward animals and people–do help us make decisions on the farm every day. Like most people who raise sheep and goats I used to castrate our rams and bucks within a few days of birth. The surgery was unpleasant and, presumably, painful for the animals. So I tried leaving them intact and separating them before they were fertile, at about four months of age. That worked fine. They miss their moms for about a day or so, then seem perfectly happy in the "boy's club." And some customers–Africans and people from the Middle East–prefer them that way. A happy accident.

My wife and I try to fairly accommodate our predatory animal neighbors–coyotes, opossums, raccoons, hawks, foxes, skunks, eagles and bobcats–by using protection animals and a secure chicken coop rather than shotguns and poison bait. The donkeys and mules work in the pastures with the sheep and goats. The dogs live in the yard with the chickens and turkeys. So far so good. We lose a chicken or a turkey once in a while, but it feels like a fair system of sharing, all in all. Once in a while I have to scare a skunk or opossum out of the chicken house myself. They generally take the hint. One tiny skunk and I had a recent confrontation in the chicken house. He didn't spray me, but he thought if he looked fierce enough I might back down. He raised his extravagant tail and bounced across the floor at me. When I didn't retreat, he scooted out the door. Imagine my relief.

When I ask myself the question of whether our life on the farm is fair for people or animals, my conditional answers don't solve any existential riddles. The question does give me a continual series of ideas about how we might change our practices to live more fairly:

1. Although the farm probably reduces the overall consumption necessary to produce the food we create, we know we could consume less. We'll continue to operate equipment as efficiently, and seldom, as possible. We'll buy local biodiesel fuel.
2. When we trade cars, we will make fuel efficiency a priority.
3. We want to generate our own electricity for our home and barn and maybe to power a new electric car when one is available.
4. We want to change the binding on our hay bales to natural, biodegradable sisal twine.
5. We try to use, and reuse, all our tools and materials to their full potential so we don't consume or discard any materials unnecessarily.
6. We will keep on trying to manage our farm to better protect the natural environment, to provide habitat for wild animals and to make it as productive as we can while protecting natural resources.
7. We'll welcome guests who want to learn more about conscientious agriculture.
8. We'll keep on writing and talking about it.
9. We want to manage our money carefully to earn more and spend less so we can give more away.
10. And we'll be actively engaged in this inquiry for the rest of our lives.

It's a great project, improving the fairness of how we live. It has captured our imaginations.

Is it Contagious?

It's a great source of pleasure and satisfaction to me that both my home and my business provide me with constant opportunities to engage with working toward a beautiful and abundant future. At work, my colleagues and I receive hundreds of letters and emails each month to *Mother Earth News* and *GRIT* magazine from people engaged with their own adventures in self-reliance. The correspondence bubbles with enthusiasm, humor and innovation.

My business exists, in large part, because the lifestyle we promote is contagious. On every continent in the world there are large regions where a family can, through ingenuity and hard work, provide a lot of its own food in active partnership with the natural environment. And people get excited about that.

Of course most people tend to think of food production in an industrial context. And society tends to indentify industrial food production as the answer to the needs of a rapidly growing human population. People take these conditions for granted. The notion of unbridled human population growth fueled by industrial agriculture is abhorrent to me because it precludes the potential for diverse, small-scale, localized farming and gardening. The idea that food can only be efficiently produced by industrial means is both wrong and wrong-headed. The resources needed to grow a little food at minimal cost are simple: Some fertile earth and people with a little spare time.

The next time you are on an airplane, look at the land below you. Are there empty city lots down there, rural subdivisions sporting 10-acre lawns, neglected horse pastures, overgrazed grasslands? Could they be reclaimed, gardened and restored to productive health? Couldn't they grow food or enhance the view?

Around the world, vast amounts of arable land are left idle in lawns, damaged pastureland and vacant lots. The big suburban lot is most evident in North America, probably, but many nations offer their own versions. Imagine if all the lawns of global suburbia dedicated, say, 25 percent of their area to food and flower gardening.

I like the technical description "brownfield," coined to describe urban or semi-urban land left in gravel and weeds. Sometimes it is contaminated. Often it is only neglected–a potential organic garden waiting for seeds and some individual's vision. Community gardeners have redeemed thousands of brownfields in cities around the world, enhancing their neighborhoods, providing local food and strengthening the social fabric. The American Community Gardening Association publicizes research showing that urban gardens enhance property values, reduce crime rates and build healthy feelings of citizenship.[142] When you think about it, what demonstrates our citizenship more concretely than planting a garden? Even a potted tomato plant on an apartment veranda is a symbol of enterprising optimism.

Traveling across Europe by train or freeway, you'll see vast garden "allotments" on the outskirts of cities. In that version of a community garden, families are assigned individual plots, usually of a few hundred square meters, where they can garden and relax in the open air or in their tiny, sometimes elaborate sheds. Einstein called his shed on a plot outside Berlin his "Spandau Castle."[143] European cities invented allotment gardens in the 18th century, around the dawn of the industrial revolution and urban sprawl. Millions of Europeans spend their summer weekends on their allotments, and they have organizations like

Luxembourg's *Office International du Coin de Terre et des Jardins Familiaux* that represent their interests. About 3 million families belong to the Luxembourg organization that promotes garden allotments as social, environmental and economic assets to their communities.[144] Many of them are quite beautiful and there are long waiting lists for plots.

In the United States huge lawns and horse pastures symbolize the "rural lifestyle" in the countryside around our cities. According to the American Horse Council there are more than 9 million horses in the United States, about 7 million of them kept for "recreational" purposes and horse shows.[145] If the grass, hay and grain of America's least-used horses were being devoted to food animals like cattle, sheep and goats, somewhere between 15 million and 30 million carnivorous Americans could have their protein needs met by the liberated resources.

In other words, there's still lots of room for gardeners and small-scale farmers to create some food. When land can't be bought, it can often be rented or borrowed in exchange for produce. Small farms like Rancho Cappuccino can be replicated in nearly any country.

So, can humanity keep doing this in the future?

Back during the days of the early Roman Empire, Pliny the Elder reflected that, "Our fathers used to say that the master's eye is the best fertilizer."[146] Apparently by the time of Jesus it was already old knowledge that with proper attention agricultural land became more fertile and remained fertile, indefinitely. Some of the olive orchards and vineyards on which Pliny meditated are still under cultivation today. Ten thousand years ago, the land where my family grows grass and cattle grew bison, elk, camels, horses and giant ground sloths. There's no evidence that, when managed properly, it is any less fertile today than it was then.

To keep our garden and our farm productive in the future,

we only need to preserve the space and keep paying attention.

The Kansas Land Trust[147], like other land trusts around the world, helps preserve valuable land by placing it under "conservation easements." The conservation easement is a contract permanently transferring the "development rights" for a piece of property to the land trust. That means the landowner can sell the property, but neither its current owner nor any future owner can develop or subdivide it, depending on the terms of the easement. In the meantime, the farmers pay taxes only on the agricultural value of the property, not its development value. The owner who donates the easement gets either a big tax deduction for the donation, or in some cases gets paid outright for the easement. The farm stays a farm. The open space stays open. The springs keep flowing and the grass keeps growing. The easement can even prescribe specific uses and practices. So we could make sure our pastures will always be pastures, at least as long as our current legal system survives.

Of course the work of raising livestock is physical and I won't be able to do it indefinitely. As I write this, I'm recovering from a sprained knee sustained in an icy barnyard as I wrestled with a frozen bale of hay. I know that I will eventually have to give up manhandling young rams and chasing contrary cattle. Eventually, I suppose I'll give up the livestock and concentrate on the vegetables. We might move to a smaller place. But we'll try to leave this place in good condition for the next farmer. If we can afford it, maybe we'll donate a conservation easement so Rancho Cappuccino can't ever be subdivided. Maybe this farm can be a farm for a long time after we're gone.

One of the best attributes of small-scale agriculture is its durability. If the fertility of the soil is protected and appropriate land is preserved from development, all over the world people can provide their own sustenance, locally, until the human population outstrips the local resources. And, if a society decides its human populations can be held within the capacities of local farms to feed them, then our small farms can be replicated into the future, until further notice.

I think that's a very contagious idea.

Initiatives

How have the queries shaped our lives and our aspirations for Rancho Cappuccino? Mostly, the queries raise new questions that we ask ourselves each day. Should we keep fewer animals, for the sake of the pastures? Are we risking the long-term sustainability of our pastures? Or would it be more efficient and abundant to have a few more sheep and fewer cattle? Do we need to start the tractor today? Can we raise our own chicken feed?

Eventually, the queries lead to calls for action. When we ask ourselves these questions, the answers call for action. Our queries have placed a number of items on our agenda:

Generate more power for ourselves. Consume less from the grid. It will, initially, take some money out of savings, but we can generate electricity photovoltaically and, possibly, with wind turbines. During the writing of this book we installed a solar system to heat our household water. We can enhance the efficiency of our heating and air conditioning with geothermal heat exchangers. We can agitate for net metering, so we don't have to equip our system with expensive, toxic batteries.

Goals: Abundance, fairness and contagiousness.

Build a greenhouse for year-round vegetables. It's not especially expensive. It'll take a little elbow grease. Time to get busy.

Goals: Beauty, abundance, fairness and contagiousness.

Put money in savings so the mortgage could be paid off in a pinch. Currently we owe money on the farm and would have to sell it quickly if we lost much of our income. We can't afford to protect the property with a conservation easement until we mostly own it.

Goals: Abundance and contagiousness.

Share more with local food charities.

Goals: Abundance and fairness.

Improve our goat herd and our hay. Our cattle and sheep thrive on a diet of grass hay in the winter, but the goats grow thin and suffer from the cold. We have been supplementing their diets with a little grain, which costs money and requires cultivation. If we bring in new bloodlines and manage our hay for goat nutrition, maybe we can wean ourselves–and the goats–off the grain.

Goals: Beauty, abundance and contagiousness.

Plant more trees. We need trees in the pastures to provide shade for the livestock. And we could use more trees in the yard, evergreens to block the north wind in the winter and deciduous species to shade the south exposure in the summer.

Goals: Beauty, abundance and contagiousness.

Fix the ugly arbor on the chicken house. I didn't do a good job when I designed it or when I built it. I'm going to plant some aggressive vines around it and hope they give it a leafy makeover.

Goals: Beauty. Maybe abundance and contagiousness, if I can get grapes to grow on it.

The photovoltaics and the geothermal may have to wait until there's more money in savings. We're still working on those decisions. The trees, the goats and the hay are all long-term projects that will evolve slowly. We can share more with the food banks now and we have started on the greenhouse and the trees. We have our work cut out for us for many years to come.

And for that, we're grateful.

CASE STUDY TWO

The Biz, Ogden Publications, Inc.

In 1996 we moved our family to Kansas when my employers acquired a small company in Topeka and asked me to run it. At that time it included *Capper's* magazine, *GRIT* magazine and Capper's Insurance Service, which sells insurance mostly to the subscribers of the magazines.

My colleagues and I hoped the small, unconventional company would provide a platform for something bigger–something that could grow. In fact, it has. Today Ogden Publications employs about three times as many people as worked in the business when we started. I feel very fortunate to have shared this business adventure with my colleagues.

One of our first–and best–ideas was that a media company could focus on the idea of sustainability. I thought that the converging interests of the baby-boom generation, which had always been interested in protecting the environment and the millennial generation born 30-40 years later would create a new surge of interest in lifestyles that preserved valuable traditions of self-reliance while minimizing humanity's negative impact on the environment. I was working on that theory in the form of a business plan when we had the opportunity to acquire *Mother Earth News* near the end of 2000 and my colleagues and I put the theory to work.

Success in business is always relative. By some standards Ogden Publications has been very successful. Our company is a solid, growing business, but our growth rate pales in comparison with the juggernauts of Silicon Valley. Our business has supported itself, grown and returned benefits to its shareholders. Today we have nine magazines, our websites are the fastest growing aspect of the business and our properties are arguably the largest media presence in the field of sustainable lifestyles. That category makes up about 80 percent of our media business.

Today the magazines are *Mother Earth News*, *Natural Home*, *Utne Reader*, *The Herb Companion*, *GRIT* magazine, *Capper's* magazine, *Motorcycle Classics* magazine, *Farm Collector* magazine and *Gas Engine Magazine.* There are some smaller entities–magazines, books, websites, e-commerce enterprises, merchandise–but those nine brands make up the bulk of our business. We have offices in Kansas and Minnesota, plus full-time colleagues in Colorado, Illinois, Oregon and New York.

IS IT BEAUTIFUL?

There is no objective standard for beauty, in a farm, a magazine or a website.

So maybe we should rephrase the question: "Are we aspiring to beauty?"

In every media business, managers have to decide how much to spend on aesthetics. The movie director makes decisions about the costs of sets and lighting. The magazine publisher decides how many art directors to hire and how much to spend on photography, paper and printing.

We spend a lot less on our appearance than the big fashion magazines. A bit more, probably than some of our competitors who publish magazines about solar energy or farm machinery. We try to strike a balance. For us, we must admit, contagiousness–and its product, profit–are higher priorities than "beauty." But that doesn't mean we don't aspire to be beautiful.

The photographs we feature in the magazines and on the websites must be beautiful to our audiences. The subject matter is the principal element of beauty. Our production values need only be beautiful *enough*. One reader might find a Scottish Highland bull quite beautiful. Another admires a Minneapolis Moline tractor or a classic BMW motorcycle.

It's our job to reproduce photographs, art and video footage beautiful enough for our audiences to appreciate. We recalculate that balance every day.

We also have an office, of course, where we have the opportunity of enhancing appearances. We could hang more art and cultivate more houseplants. We could maintain the outside of the building a little better. Our building is a very simple commercial structure in a very plain industrial subdivision, but every little bit helps. This year a group of my colleagues planted two plots of vegetables in front of the building and they made us much more beautiful. Someday we might even renovate a more elegant older commercial building, make it energy-efficient and invest more in aesthetics. Someday, maybe.

In the meantime, yes, we aspire to beauty. And we create some beautiful things, judging with our own eyes and the eyes of our audiences. But of course it's only through the ongoing daily aspiration to beauty that beauty is achieved. So, we keep it up.

Does it Create Abundance?

We try to help people create abundance by both possible methods: by conserving existing resources and by propagating new resources. In other words, the two basic tools at our disposal are *conservation* and *innovation*. We try to promote uncomplicated sources of pleasure that give our audiences tips for a fulfilling life created from relatively simple things. And we support new technology that generates energy–that most fundamental of all assets–from more ubiquitous and renewable sources.

You might even say that the creation of abundance–or a sense of abundance–is right at the core of our mission. We advocate the creation of abundant food from our gardens, abundant pleasure from simple projects like the construction of a bench or the renovation of an old tractor, a sense of abundance in the realization that we are born on a planet rich in resources and diversity, both human and biological.

The question of creating abundance, in the global sense, is more relevant for us than it might be for most businesses because the issue is woven into our subject matter. But every business is dedicated to the creation of abundance–ideally for its owners, its employees and its customers.

In business, just as in the rest of the world, abundance is created both through conservation and through innovation.

Most business managers seem to be more reliant either on conservation or innovation. Many entrepreneurs build careers on their ability to invent and innovate, but never master the techniques of cost control. They find it difficult to run a stable, profitable business. Other businesspeople are overly reliant on frugality and fail to innovate. They may watch their highly efficient businesses decline and fail because, when the environment changed, they were unable or unwilling to gamble on new sources of revenue.

Like businesspeople everywhere, we try to find a balance between these two approaches. We try to invest wisely and manage our money frugally while remaining alert for new opportunities. We balance our efforts between conservation and innovation.

Is it Fair?

It is, perhaps, the principal philosophical quandary of the Industrial Age, "Is capitalism fair?"

Resoundingly, our experience sends back the answer: "Sometimes, yes. Sometimes, no."

I'm reminded of Winston Churchill's speech in which he acknowledged that democracy could be said to be "the worst form of government except for all those other forms that have been tried from time to time."[148] Capitalism may be an unfair economic system, but it may also be the fairest that's been tried. It can, at its best, reward ingenuity and hard work. At its worst it provides a rationale for the routine subjugation the powerful have always exercised upon the weak.

I'm not remotely prepared to argue the abstract virtues of capitalism against any other economic system. I am prepared to assert that capitalism has been a highly successful philosophy in recent centuries. If you want to get anything done in the world today, you had better know how to engage with capitalism.

A long time ago I decided that capitalism could be fair, and so it was a good enough place to exert our efforts. I don't consider business a superior enterprise to government or charity work. Nor do I consider it inferior. When an individual or a company engages with a system like capitalism, we tap into its power.

Capitalism is enormously powerful. It has tremendous potential to spread opportunity in the world by stimulating and rewarding innovation. The fact that some of its products fall short of that potential does not diminish it.

Capitalism can, for instance, be very generous to its storytellers. Capitalism rewards them even when they are disrespectful of the capitalist institutions on which they depend. NBC pays Jay Leno very, very well even when he's spending his time ridiculing NBC. Producer Oprah Winfrey, comedian Larry David and *New York Times* economics columnist Paul Krugman are likewise paid (well, very well or unbelievably well) for communicating messages that are sometimes critical of the capitalistic institutions they serve and sometimes derisive in their tone. They are allowed this privilege because they attract audiences, and audiences pay money–both directly through their subscriptions and indirectly through advertising revenue.

Our business works the same way. Our writers sometimes criticize the system, but everyone understands that the system makes our existence possible. And the more successful our company is within the system, the more influential our work becomes. When our stories are interesting, we and our colleagues prosper. If we fail to compel an audience, the enterprise fails.

That's fair, I think.

So our business competes in the marketplace–for audience, for advertisers, for people and for allies. When we are successful, we can create prosperity and personal growth for the people associated with our enterprise. The stakes in this game are pretty high. We're trying to make sure they are won fairly and distributed fairly.

The distribution of resources is, perhaps, the most complex problem in any business that employs more than one person. Some managers like to claim that it is simple. They'll assert that you just have to pay the market rates for payroll, goods and services. Surpluses are distributed to shareholders. Easy as pie.

But what is the market-rate compensation for a highly motivated, creative and disciplined manager? At a small manufacturer in the Midwestern United States that number might be 1 or 2 percent of the market rate for the same individual at a Wall Street investment bank. I believe I've known highly intelligent individuals working and succeeding at small enterprises across the country who would compare favorably in every criterion—intelligence, creativity, work ethic, loyalty, dedication–to other friends of the same age and same qualities working on Wall Street. Nevertheless, the factory manager in rural Minnesota makes 1 percent of the Wall-Streeter's salary.

Can that possibly be fair?

My friends in Kansas and New Mexico and Utah seem to be at least as happy, on the whole, as my friends working in the skyscrapers at the southern end of Manhattan Island. They are, from what I can tell, very engaged in their pursuits of building agricultural scales, mining potash or raising dairy cows. And they are conscious that they could have, if they had wished, pursued more remunerative careers. Why didn't they? For that matter, why didn't I?

For some, there were geographic considerations. Most people don't want to sever their geographic and familial roots. Others discovered a sense of purpose or a personal passion for a vocation such as farming or engineering or journalism. But all of us share one characteristic that determined our fates, economically speaking: Money isn't the most important thing we want from our careers. Our career choices weren't determined by rates of pay, mostly, or we would have chosen differently.

Sometimes when we're struggling to pay the rent it's hard to remember, but most of us chose careers that we knew weren't likely to make us rich.

So is it fair that we didn't get rich? Sigh. Yeah, probably. If our stars align so that we make some money, do we feel gratified? Of course. Should we wear our affluence as a badge of superiority? Certainly not. If we don't get rich, will we judge ourselves failures? Hell, no.

The question of whether Wall Street bankers are paid too much is a question, I think, of efficiency, not fairness. Maybe entrepreneurs should open more investment banks in South Dakota and Idaho to see if some down-to-earth organizations can't supply the same services at a lower cost.

With all this in mind, how is an employer to decide whether he is compensating people fairly? I believe that, first, every employer should define compensation more broadly than pay. The payroll check is only one facet of a large, intricate compensation formula.

After pay, benefits are the second-most-obvious element in a compensation package. In the United States today, no mindful individual can feel financially secure without health insurance. Most employers have acknowledged this fact and make group health insurance part of their standard compensation packages. Likewise vacation time, sick leave and some form of insurance against disability are important to peace of mind. Holidays and some flexibility in scheduling enhance family life and help employees create balance in their lives.

Beyond salary and benefits are the more abstract but equally important elements that make an employee feel valued. Does the staff have access to management? Do managers listen effectively? Does the management, in turn, share meaningful strategic information with the staff? Are all employees aware of the company's philosophies, strategies and tactics? Are achievements acknowledged and celebrated?

More controversially, are standards for productivity and demeanor established and upheld? Nothing undermines the morale of dedicated employees more insidiously than a general tolerance for a lack of dedication. Great team members want to be held accountable. And they want to work with other people who feel the same way.

In discussions of compensation we shouldn't neglect the shareholders. The business' owners, whether they are scattered across all the equities markets around the world or in the office next door, need to be fairly compensated for putting their capital at risk. How do managers and stockholders define a fair return? Generally, it's defined by what the shareholders require.

For better or for worse, the question of whether a business is fairly compensating its stakeholders–owners, employers, suppliers, etc.– is determined by whether those stakeholders FEEL they are being compensated fairly. Compensation is a compilation of many different resources transferred through a business. If the employers, managers and owners–all the stakeholders–feel good about their participation, then I think the compensation can be judged fair.

Some managers will succumb to the temptation to create this sense of fairness by overpaying shareholders, employees and suppliers. One can often silence criticism, at least temporarily, by paying a little more. A lot of people have ruined businesses that way. When costs run amok and a business fails, none of the stakeholders is pleased with the outcome.

My colleagues and I have to define fairness in our own business through the traditional process of negotiation. We are called upon to negotiate rates of pay with our employees, to resist demands for raises unless there is evidence those raises create value for the enterprise, to negotiate aggressively with suppliers to get the best possible prices and to persuade our shareholders that ongoing investment in the business will create more value in the long run, even when it reduces dividends this year. The definition of fairness is renegotiated every day in uncountable different conversations all over our offices and boardrooms.

In this process and in the very fundamentals of capitalism, some people find a kind of violence. When we're negotiating, we are attempting to move resources from one place to another through force of personality, intelligence and strategy. It can be compared with war, although my colleagues, suppliers and competitors are generally not killing each other.

Capitalism distributes power in the form of money. People with money have more power then those without. It's not the only source of power in our society, but it may be the primary power source.

So if we compare our capitalist society with a model society in which power is distributed equitably, then we are disappointed. The distribution of power and money is not perfectly equitable. There is even a kind of violence in the way entities compete for money and power.

But where can the historian find a perfectly equitable social structure? Small tribes may have been run by consensus, here and there, and some people may idealize the stone-age lifestyle, but if you were a member of a competing tribe and happened to stumble into their circle of firelight some evening you might find the welcome less than equitable.

Communism and socialism are idealized, too. The fair and equitable distribution of resources is the unifying tenet of communism and socialism. But in practice people in socialist societies have competed for party rank and favored positions within the bureaucracies. They have redistributed resources based on rank and position. They have harmed each other to achieve rank and position. Where human beings compete for power and resources, fairness is always questionable. I challenge any student of history to cite a perfectly fair and equitable human society at any time since Adam and Eve.

Our form of capitalism is, at least, dynamic. It provides the opportunity for enterprising people to improve their lives. It is not unique in this quality, but its potential is proven. So if our specific capitalistic enterprise is not fair in every detail, it at least provides us with tools for pursuing fairness. When an individual or an organization asks, "Is it fair?" the answers can provide a bunch of opportunities for constructive engagement.

Is it Contagious?

One of the best-proven characteristics of our system of business is its contagiousness. Generation after generation, entrepreneurs have invented new enterprises across hundreds of nations and myriad cultures. The system has proven itself repeatable and contagious across both time and space, across centuries of time and every continent.

For better and for worse, some cultures have proven themselves more adept than others at the pursuit of capitalist success. Those less adept have been exploited and sometimes erased by the more successful.

Nonetheless there is hardly a corner of the world where money is not changing hands right now, or where someone isn't socking some of it away for a rainy day or some future investment opportunity.

Our particular business was built mostly on the practice of publishing magazines–printing stories and photographs on glossy papers, selling subscriptions to readers, and selling advertisements to businesses who wish to put their products in front of those readers. The capital with which we started the businesses and expanded was provided by a family whose seminal business was publishing newspapers–printing stories and photographs on inexpensive paper daily for local audiences. As I write this in 2010 the media are full of speculation about the future of these two businesses–magazine publishing and newspaper publishing–or the lack of a future. Some experts believe the digital media will completely replace newspapers and magazines. Readership and revenue are falling. Cooler heads predict a realignment but not an extinction.

My colleagues and I see it as neither. We believe our core business–building audience around content–is merely shifting its emphasis from one medium to another. It's true that today about 80 percent of our publishing revenue is generated, one way or another, through the printed products. About 20 percent is generated online. But just five years ago our online revenues were less than 4 percent of the total, and total revenues have grown by about the amount of the digital business. So in one way of looking at it, our printed business has been static, but it has provided a platform for a growing digital media business.

Strategically, we try to look at the business in abstract terms. We'd rather not describe it as a publishing business or an advertising business. We say we're in the audience aggregation and content generation businesses. The core of our enterprise is built around audiences. Readers come to *Mother Earth News* for information on a specific set of topics: self-reliance, sustainable lifestyles and rural lifestyles. For 40 years the magazine–as well as its books, radio shows, newsletters and websites–has been fascinated with that specific set of topics. It has shared that sense of fascination with millions of people. Likewise, *GRIT* has shared stories of rural American life and attracted rural American audiences since 1882. *Farm Collector* shares its fascination with agricultural machinery.

How long will we print our stories on paper and distribute our magazines through the mail? Who knows? Technology and consumer preference are difficult to predict. Will we be able to run businesses based on the distribution of engaging content to passionate audiences? We think the answer to that question is a resounding, "Yes!" It seems likely that we should be able to continue attracting audiences with our stories–if we tell them well–regardless of whether we deliver those stories at the campfire, in a printed magazine or on an electronic reading device. And if we hold readers' attention, it seems equally likely that we, and our advertisers, will find ways of selling valuable things to those audiences.

And, in fact, over the past couple of years our audiences–both print and electronic, have grown nicely.

In business, contagiousness is one of the critical indicators of success. Businesses aspire to expand and grow. The day our enterprise is not contagious is the day we admit failure.

It is repeated in nearly every country, so let's call our free-enterprise model contagious across time and across space.

Could it be more contagious?

Well, every stage of commercial success is a step toward greater contagiousness. If we grow and become more profitable, we can do more of the things we do. We can promote to larger audiences. We can proliferate our messages across new media. So we are working all the time toward greater commercial contagiousness.

Like every commercial business we also consume resources in ways that are not repeatable forever. We burn petroleum products and print on paper. We've traded for carbon-offset credits to replace the coal-generated electricity we consume with power from renewable sources. The benefits of carbon-offset trading are debated, but we believe it's at least a gesture in the right direction.

In fact, most of the things we do to conserve resources and protect the environment are subtle:

- We've added insulation to our building.
- Installed skylights to replace electric fixtures.
- Installed the most efficient fixtures, ballasts and bulbs we could find.
- Assigned prime parking spaces to commuters who arrive via carpool, bicycle or motorcycle.
- Bought passes for employees who come by bus.
- Switched to postconsumer recycled copy paper, note pads and other office papers.
- We reuse nearly every box and all the packing material in our warehouse.
- Replaced office Styrofoam with washable mugs and glasses.
- We try to buy the most energy efficient models when we need new equipment.
- Set all computer power settings to the most efficient settings.
- Provided a recycling bin at every employee's desk, and placed recycling separator bins in public spaces.
- We try to recycle any recyclable materials that pass through the organization.
- We compost coffee grounds and food waste taken from the break room.
- Sponsor recycling drives for employees who bring in recyclables like home computers and worn out tennis shoes.
- Print most of our magazines on 100-percent post-consumer recycled magazine paper, all chlorine-free. When we use paper made from virgin pulp, we make sure the paper is certified by a reputable conservation agency, usually the Forestry Stewardship Council.
- Use inks that are 29 percent soy, rather than petroleum.
- Try to eliminate unnecessary steps in all our transportation,

communication and production activities to save fuel and reduce the release of toxic chemicals into the environment.

- Try to eliminate promotions based on paper media–direct mail, insert cards, etc.–and substitute digital promotions. We have a long way to go on this one.
- When we promote on paper, we use recycled paper for the promotional pieces.
- We offer auto-renewal subscriptions that eliminate the need for mailed renewal notices.
- We keep looking for new ways to do better.

And we remain acutely conscious that all this, combined, still doesn't make us a truly sustainable business. We have a long way to go. But we're trying to get there.

Initiatives

At work, as at home, the queries have helped us add a number of constructive items to our agenda.

Expand digital and web-based products. Most of the resources we consume in pursuit of our business are tied up in paper, printing and distribution of the printed products. Theoretically, we might someday completely replace our paper media with digital products for the Internet, e-readers, cell phones and other devices. When electricity is generated from clean, renewable sources of energy, the electronic media distribute information much more efficiently and sustainably than paper media, conserving both fuels and forests. For now, a lot of readers prefer paper but the digital possibilities are more compelling every day and we'll try to stay up to date with the technology.

Goals: Beauty, abundance and contagiousness.

Push the Suppliers. Every consumer has the opportunity to influence innovation. Businesses have even more opportunities. By demanding new products that lessen the negative environmental affects of our enterprises, we inspire the invention of more conscientious new products. By asking our suppliers for recycled or environmentally responsible papers, energy from renewable sources and durable equipment we help those suppliers justify their investments in new techniques and technologies to deliver the goods.

The specifics are less important than the intent. The networks of manufacturers, suppliers and modes of transportation on which we depend are extremely complex and sometimes it's difficult to sort out the effects of our buying decisions. Recycled paper isn't always the best choice. Virgin pulp grown in a responsible manner can have, in some cases, more benign effects than the collection and processing of repurposed paper, depending on the sources and systems we use. Sometimes products can be delivered from Europe or South America more efficiently than they can be trucked cross-country from Wisconsin or Maine. It's dangerous for us to commit, mindlessly, to any given scenario.

To run a business responsibly, we need to do our homework. We need to study the options and choose responsibly. And once we've chosen, we need to push our suppliers to provide the best option, even if it requires an investment to do so. When we push for innovation, suppliers have an opportunity to take market share by delivering innovative products and services. Our suppliers have done a good job of finding affordable recycled paper, tree plantations run in responsible and innovative ways, relatively nontoxic inks and more efficient methods of distribution. Would they have found these resources if we hadn't asked for them first? Possibly not. In fact, probably not. We create change by bringing our conscience to the market.

So rather than get too detailed in the discussion of the most environmentally responsible ways of running a media company–a worthy topic of a book unto itself–let just say that all of us, in any business, should be studying the alternatives and demanding the best of our suppliers.

Goals: Beauty, abundance, fairness and contagiousness.

Implement Video-Conferencing. After manufacturing and distribution, business travel probably consumes more energy than any of our other activities. Technology is making it much easier and much less expensive to connect with clients and colleagues in videoconferences. The laptop computer on which I am typing (coincidentally, in the departure lounge of an airport terminal) has a built-in camera that can show my face, chatting away in real time, to my son in Hawaii, my friends in England or our suppliers in India, China or Spain. That way, we consume a few electrons rather than hundreds of gallons of jet fuel.

Goals: Abundance and contagiousness.

Push for Expansion. Since part of our mission as a company is to promote sustainability, our success can have positive implications. Any conscientious company has a bigger positive impact when it grows. We want to build bigger audiences for our message. That's part of the inspiration for this book.

Goals: Beauty, abundance, fairness and contagiousness.

Explore new facilities. Our building is full, so we're looking for appropriate locations where we could expand our footprint. We hope to find a neglected existing structure that we can retrofit for better energy efficiency and to integrate on-site power generation. We've taken most of the practical steps toward energy-efficiency at our current site, which we acquired with the business. If we chose a new building with energy-efficiency in mind from the beginning, we could accomplish more. We want our offices–as well as our homes–to be efficient and self-sufficient.

Goals: Beauty, abundance, fairness and contagiousness.

Stay skeptical. Businesses tend to drift into a state of inertia, especially when they are profitable. We try to keep questioning every aspect of our organization–the businesses we're in, our sources of goods and services, our equity structures, our personnel policies, our payroll structures and our strategic goals. It's through this process of questioning that enterprises improve. If we are aggressive enough, maybe we can accelerate our innovation to the pace of change in the marketplace. That's critical, but it isn't easy.

Goals: Beauty, abundance, fairness and contagiousness.

CASE STUDY THREE

The Juggernaut: Google Inc.

Google's famous unofficial motto is "Don't Be Evil."

The decade between the turn of the millennium and 2010 might justifiably be called the Google Decade. The company may have built more influence in less time than any other human endeavor in history. If you consider the number of people interacting with Google each month (about 150 million unique visitors at the time of this writing, according to Compete.com), the company's worldwide computing power (more than a million[149] servers processing a billion search requests[150] and 20 petabytes—a petabyte is 1000 terabytes, or a quadrillion bytes—of data every day[151]) or its raw economic might, Google must be considered the biggest media company of all time, exchanging more information with more people than could have been imagined just a decade ago.

The founders raised about $25 million to get their company rolling in 1999. Five years later their initial public offering raised $23 billion. In other words, between 1999 and 2004 Google's market value appreciated at an average rate of about $12 million a day. In 2007 the company generated about $16.6 billion in revenue. In 2008 Google's revenue swelled by 31 percent to

$21.8 billion. In 2009, during one of the worst downturns in the history of the advertising industry, the company's revenues, which come almost entirely from advertising sales[152], grew another $2 billion, in round numbers, to $23.7 billion.

One of the moments that define Google's corporate personality, and possibly the reason it has dominated its highly competitive industry, is described in Ken Auletta's best-selling 2009 book about the company.[153] Google founders Sergey Brin and Larry Page were meeting prospective investors in 1998, including Yahoo's Jerry Yang and David Filo. They were discussing Google's search results and the fact that they were more relevant than Yahoo's. That put Google at a disadvantage, the Yahoo founders told the Google upstarts, because the revenue model for search engines is based on advertising sales. The more pages a search customer sees, the more advertising can be sold. Google's more relevant searches meant that fewer pages would be displayed for advertisers, ergo, Google would make less money. Brin and Page said they didn't care. They wanted to build the best search engine. They wanted to deliver the most relevant results for their users, faster than their competitors.

An investor in the meeting described Google's strategy as "disruptive," and put his money in. A few months later he introduced Brin and Page to Amazon founder Jeff Bezos, another customer-focused entrepreneur who became one of their first few investors.

"I just fell in love with Larry and Sergey," Bezos is quoted as saying. "There was no business plan. They had a vision. It was a customer-focused point of view."

The fact that one of the greatest success stories of the digital era was conceived based on a collective vision of customer satisfaction–rather than a business plan–speaks to the power of a collective vision. Google's success may be, in part, a demonstration of the economic potency of conscience. Google has succeeded at least partly because its founders kept their priorities straight. They focused their organization's achievements on delivering the best product–the most efficient search. Their "Don't Be Evil" culture reinforced their business strategy. In their view, the most enlightened, least Machiavellian approach to business was to provide the best product by the most conscientious means possible.

Not everyone was impressed by the company's informal strategy, or its culture of nerdy conscientiousness. For every early investor who fell in love–like Jeff Bezos–there were hundreds of important technology capitalists who steered clear. Media mogul Barry Diller tells the story[154] of meeting the Google founders in the early days. At the time, Diller controlled Ticketmaster and Expedia. Brin arrived late, on rollerblades. Page wouldn't look up from his PDA, even after Diller asked him if he was bored. According to Diller he said, "I'm interested. I always do this."

But Google's culture appealed to two audiences who, in the end, proved themselves to be more valuable than investors. Users approved of the search engine's efficiency. Traffic and revenue grew hyperbolically. And the best and brightest young minds in Silicon Valley were drawn to the company's style and its perks.

On its website the company describes its culture: "Our commitment to innovation depends on everyone being comfortable sharing ideas and opinions… We are aggressively inclusive in our hiring, and we favor ability over experience." Then the website describes the company's offices around the world, "Bicycles or scooters for efficient travel between meetings; dogs; lava lamps; massage chairs; large inflatable balls. Googlers sharing cubes, yurts and huddle rooms–and very few solo offices. Laptops everywhere–standard issue for mobile coding, email on the go and note-taking. Foosball, pool tables, volleyball courts, assorted video games, pianos, ping pong tables and gyms that offer yoga and dance classes... Healthy lunches and dinners for all staff at a variety of cafes. Break rooms packed with a variety of snacks and drinks to keep Googlers going."[155]

Conscientiousness is also woven into the company culture, quite intentionally. Free bicycles are scattered around the "Googleplex" headquarters and plug-in hybrid cars are provided, on a shared basis, for short journeys. When not in use, they sit under a carport, charging with solar power. Biodiesel shuttles bring about 1,500 people to work every day, local food is served in the cafeterias, food waste is composted and Google buildings are showcases for green building materials and energy efficiency. Google employees are eligible for special discounts on solar equipment for their homes. People who use human power to commute, "bike, walk, pogo-stick, unicycle," etc., earn points that Google translates into donations to the employee's chosen charity.[156] At the California headquarters, 9,000 solar panels produce about 1.6 megawatts of electricity.

Through investments and grants from the company's nonprofit arm, Google.org, Google is promoting utility-scale renewable energy from solar, wind and geothermal power sources. The company is also providing incentives to car manufacturers who are developing plug-in electric and electric-hybrid vehicles and is working to develop its own Google PowerMeter to track home energy usage.[157]

Of course you don't power a billion searches a day without burning some electricity. Most of the energy Google consumes isn't related to commuting employees.[158] Even though they reportedly run data centers very efficiently, consuming about half the power of similar "server farms" owned by other companies, recycling water and equipment and lobbying the industry to do better, a lot of power still goes into the Google servers. Google says each search uses .0003 kilowatt hours (kWh) of electricity.[159] Multiply that by a billion searches a day and you have about 300,000 kWh a day flowing into Google servers, more than 100 million kWh per year, about the same as the entire nation of Cambodia, or Belize, or Rwanda.[160] That's a lot of juice.

And the Google executive team, in spite of its proletarian wardrobe, doesn't completely eschew the trappings of great wealth, including aircraft. Founders Brin and Page with CEO Eric Schmidt control a company that owns, at last report, a Boeing 757 airliner, a Boeing 767, two Gulfstream V business jets and, just for fun, a two-seat European fighter plane called a Dassault/Dornier Alpha Jet. [161]

Quite rightly Google websites point out that the electricity used by its servers represents a tiny fraction of the energy that would be consumed if all the same information was being distributed to people who drove to libraries or bookstores. And the leaders of giant multinational corporations have legitimate travel needs that can't be met by the commercial airlines. In comparison with most giant corporations, Google is a highly conscientious institution. The Google executives are responsible citizens who do a lot for people and the planet. They are also billionaires, of course.

And since the days of the ancient Greeks, human societies have understood the code of *noblesse oblige*. Those who enjoy great privileges bear great responsibilities for making a positive difference in the world.

Journalists criticize Google for devaluing content. Activists want the company to pull out of nations that don't recognize rights of free speech. Lots of people worry that Google's technological eyes and ears reach into their homes and invade their privacy. The more prosperous and powerful the company becomes, the more strident the criticism. Any institution as powerful as Google has great potential for evil, and for good.

Is it Beautiful?

Google's mission is making information available. That includes all the beauty in the world (along with everything else, of course). Without question, our ability to craft a collective vision of beauty depends on the existence of a "collective." Today the global collective depends on efficient Internet search more than any other source of information.

When my wife and I get ready to plant some flowers around the farm, we sometimes use Google or one of its competitors to track down the varieties we want. When we redecorate our home we search the Internet. We found the company that provided our cork flooring through Google. Our drapes and our newest lighting fixtures we found, initially, through Google.

More importantly, a beautiful new image or idea can be distributed, around the world, more quickly by Google than any other institution past or present.

That's a lot more important than the architecture at the Googleplex.

Does it Create Abundance?

That's an easy one. Abundance is the most fundamental building block in the Google DNA. The founders called it Google in honor of a very large number, googol, which is represented by a 1 and 100 zeroes, or 10^{100}. Googol has been used to illustrate the difference between a very, very large number (googol), and infinity, which is immeasurable. Giddy with the notion of all the information out there on the Internet waiting to be indexed and searched, Brin and Page named their company "Google."

If you are interested in, well, anything, Google offers a cornucopia of information, a digital horn of plenty. Without Google, or something like it, writing this book would have required a thousand trips to the library or a staff of three people, or both. Not long ago writers like me spent hours poring over the card catalog and wandering through the stacks at libraries. We hired researchers and personal assistants. Now, when we need a bit of obscure information, we just "Google it."

Is It Fair?

Google's unofficial motto, "Don't Be Evil," could be expressed as easily in the positive, "Be Fair." The premise to which the company's founders refer frequently–the notion that information should be easily accessible and freely available–describes the essence of fairness. Google stresses its meritocratic culture. The company hires and promotes people on the basis of their capabilities rather than their background or experience. Again, the essence of fairness.

Don't Be Evil is actually only a translation of one small part of the official Google philosophy, which is summed up in 10 points on the company's website:

1. Focus on the user and all else will follow.
2. It's best to do one thing really, really well.
3. Fast is better than slow.
4. Democracy on the web works.
5. You don't need to be at your desk to need an answer.
6. You can make money without doing evil.
7. There's always more information out there.
8. The need for information crosses all borders.

9. You can be serious without a suit.
10. Great just isn't good enough.

The company is regularly recognized as one of the world's best companies to work for, by *Fortune* magazine among others.[162] *Fortune* has also named it one of the world's "Most Admired Companies." In *Fortune's* 2010 list it was ranked second right behind Apple.[163]

Of course the company has its critics. In many parts of the world Google's open access model is considered a vehicle for alien values: capitalism, liberalism, and immorality. Journalists believe some of the company's practices violate their intellectual property rights by reproducing their work without paying for it. Media companies sometimes complain that the search program's valuation of content devalues high-quality analysis and opinion in favor of the sensationalistic and the popular.

And some of the information so highly valued by Google is information about individuals. The giant communications company is looking everywhere, all the time, for clues to make its searches, its maps, its photos and stories more relevant and useful. In the process it sometimes looks into people's private lives. Most recently Google collected about 600 gigabytes worth of users' emails, passwords and other "tidbits of information" from computers hooked up to wireless networks.[164] When something like that happens, Google says it happens accidentally. As Google becomes more powerful, the concern that it might use its insights to exploit individuals becomes more troubling.

Founders Sergey Brin and Larry Page have accumulated great wealth over the past decade or so. They have also made thousands of their employees wealthy. When the company went public in 2004, at least 1,000 Google employees became millionaires on paper, including the woman who had been the company's masseuse for five years.[165] Brin emigrated from Russia when he was 6 and grew up in middle-class Maryland. Page came from a middle-class family in East Lansing, Michigan. Both founders have parents who are professors in technical fields and both went to Montessori schools.[166]

In other words Brin and Page had intellectual advantages but no particular economic advantages.

Through it's own nonprofit, Google.org, Google Inc. has pledged to contribute 1 percent of its equity and profits to charity "to address some of the world's most urgent problems."[167]

A single percentage point of its leviathan profits might not seem overly generous but it added up to about $100 million in grants and investments over the nonprofit's first six years. As a percentage it is below average. The average big corporation tracked in the U.S. over the past 40 years gave about 1.2 percent of its profits away.[168] U.S. individuals gave away about 1.8 percent of their income over the same period.[169]

The unanswerable question remains: Is it ever fair for anyone to have billions of dollars in net worth, private jets, palatial homes and an excess of every personal resource in a world where other people lack sufficient food, just because they were born in a poor part of the world?

Perhaps not. But Google has succeeded in a game with clearly defined rules and it has, apparently, played by those rules. The company's founders have become wealthy by playing the game of business more astutely than their competitors. Their employees have prospered.

Inarguably, Google has been a powerful engine for creating prosperity. Search engines like Google have made information more widely available than ever before. If its inventors hadn't seen an opportunity to become wealthy, would the Internet be as efficient and useful? Probably not. Google, Microsoft, Facebook and Apple were all built in a capitalistic society by entrepreneurs out to make a bundle. That wasn't an accident. Economic incentives compel human creativity and innovation.

Is It Contagious?

In each decade new institutions of power arise in the world that appear to have a stranglehold on free enterprise. The mighty metropolitan newspapers once controlled the flow of information to the mass audience. Their era is over. When I was a kid, the oil companies and television networks seemed to run the world. They are still powerful, but a lot less powerful than they were in 1965. In college I heard people fret about IBM's monopolistic control of high technology. "Big Blue's" wing-tipped minions ruled the computer industry. That didn't last.

In fact, the dominant global businesses in each decade of my life have followed the same pattern of growing power followed by decline.

Google's dominance won't last forever. Some upstart with a bright new idea will take its place. But the company's founders seem to be as proud of the company's culture as they are of its financial success. Can the Google culture persist when the company's economic power declines?

More seasoned executives might say that it's simple to supply free food and video games to your employees while you're one of the world's fastest growing companies. It's easier to have fun at work when the company is making lots and lots of money. As the company and its industry mature Google's culture will probably become more conventional unless its managers and shareholders make continuing investments in that culture. And as company resources become more constrained with the maturing of its industry and its business model, those investments will be harder to make.

Still, managers in every industry should take note of Google's ability to attract excellent employees with a combination of personality, conscience and equity. The opportunity of joining an attractive culture, building a business and sharing in that business' economic success makes for an attractive offer. When Google's growth slows, retention of great employees will be more important than attracting bright new stars. That may require some redefinition. What components of the Google employment contract are valuable after the stock options stop appreciating so rapidly?

Google's cultural innovations are probably repeatable in companies around the world. Most of us could invest more in the corporate lifestyle to attract good people. Most companies could be a little better at citizenship, and could publicize their citizenship a little more effectively. And most companies would benefit from investing more in culture and citizenship.

Google has made its citizenship an integral facet of its product. Consumers today implicitly consider a company's conscience a part of its value proposition. The consumer's new mindset is probably here to stay. And workers worldwide are aware of the quality of life the staff enjoys inside the Googleplex. To compete for high-quality workers all employers must, on some level, compete with Google. Plus, the children of today's workers won't willingly accept a lower quality of working life. So we'll keep on meeting these new standards in the future.

Initiatives

Google can be the most enlightened power-user on the planet. Because it is so successful, and because it uses a lot of electricity, Google has the opportunity to set a new global standard for clean power. The company already makes a noticeable contribution to clean energy through its efficient computers, the headquarters' solar array, its dedication to electric and electric-hybrid transportation and its research projects. Google is studying utility-scale renewable electricity, plug-in vehicles and smart metering for businesses and households.

True to Google's engineering culture, the company's contributions so far are relentlessly practical, made with an eye to efficiency.

What if Google set a new standard of consuming electricity for its operations worldwide only from renewable sources?

Imagine a thousand server farms bristling with photovoltaic panels and wind turbines. It would cost something, but Google can afford it. It might not be practical or repeatable for the majority of companies today, but imagine the ripples of influence the new standard might send out across businesses around the world. Imagine utilities vying for Google's patronage with their own renewable-energy solutions in every country where a Google computer is plugged in.

Imagine competitors scrambling to do the same thing when conscientious computer users focus their activities on the Google sites.

Google's commitment would set a new standard that could catalyze a drive for more contagious and abundant power everywhere.

Goals: Beauty, abundance and contagiousness.

Amp up the charitable giving. Google is many orders of magnitude more successful than the average company, but its charitable giving is below average. Google commits to giving away 1 percent of its profits. The average company gives away 1.2 percent. Why not commit to at least meeting the average?

Or, better yet, why not match the 1.8-percent average for individual U.S. taxpayers? While they're at it, why not make it an even 2 percent for simplicity's sake?

Because Google is so visible, a commitment like that could increase corporate giving everywhere.

Goals: Abundance and fairness.

Play Favorites. Google is justifiably proud of its search engine's impartial results, refined to deliver the most useful and efficient information. But the company that handles more information than any other entity in the world is in a unique position to support the causes judged most worthy, either by Google employees or Google users. Google could create a partition within its search engine for the sites that it determines do the most good in the world. In the way Google Health helps users organize their medical records or Google Finance provides special money-management tools, *Google Good* could promote tools for people who want to give their money away based on the best available information about charities. It could also provide useful information for job seekers in search of especially meaningful work in mission-driven organizations.

Goals: Beauty, abundance, fairness and contagiousness.

Maintain the pressure. In March 2010 Google began redirecting all Google China's traffic to its servers in Hong Kong[170], allowing uncensored search results to appear on the screens of its hundreds of millions of Chinese users. China censors pornography and content it judges likely to foment social unrest and Google initially submitted to that censorship. Google searches explicitly stated on the screen that the search results had been censored. However, when Chinese human-rights activists had their Google Gmail accounts hacked–and it appeared that the Chinese government was the most likely perpetrator–Google retaliated.

In 2010 the world's largest search engine bypassed the censors by re-routing searches to Hong Kong, a special jurisdiction where Chinese laws are more liberal.

Google walks a fine line in China and in other countries where information is aggressively censored or where governments want information about Google users. In April 2010 the company published a new "transparency" tool on its website designed to identify countries that either ask Google to remove certain content or request access to user data[171]. China considers its censorship practices a state secret–it's the only country listed that does that–so the site doesn't report much of anything about how China limits its citizens' access to Internet content. Brazil submitted more "removal requests" than any other country. Germany, India and the United States were in second, third and fourth place at the time of this writing. Brazil also requested more data on Google users than any other country, followed by the United States, the United Kingdom, India and France.

So far Google's "transparency" doesn't report where countries are simply blocking content. Those countries obviously don't need to request the removal of content. The website reports that Google is working on a tool to show where content is blocked.

With access to unprecedented amounts of information, Google can have an unprecedented impact on public knowledge. If you believe that the access to knowledge is important to creating and maintaining democratic societies, then Google is in a unique position to push for open access to information. Or to provide tools that give access in spite of censorship.

Goals: Abundance and fairness.

CONCLUSION

The Great Privilege

As I wrote these case studies the same thought kept occurring to me: These are some of the best puzzles ever! Applying human objectivity to the biggest, most intriguing and most definitively human problem, ever, is quite an endeavor. And we're in that endeavor. We're part of that enterprise.

I notice a lot of people my age–in their 40s and 50s–saying they don't know if they would want to be young today. They feel overwhelmed by our challenges. For some the challenge of global cultural conflict seems insurmountable. For others it's the prospect of economic stagnation that overwhelms them. Then, of course, there are planetary environmental problems.

If I just sit around and think about problems like these, I sometimes feel a little intimidated myself. But if I get off the couch and do something–write something, grow something, fix something that needs fixing–I feel a whole lot better. In fact, when I'm busy I often feel energized by the *importance* of the projects our species is tackling today. Old-fashioned biological expansion was automatic. Our previous technological triumphs were exciting, but they were, ultimately, the products of our primitive desires for more power, more speed, more food and richer entertainment.

Now we're inventing something new–a path toward prosperity of a particularly human kind. To expand and grow stronger is the animal impulse. To calculate our natures and build a world to suit those natures–a world designed for the long term–is an achievement to which only a human being can aspire.

We're working on the best human project of all time.

What a great privilege.

The Ghost Turkey and Other Miracles

For a long time I disrespected turkeys. Over the years we've probably owned 20 or 30 of the big birds. None of them has ever made it to our dinner table or provided any other useful function except, maybe, entertainment. They do OK for a while. They stalk around the yard gobbling grubs and grasshoppers. They've even raised clutches of babies in our coop. Somehow each of them has contrived to be killed by one predator or another–dogs, coyotes, hawks, opossums, skunks, owls or bobcats before they had been here 6 months. In the morning I might let six turkeys out of the coop. In the evening only five come in. Sometimes I find a pile of feathers. Chickens thrived alongside them, but the turkeys just couldn't seem to stay alive.

I figured they just didn't have the intelligence or the survival instincts to make it in the open. I lost respect for domesticated turkeys.

Then I met the Ghost Turkey.

She was one of a half-dozen turkeys we got from a breeder promoting "midget whites," an heirloom variety bred for better taste and smaller meals. The midget whites didn't last any longer than our other turkey experiments. Soon they all had disappeared.

One of the more memorable midget whites was a shy little hen with an unusual red tinge in her tail feathers. One evening she wasn't in the chicken coop when the sun went down. That left only a white midget tom and a bigger hen from a breed called a royal palm. Pretty soon the tom was gone also.

Six weeks later I was working in the garden on a Saturday afternoon when, out of the corner of my eye, I saw a white bird larger than a chicken sneaking through the shrubs around the henhouse. It was a white midget turkey hen with red in her tail. I watched her slowly make her way through the bushes and around the corner into the henhouse. Ten minutes later she came out again, took a careful look around, and then walked across the yard. She threaded her way through three fences and into the woods a quarter-mile north of my house on a neighbor's property.

Since then I've seen her a dozen times, always in the middle of the afternoon. She doesn't vary her routine. She follows her standard route past the corners of the gates and through a tear in a wire fence, visits the coop for a quick meal and then returns to the woods.

We're proud of our hardy chickens. We congratulate ourselves on breeding a flock that ranges freely and thrives in spite of predators and the weather. We always thought our turkeys just couldn't make the grade.

But, miraculously, the Ghost Turkey survives.

It isn't the first time one of our animals has done something astonishing. When the cat settled comfortably into the chicken house we were surprised. When we found him sheltering baby chickens under his furry belly on a cold morning, we were amazed. Asnath the goat was impossible to catch but confidently moved herself out of the billy-goat pasture and into the pasture with the other does and babies the evening before she gave birth. Duke, our first ram, was inexplicably the most popular animal on the farm–physically affectionate with people, mules, donkeys and even the other rams. We've never seen another that we could so much as touch, much less scratch his belly the way Duke liked. And he came from the same farm that provided almost all our breeding stock, raised in the same rambunctious flock.

We are surprised, nearly every day, by some personality quirk or ingenious solution dreamed up by a chicken or a baby goat. Our farm is not only our hobby and our sustenance, it's also a big part of our social life. Our animals are inventive and interesting. They are, generally, good company.

Seeing nature from this perspective, I don't worry about nature adapting to new conditions. If we are having a permanent impact on the planet, nature will adjust its methods to the changes. Nature is good at that. If a white midget turkey hen can survive alone in the woods for months, nature's diverse citizenry will find new ways of thriving on a warmer planet, a wetter planet, a drier planet or a colder planet. They've done it before.

I'm not concerned about "saving the earth." The earth is pretty tough.

But I want to make sure people are here to see the next wonderful thing. I want people to be here to gape at the great waterfalls, the big rocks rising out of the desert and the glaciers flowing down off the mountains into the ocean. I want my children's children to see this planet and to marvel. I want poets and composers to record their inspirations in books and symphonies. I want our species' love affair with its beautiful, abundant planet to go on for a long, long time.

EPILOGUE

As I See It (Idealistically, Unrealistically...)

This is a book about forming a collective vision. It is not meant to be a book about my vision of the future and the first version of its manuscript didn't include this epilogue. I didn't intend to get into my own idealized, unrealistic view of the future. Then a wise friend read it and pointed out that I've asked readers to go out on a limb without demonstrating that I'm willing to do the same.

Fair enough.

I want my great-grandchildren to live in a place that is...

Beautiful.

Anyone who has traveled in the developing world during the past 30 years has seen the vast slums that engulf the cities. Slums occupy decaying sections of old cities and newly built shantytowns that often surround more affluent urban areas. About a billion people, worldwide, live in slums today and the United Nations expects that number to double by 2030.[172]

Slums are densely populated aggregations of minimal human shelter. Generally speaking slum dwellers are barely protected from the weather. Their sewage is not treated. Their children are not educated. Increasingly, the world's slums host a variety of toxic occupations such as recycling used computer parts and scavenging landfills.

Slums are not beautiful. I'm sure their residents find some beauty in them, but ugliness remains one of their defining factors. The slum's residents want to make it smell better, look better and provide better shelter.

An absence of beauty often indicates an absence of health, and the slums metastasizing around the world are indicators of a profound economic disease. As we've enhanced the lives of the world's riches human beings, economic disparity has advanced like a cancer. It's not that the poor live a lot worse than ever. As far back as recorded history can take us, there were unfortunate people who lived without shelter, clean water or adequate food. Their condition hasn't changed appreciably in the entire span of human history. The richest residents of the 21st century, on the other hand, live lives of luxury that kings and emperors couldn't have imagined until very recently. The rich need not ever smell an unpleasant smell or see an unpleasant sight. From birth to death they have access to temperate air, clean water and beautiful things. They can reach any terrestrial destination that pleases them in a few hours. They have drugs that soothe almost any pain. Almost any form of entertainment is available to them at the touch of a button.

And they live, quite often, within walking distance of a slum.

The ugliness of the slums is striking for its proximity to wealth and beauty.

To spread beauty in my vision of our human future, the poor must be elevated.

I don't imagine a world in which economic disparity has been eliminated. I think that would be a bad idea. Economic disparity and the opportunity of improving our individual standard of living is a tremendous source of energy fueling enterprise and innovation. It's a motivator.

But I envision a human world that no longer tolerates "in-human" conditions. I see a world in which people don't go hungry, because we no longer put up with starvation. Today we have enough food to eradicate hunger, but we lack the collective will to do so. We could feed every hungry person tomorrow but we haven't collectively decided to do so.

In my beautiful vision, we would tolerate nothing less.

The poor will, by some definition, always exist. But we have the power to change the definition. The poor should have food in their pantries, doctors in their neighborhoods and beauty in their lives. In my vision, no nation in the world will tolerate anything less, even for its poorest residents.

But perhaps I'm not setting a high enough standard. Perhaps I'm being too realistic. Raising the lifestyles of the poor is a relatively simple matter of reallocating resources we already possess. I'm not meeting my own standard for an idealized, unrealistic vision.

So I think the poor, and everyone else, should also have access to beautiful, unaltered nature.

In nearly every literary tradition across the world, untrammeled nature remains a standard for beauty. A Libyan novelist writes movingly about the virgin sand dunes of the deep Sahara. A Canadian poet describes a frozen lake in the north woods and a pygmy storyteller sings of the subtle, changeable beauty of the African jungle.

Nature's beauty is, often, the standard against which we measure manmade art. Art elaborates on nature's image. Without reference to nature, could we even define beauty?

I have been privileged to visit most of the planet's ecosystems: from subtropical deserts to the floor of the ocean; from the grasslands to the tropical rain forest, the temperate rain forest, the temperate deciduous forest, the alpine tundra and the northern boreal forest called the taiga. Each and every one of them was beautiful. I haven't yet seen the arctic tundra or a polar ice cap in person, but I'm certain they are beautiful and I hope I get the chance.

Every natural environment is beautiful in ways we cannot imagine. We must preserve natural beauty for precisely that reason, because we could not conceive of natural beauty on our own without nature's inspiration.

People who design modern zoos use a criterion they call "flight distance." Most animals have a prescribed distance they would run, if frightened, before they turned to look back. If a zoo enclosure is built at least a little larger than the animal's flight distance, zoo creatures are calmer and healthier. If designers don't allow for flight distance, the animals are neurotic, combative and less healthy.

Besides beauty, wilderness also provides us with the psychological flight distance. As long as there are empty places on the planet, our minds can flee to those empty places when they have the need.

So in my vision, every unique ecosystem across the globe would be preserved in its natural state. Perhaps we could reserve at least 20 percent of each nation's landmass for wilderness, allocated to each biome, each ecosystem. In the United States 20 percent of our grasslands, 20 percent of our forests, 20 percent of our swamps and at least 20 percent of our deserts would be permanently preserved as God created them, open to visitors but not vehicles. Whatever natural resources they contain would remain unexploited, by popular consent, forever, as a testament of our commitment to beauty, and to abundance.

Because I want my great-grandchildren to live in a world that is beautiful and…

Abundant.

As I've pointed out repeatedly in this book, there are two variables affecting abundance in our world. The first is supply. We depend on the planet's natural resources. Those resources are, by definition, limited. The second variable is demand. Demand we can control.

Demand for resources is also influenced by two primary variables. The efficiency of our usage determines how much of the world's natural bounty each of us requires. We can improve efficiency, to some extent. The second variable affecting demand is population. No matter how much we improve efficiency, there will still be an ultimate limit to how many people we can support.

Once I acknowledge that limitation, I find myself thinking, well, why are we talking about a maximum human population? Why not aim for an ideal population, instead.

Since I've already set aside 20 percent of every earthly biome for wilderness, in my mind, I might set my own ideal human population at 20 percent less than our current population of about 6.9 billion people. That would put us at about 5.5 billion people. That was the world population in the early 1990s.

What the heck. While I'm idealizing why don't I allocate a little more room for solving the world hunger problem and take us back 30 percent, to a total human population of 4.8 billion. Just about like 1984, when I celebrated by 25th birthday. That's a shocker, isn't it? Our population was 30 percent smaller when Ronald Reagan was elected to his second term as President of the United States.

When I suggest something like this in public some idiot always asks me whom I'm going to kill. I get letters from people who ask me which of their children should they give up. Let's kill no one. Let's keep all our children. But if each of us reproduced ourselves once, if each human couple had two children, from now on, then the total human population would soon begin to decrease. Of course we will not prescribe death or childlessness for anyone. We don't need to. We can simply agree, as a species, that two parents and two children make a great family.

We could have wild elephants and mountain gorillas in a world of 5 billion people. We could have oceans teeming with fish and vast grasslands where bison and wildebeest roam wild, forever. We could provide clean water for every human baby, food for every new mother and a warm, comfortable bed for every old man, always.

Well, why not?

If we commit ourselves to abundance, we can halt the irreversible tide of species destruction. We could celebrate the diversity of life and set a standard of preserving it, by the mutual consent of people around the world. All our food could be naturally wholesome and nutritious, except when we'd rather it be otherwise. We could live on farms or we could live in cities, as we wish. We could live at the edge of the mountain wilderness, or the edge of the ocean. Some of us would no doubt choose to work very little. Others would work hard to achieve something – new discoveries or greater personal wealth.

In a stable human population, corporate success will be determined by some criterion other than the greatest number of products at the lowest price. The value of scale will be reduced; the value of quality will be enhanced. Products and companies that support our shared values of beauty, abundance and the preservation of nature will earn more. Quality will be defined, in part, by how well a product or a company supports those values. Innovative, conscientious companies will succeed. Less innovative companies will try harder. Our possessions will be more beautiful and more durable.

As our population declines, territorial conflicts will become absurd. With more land, more energy and more food available each year, military conflict will seem more wasteful and more stupid than ever. We can decommission most of our armies. Rather than competing with faster jets and more powerful bombs, we will race to see who can preserve more natural beauty and attract more tourists. Who can print the most beautiful books? Who can build the most reliable and elegant machines? Who has the best skiing? Who has the best beach?

A few hundred pages back at the beginning of this book I challenged you to form a personal vision that idealizes our future. I challenged you to be unrealistic. Now I find I've failed to meet my own standard. Why is it unrealistic to believe we can agree that clean air and water are important and limited resources? What's so crazy about wanting a couple of kids, and no more? How insane is it to think we could imagine a world of beauty and abundance?

That's what I'm going to aim for.

Appendix

A few excerpts from the manuscript for this book were published in Mother Earth News *during the year leading up to its original publication. The essays attracted a lot of feedback, particularly the sections that discussed human-population issues. For the record, I've never advocated mandatory population control, and I can't imagine that I ever will. Still, the mere mention of overpopulation kicks up some dust on both sides.*

All of these notes were submitted to the magazine for publication, but very few of them could be reproduced in the pages of Mother Earth News. *I thought they might provide an interesting perspective on the challenges we face in forming a collective vision.*

— *Bryan*

I deeply appreciate this thoughtful article. The overall message of the need for a positive vision resonated with me. We must not completely discount, however, that some people may only be motivated to make fundamental changes to their behavior through fear of loss. We need to both strive for abundance and beauty and be mindful of what is likely to befall us all if we don't change our current ways.

I think the first question—Is it fair? —is a deeply philosophical one. What is fair, anyway? Is it fair that individuals should be able to keep the fruits of their labor? Is it fair that some should starve while others live a life of admitted overconsumption? We all know that some places and some people are inherently blessed with more resources than others. What is the fair response to that? I don't have an answer—but I am glad that this article is stimulating me to think about that today.

— H. Martin

We are wrestling with a false dichotomy. Frugality is not impoverishment. Consumerism is the path to poverty, not abundance.

Reducing our energy consumption, converting our lawns to gardens, switching from chemical cleaners to simple household provisions like vinegar and baking soda—these things all lessen our financial burdens, enabling us to either enjoy more discretionary income or reduce the hours worked for wages.

Yes, the author is right. The path to earth-friendliness is the path to abundance. It's the updated version of the salty old New England wisdom, "Waste not, want not."

— Lee

I disagree from a semantic perspective. Maybe there is no disagreement in concept, but semantically it's huge. Conservation and abundance go hand in hand. Wild nature is all about abundance, not surplus. The oak that produces thousands of acorns does not create surplus. Each acorn has a life and a purpose. Some, a very few, will become oaks; some will be food for wildlife and some for the soil. There is no waste and no surplus. My dictionary defines "austere" as "severely simple; unadorned". A walk in the wild will quickly dissuade any thought that conservation is austere. Wild nature inspires so much that we are driven to care for it, so we can enjoy it over and over.

— Katey

I believe there are many people who want sustainability but don't know where to begin. Education is a remarkable tool. In the area where

I live, there are small pockets of people teaching the benefits and pleasure of farming. Perhaps if we could get more people showing other people how to begin, then we could do this properly.

— *Julee*

I wholeheartedly agree with your emphasis on inspiration and beauty. Certainly, we need to be aware of the depths of the ecological and social crisis we face, but guilt and fear will never prove to be sufficient motivation for the radical changes that are required in the way we live. Love, beauty, creativity and joy must be at the heart of meaningful transformation.

— *Mark*

Someday people will realize that government is the greatest threat to sustainability because it takes away more and more of the fruits of our labor, dragging us down to subsistence levels as we try to pay for all its programs. The English philosopher John Locke knew in the 1600s how important life, liberty and property are to the sustainability of civilization. His writings were well read by our Founding Fathers. The innovation to solve our problems depends on minimal interference.

— *Pat*

Those who balk at the idea of population control, claiming that it's not how many that live but the way they live that's adversely affecting our world, are either overly optimistic or downright foolish. By sheer mathematics alone the Earth cannot sustain an infinite number of people. Say, just for example, we have a field that can produce a hundred ears of corn per day—no more, no less, and this field of corn is the only source of food for the village of 100 people it serves. The field cannot be expanded without tearing into the local forest. So, each person gets one ear of corn per day. But if even just one person were added to the mix, that means some people will have to share their corn rations. Now everyone is a little hungrier. Add 10 people and more people will have to share more corn.

Sooner or later, the people will either starve to death, be forced to genetically modify the corn, be forced to cut down habitat, or be forced to overharvest wild resources—because how else will they find enough food to feed the burgeoning population? It's not about caring for the land; the land is giving all it can. And where will the village find homes for all these people? By either tearing down more habitat or by depleting a large portion of resources in building taller, stronger houses. You can care for the Earth as meticulously as you want, but there's still only so much it has to give!

Don't get me wrong. I don't use the word mathematics to imply that I am coldhearted. I, too, highly value the sanctity of life. But not just human life; all life.

— *Rachel*

Population control? Are you kidding? Are you aware that the European countries are dying out and that many countries now offer financial incentives to couples that have more than one child? Population control? Under whose control? China, with its one-child policy, forced sterilization and forced abortion, has one of the worst human rights violation records in human history. Pushing a geopolitical agenda such as population control in this type of journal is going to cost you a lot of your subscribers. Overpopulation is a myth. Greed, selfishness and elitist racism along with ignorance perpetuate this myth.

— *Sharon*

China has been in the forefront of population control since the 1970s with a one-child-per-family mandate and an aggressive birth-control policy. The fruit of that policy: an aging population unsustainable by the current birth rate. The policy is also partially responsible for the disproportionate number of male births (due to selective abortion of female fetuses: why waste your one shot on a girl?). Is this where we want our country headed?

— *Mary*

It's do or die! The Earth will cleanse itself if we do not do something! Our population is out of control, and it will only take one major calamity, such as a drought, flood or earthquake, to reduce the food supply. This will cause war, and cruel and inhuman deaths will follow. In fact, they already are occurring.

As for those who simply expect God to provide us more, who act like spoiled brats used to always getting what they want—well, sometimes parents tell their children no, don't they?

Congrats to *Mother Earth News* for raising the issue and shedding light on a subject that should never have been in the dark!

— Leia

Sooner or later, as unwanted a debate it may be, we have to realize that we are living on an island. A large island, no doubt, but an island nonetheless. You can believe whatever you want about God and his will for you, but that will never give you the right to take away another's right to live in peace and harmony.

I have heard it said that "if you have faith, God will provide." God has already provided. He gave us a wonderful place to live in peace and harmony. If we continually screw it up, it is our fault for refusing to use logic, goodness and the peacemaking abilities that God gave us.

So don't exercise stubbornness, selfishness and stupidity and then use God as your excuse for causing endless problems and suffering.

Other than that, feel free to believe whatever you want!

— Mark

I have never read such unimaginative "solutions" for a sustainable world as in "Three Mountains We Must Climb" and, quite frankly, I was staggered by your sincere lack of creativity, intelligence and wisdom.

It is clear that you have no true belief in humanity or people's innate right to make their own way in the world. Instead, you promote solutions that would chop individuals' legs off at the knees and then "solve" their problems by issuing state wheelchairs to the formerly healthy people you have crippled.

Your "simple" approach to population control is reminiscent of the Nazi idea to eliminate the "feebleminded" and institute mandatory sterilization. And your solutions for economic reform show that you have no real bearing or understanding of what the words "socialism" or "communism" even mean, as your solutions are simply to rename these social systems that have already proven to be failures.

— *M. Hancock*

I base my life on the teachings of the Bible. It gives me the basis for my work ethic and the way I treat those around me. It tells me to help those in need. It tells me to be kind to all of God's creation. That includes the animals that aid in our survival. It tells me how to treat the land on which I live. It gives me ethical guidelines, such as directing me to be honest and to not steal from others. It even talks about ways to control population growth. It tells me to be a good steward with what I have been given.

I could go on and on, but I think you get the point. Those of us who are truly "religious" will be the ones who will be going about our days taking as much care as we can with what God has given us. The words "religious" and "conservationist" should go hand in hand.

— *Rebecca*

Thank you for raising the critical issue of population stabilization. Simple math will demonstrate that at some point the human race will exceed the Earth's capacity to feed it, and what Malthus called "positive controls" (such as war, famine and pestilence) will kick in. This fact is inescapable, and any debate on the topic is limited to the question of "when."

For my part, I think we have already reached a point of overpopulation, as evidenced by climate change, species collapse, and food and fuel supply instability,. I say we should begin to discourage population growth now, rather than wait until the Grand Canyon is filled with condos.

Make no mistake, if the human race continues to expand, the day will come when the draconian measures that China has enacted will seem quaint and benign. Let us try to forestall that day by first establishing that having huge families is socially unacceptable. Let us stop fawning over some irresponsible fool who whelps a litter of five, six or even eight babies through artificial means. Let us establish that implanting more than three or four embryos at once, or assisting those who already have three or more children conceive, is unethical medicine.

Then let us stop subsidizing huge families (with an exemption for adoption) by reforming the tax code. We could provide a deduction for the first two children, then perhaps a half deduction for the third, then no deduction. (Personally I would *increase* taxes after three children, but that can wait a few decades until the crisis deepens, as it will!)

If you consider this position selfish, so be it. My wife had two children from her previous marriage, and so I elected to be sterilized. I feel I have done my part, and I refuse to surrender any of my rights, freedoms or the beauty of this world so some jerk can have a fourth or fifth baby.

— *Rick*

You were right when you stated that "population control is perfectly unavoidable." God knows exactly what he is doing and in his perfect word, the Holy Bible, it is his mandate that "you, be ye fruitful, and multiply." This is one area that we need not mess with. We have seen politically how this whole thing of planned parenthood goes totally against the word of God.

Also I would like to say that if anyone thinks that our land cannot sustain us in the near and far future, just take a plane ride across the country and look out the window. It will amaze you, just as it amazed me, how much usable land is available for food growing. The problem is not population-related as much as it is that we as Americans are buying so much of our food from foreign countries rather than growing it here. Let's get back to supporting our farmers and let them grow the crops we need.

God has created this land. Let him decide how *he* wants to populate it.

— *Kelly*

Scientists agree the Earth cannot indefinitely support our current population of 6.7 billion people, especially as the less-developed nations catch up with the consumptive lifestyles of the developed world. I believe it is only economists and folks looking out the windows of airplanes who disagree with this.

One needn't look too hard through the news to find the evidence that we do need to climb all three mountains. We've got fisheries collapsing, fertile topsoil declining rapidly, desertification, water shortages, climate disruption and mass extinction. Peak oil, peak water and peak food have come and gone. All the growth-boosters can offer is a hope and a prayer that we can perpetually increase our population and economic throughput if we just try harder to feed all those people!

A special bravo for pointing out that our growth-obsessed economic system must be overhauled. Few people are willing to facilitate open, honest dialogue about overpopulation. Fewer still are open to discussing the fact that our worship of economic growth in part drives our population growth, and is also responsible for killing our planet.

— *Dave*

I do think that conservation and working together to improve our economy are worthy goals, but I definitely disagree with Bryan Welch on the need to limit the population.

Japan and Italy have drastically reduced their population growth and now they have a crisis: a lack of younger working people to support and provide medical care to the large population of older people. China has drastically reduced its population and will have a disproportionate number of old people in the future, with the same concerns for support and medical care. A large working population has always been needed for economic growth. The United States has only escaped this problem of disproportionate numbers of old people because of immigration. We are already concerned about sustaining Social Security and Medicare in the near future; we too will have a crisis if immigration should slow.

I believe that the Earth has enough food and shelter to sustain its people. We just need to do a better job of raising food, improving crop seed, teaching people effective methods of raising food, distributing food more equitably and helping people in developing countries to have sufficient food. One need only look at the example of Malawi in Africa: Its admirable improvement in raising enough food for its people has been due to donations of seed and fertilizer from developed countries, as well as the encouraging of people to adopt sustainable farm practices.

Finally, as a Mormon and Christian, I believe that we are children of our Heavenly Father. He has many more children who are waiting to come into this world and if we limit the number of children we have, we thwart his plan. The planet has enough for all as long as we share what we have with others and use our intelligence and technology to provide enough food and shelter for other people.

— *Peggy*

I applaud *Mother* for introducing the concept of population control as a means of improving sustainability to its readers. The subject is a political hot button that most media and environmental outlets are obviously avoiding. Frankly I am disappointed in your readers who threaten subscription cancellation at the mere mention of the issue. Instead of a closed-minded reaction, let's bring on rational discussion. I'm looking forward to the future fact-based presentation of the issues. Thanks for going out on this unpopular limb.

— *Laura*

The article "Planning for a Sustainable Human Future" was excellent. I support many environmental protection organizations, human rights groups and sustainability movements. Few of these groups are willing to even discuss the extremely vital issue of human population growth. Without consciously and collectively working to maintain sustainable populations worldwide, we will inevitably face ever-increasing food shortage, starvation, wars over resources, environmental devastation, epidemic diseases and poisoning of the life web and environment. Population stabilization could easily be achieved through education coupled with free and easy access to various methods of birth control.

Compassionately and creatively dealing with this problem now

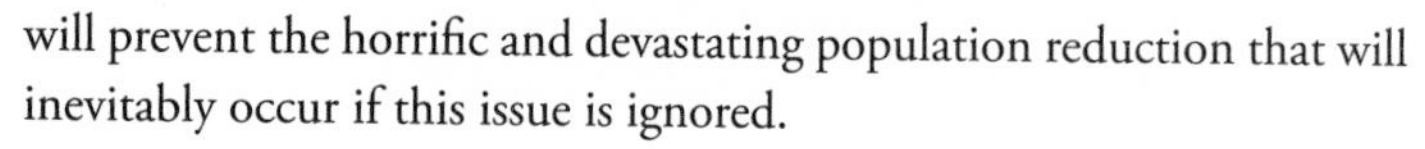

will prevent the horrific and devastating population reduction that will inevitably occur if this issue is ignored.

— Rand

The claim that the world will be a better place if families are encouraged to only have two children is misplaced and offensive, particularly in a free society. While I think that overpopulation is a myth, at best it's a theory, which should be debated and supported with evidence rather than treated as a hard fact that must be dealt with to solve the world's problems. Being good stewards of our planet also means respecting the human life that abounds here.

— Toni

I am appalled and disappointed in your stance for population control. Let's call it what it is: abortion, artificial birth control, embryonic stem cell research, euthanasia—in a word, murder. Not everyone ascribes to the culture of death that your magazine does.

When I was a child I saw an old black-and-white war movie on television, in which the Nazis used children to give blood transfusions to wounded soldiers … and the children died. Isn't this what we are doing today? We eliminate and use up the small and innocent so that the elite can survive.

Save the planet, but kill the babies. Save the whale, but kill the babies. Save the baby seals, but kill our human babies.

— Jennifer

Despite what people may believe, overpopulation is a serious issue and contributes exponentially to the problems facing the planet. Given that our planet is finite, just how many people do we think it can support? We can't go on with our heads in the sand like ostriches, ignoring the facts around us.

Present government estimates are that each person in the United States generates about 4 pounds of trash per day. As the population multiplies, so does that number. Where does that trash go? Most people don't seem to care, as long as it's out of sight and out of mind. As long as they don't see the trash and other side effects of human presence on the planet, they see nothing wrong with a growing worldwide population, and as long as they don't experience immediate effects of pollution or toxins in our environment, they think there must be nothing wrong with the way we live. But by the time we actually notice any of this in our own lives, it will be too late.

Whether you believe in global warming or not, it's impossible to ignore the environmental challenges facing us today. I believe it is incumbent upon each of us to make significant changes in our lives to help ensure that we have a healthy planet to pass on to future generations. There is, I believe, a moral imperative for each of us to live in ways that assure enough food, water and energy to sustain the world's population; to live in ways that restore the health of our soil, air and water; and to live in ways that teach our children the value of Mother Earth. And if those lifestyle changes also help abate a global warming situation that people think is a hoax, so much the better.

— Lynda

I was pleased to see that you are not allowing your magazine to be bullied into stopping the discussion on population control. I have been trying to make people understand since the early '70s that we are no different than any animal if we blindly allow unrestricted populations in this country and around the world destroy not only ourselves but every other living organism. It has started already, with thousands of extinct species of plants and animals. Your courage in this is admirable and appreciated.

— Deb

I believe you and the majority of your readers (and letter writers) have a worldview that is contrary to my own. For example, you support control of population growth. I know that is liberal-speak code for abortion on demand, at the least, and possibly forced sterilization and other so-called progressive social-engineering schemes. In fact, social engineering is one of the primary problems that those of us whom you call "conservative" find with the liberal worldview.

I believe that, even if we agree that it might be a good thing if the world's population growth were to stabilize, that would be better accomplished by free markets and by more opportunities available to more people. The latter happens naturally in the absence, not prevalence, of social engineering. One need only look at the most free nations to see that, indeed, population growth slows when democracy, opportunity and free markets are the norm.

— *Brad*

The fact is that there are too many people having babies who should not be, such as teens, singles and the promiscuous. The only real, safe and responsible way to solve this problem is to teach chastity to our children and to the world.

Overpopulation is an overstated problem. My husband and I have five beautiful children who were spaced three to four years apart by natural methods (not by artificial methods with unhealthy side effects).

We are able to feed, clothe and shelter them on one blue-collar income. We do not live beyond our means, but we are comfortable. And we try to help those in need. Overpopulation is not a problem. We can learn to help the poor and needy of the world. And we should not be forced to give; we should do it out of the kindness of our hearts.

The countries of the world do not need to be forcing sterilization, contraception and abortion; they just need a good dose of Grandma's moral values and healthy living.

— *Georgette*

I just want to say how much I love your magazine. My family is in the process of trying to be more self-sustaining. Your magazine has been a great help. Your articles are well-written and easy to understand. Since I have been a subscriber (not even a year) my husband and I built a clothesline, built a compost bin and put a rainwater system in our organic garden. We used biochar in our garden this year and several other things. My plants are huge this year!

I also want to commend you for tackling some tough issues, such as population. It's alarming that we have more people than our planet can sustain. It really scares me to think of how many would starve if we took all the processed foods off the shelves.

If something happened and we had to rely on farming and hunting to survive, how many people would know what to do? I cannot believe that people are cancelling their subscriptions.

Our planet is going to die if we as a people do not make some changes in the way we are living. It is truly frightening to me. Here in America we waste so much. I want to encourage people to look at their lives and see what changes we can make, no matter how big or small. I want to thank everyone at *Mother Earth News*. You are amazing, and you are doing so much to help our planet. Please know that your articles are helping to teach people how to make earth-friendly changes in their lives. Keep up your great work, and thank you, thank you!

— *Sarah*

If the sample of letters on the topic of global warming and human population numbers is reflective of the readership's opinion then much more awareness-raising is needed, and I'm encouraged to see *Mother Earth News* contributing so admirably.

For the doubters still subscribing, consider the following:

The Commission on Population Growth and the American Future (Rockefeller Commission Report) in 1972 stated, "After two years of concentrated effort, we have concluded that, in the long run, no substantial benefits will result from further growth of the Nation's population, rather that the gradual stabilization of our population through voluntary means would contribute significantly to the Nation's ability to solve its problems. We have looked for, and have not found, any convincing economic argument for continued population growth. The health of our country does not depend on it, nor does the vitality of business nor the welfare of the average person."

Physicist Al Bartlett, a professor emeritus at the University of Colorado, puts it this way: "Can you think of any problem in any area of human endeavor on any scale, from microscopic to global, whose long-term solution is in any demonstrable way aided, assisted, or advanced by further increases in population, locally, nationally or globally?"

We need to raise our awareness of global issues and strongly advocate for our grandchildren's sake while tending our gardens.

— *Wolfger*

I've been following the population-control debate these past few months closely, and what surprises me most is that this issue is even being debated at all. Didn't we learn enough from the last century's policies that decided who should be allowed to live? Deciding who should be allowed to be born is no different.

Those who would justify such policies in the name of the greater good for the planet are treading a slippery slope towards an Orwellian goal.

— *Matthew*

As another reader wrote, folks should toughen up and not feel threatened every time they read or hear something that doesn't agree with their personal worldviews. This is one of the reasons why I love *Mother Earth News*, because it *is* diverse. I can take what I want, and leave the rest if I choose.

Overall, it is a catalyst for change, one way or the other.

On that note, I wanted to point out something obvious that has been overlooked in regard to heated discussions on population. I've read numerous arguments since the articles were printed. But today, I caught myself giggling at the elephant in the room. Here I was, reading a magazine called *Mother Earth News*, yet no one considered that our Mother Earth might actually take care of population on her own, with or without our consent. She always has before, and if we consider that the earth is millions of years old, according to scientists, the fact that the population isn't bigger should speak for itself.

So why get wrapped around the axle about what we should or should not force everyone to do? Some people don't want children, some only want to adopt, some only want one or two, and some want huge families. There is room to accommodate everyone, and when that room is used up, Mother Earth will naturally balance us out.

The greater argument should be, is she selective, and how does she decide who stays and who goes? So perhaps we all should live better, respect others, let everyone make their choices as they see fit, and leave the decisions to our Mother.

When Mom comes to sort things out, all she wants to know is "what did *you* do?"

— *Erin*

I have been subscribing to *Mother Earth News* for one year and have just received my fifth issue. Excellent material as usual. I feel like I have found a lost friend and a community that I can relate to. I enjoy the informative articles and the opportunity to learn new techniques and points of view.

I also like to read the subscriber comments. My first issue contained the article "Three Mountains We Must Climb," which showed three obstacles that humanity has to face. I thought the article was a much needed wake-up call for all. Not only did it broach the taboo of discussing overpopulation, it gave some solutions to each obstacle.

It has amused me to hear some of your readers are not going to renew their subscriptions because of that article or some other controversial article. That just shows me and the rest of the *Mother Earth News* family that we are supporting the right causes.

Overpopulation is the root of all of humanity's problems and family size needs to be limited to two children, one child or no children for a sustainable future.

Some of our brothers or sisters disagree with that because of religious ideation and a belief that God will fix it. I am here to tell you that is pure and utter ignorance. We procreate and we need to challenge our beliefs that it is OK to have as many children as we want to. I am 43 years old and have given up my right to have a child, because of overpopulation.

Human population doubles approximately every 40 to 45 years. In 1900, the human population was 1.6 billion and now the human population is pushing 6.5 billion. You do the math and tell me what kind of future your child or grandchild is going to have?

In all honesty I would love to have a boy and a girl, but I know too much. I cannot bring them into an overpopulated, polluted, exploited, war-torn planet in good conscience.

Thank you to everyone at *Mother Earth News* for doing a great job!

— *Christopher*

Unlike the mainstream media, Bryan Welch and *Mother Earth News* speak the truth ("Planning for a Sustainable Human Future"). The current and next two generations are facing the most colossal challenges that have ever confronted mankind and the totality of life on Earth—the need for human conservation, population stabilization (orderly decline) and sustainable economies. All three are closely interconnected, and all three are absolutely necessary for a sustainable world.

This essay is right on and says it all. Thank you, thank you, thank you, Bryan Welch and *Mother Earth News*!

— *Robert*

I have stewed over the replies to "Three Mountains We Must Climb" for two months now and I have decided to finally spout off myself.

The problem with controlling human population is based in archaic religious beliefs that (1) Humans are the most important thing in the universe other than the omnipotent being too many of them believe in and (2) Humans must breed uncontrolled and cover the earth.

It was necessary to have many children because of high mortality rates 2,000 years ago. As recently as the 12th and 13th centuries the human race was near extinction because of disease, famine and war. Since then there has been only one close brush with extinction, the Cuban Missile Crisis. Maybe it should have ended differently.

Why is there war? It's a human thing. Why is there a water shortage? Because there are 6.7 billion bags of water walking around on our planet. Why is famine and disease on the rise? 6.7 billion humans. Why is there pollution? 6.7 billion humans. Why why why why why? 6.7 billion humans.

— *Thomas*

Thank you so much for addressing the issue of overpopulation and how it is affecting our planet. I have thought this a serious issue for more than four years, but hardly anyone has been willing to look at this realistically.

We are in the process of overusing, abusing and generally destroying the Earth. The more people there are, the faster this will happen.

I believe a couple should have no more than two children (the theory of Zero Population Growth). That is, one child to replace each adult. Even if we weren't destroying the earth, it is finite and the population could not increase forever.

The only thing selfish and irresponsible here is people who think they can have any number of children they want. In the end we are all in this together and what affects one will affect all.

— *Linda*

For years we were told that global warming is a myth, and now we know the truth, that it is a real threat to our planet. For years we were told that smoking cigarettes doesn't cause cancer, and now we know the truth about that too.

Today, the latest myth is that the world is suffering under an exploding population threat, yet the facts from respected authorities like the United Nations simply do not bear this out. Consider that in 1965, each woman had an average of 6 children. Today the number is 2.1. The dramatic population increase your article showed is due to the fact that life expectancy rates have drastically increased, climbing from 46 years in 1950-1955 to more than 65 years from 2000-2005.

In fact, the global population growth rate peaked around 1965 and has since then fallen. This is the real population crisis which threatens existing social security systems as our population drastically ages

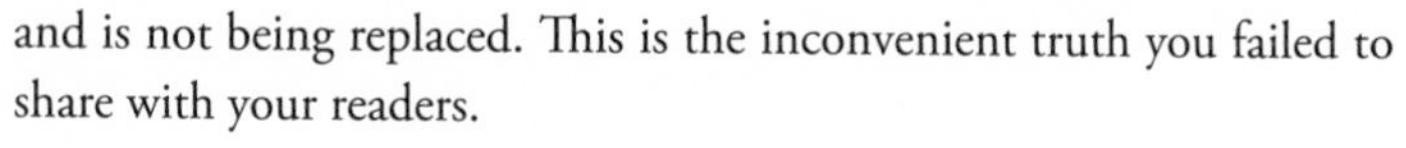

and is not being replaced. This is the inconvenient truth you failed to share with your readers.

— *Margaret*

The April/May issue (number 233) was one of my all-time favorites. "Planning For A Sustainable Human Future" was to a large degree the reason. Bryan Welch began with the motorcycle metaphor that clearly got my head around what is happening around me. He gave me talking points on overpopulation and the need for a new type of economy that doesn't require a growing population.

These are obvious points as Mr. Welch writes them. Well done. I'm a fan. I hope David Brooks, Thomas Friedman and my other favorite columnists see this article.

— *John*

Yes, our planet has too many people. Either we limit our population growth or the planet will do it for us. All animals outgrow the carrying capacity of their environment. We already have; we just don't know it yet.

I love my grandson dearly, and if I had a dozen grandchildren, I'm sure I would love them all. But we cannot save the planet by having more children, nor consume our way to prosperity.

— *Peter*

I've always enjoyed *Mother Earth News* for the great gardening articles, but your recent discussions of global environmental issues have been so concise and well-written that I'm keeping your magazine in my office to help me articulate opinions and vision with my colleagues and clients.

In particular, "Planning For a Sustainable Human Future" by Bryan Welch and "A Plan for the Solar Revolution" by Dennis Hayes in the April/May 2009 issue are must-reads for all.

Welch's analogy of visualizing success in completing a difficult athletic challenge is effective and relevant in relation to our environmental challenges. His observations regarding population balance present a compassionate and simple necessity.

Hayes lays out such a clear and comprehensive strategy that he should be our president.

Thank you for keeping the quality of discussion at this level.

— Mike

As a Christian subscriber to your magazine, I can tell you that there are many of us conservative Christians who feel a Biblical mandate to care for the Earth through sustainable living. Many of my friends try to eat organically, produce home vegetable gardens and recycle, among other things.

Your call to "defeat our biological programming—the programming that, in the words of the Judeo-Christian Bible, tells us to 'go forth and multiply'" is both hypocritical and bizarre. You advocate a return to natural living—in every area but this: Our deepest joys in life come from our families. Yet you advocate behaviors that would lead to their extinction. Two people producing only two more humans is *not* replacement value (check with demographers!).

I'm amazed that you would advocate for human extinction and for such unnatural measures. Your crusade against the Judeo-Christian Bible is remarkably intolerant of diversity!

Your time and efforts would be better spent in helping parents develop tools to teach their children sustainable living rather than crusading against what is still the most popular religion on the planet.

— Jeanine

Many of us who agree with your goals of living responsibly nevertheless disagree vehemently with your view that we should lower our population level and keep it there.

Here was the offending remark: After ceding the point that we could find ways to accommodate more people on this Earth, you then asked, "But why would we want to?"

Why? Here's why: Because each human being is unique and unrepeatable, and makes the world a better place. If we can't see everyone in the human family, past, present and future, as a gift and say, "It is good that you are with us!" without appending an asterisk that says, "but your presence is a drain on the Earth," then we simply devalue the life of every person, ourselves included.

Our inherent dignity is not dependent upon our carbon footprint. Even Mother Teresa, no stranger to the problems of overcrowding, once said, "How can you say there are too many children? That's like saying there are too many flowers!"

Population control fatalistically turns humankind against itself and says, "We're not worth the effort."

— *Dan*

Thank you for your attention to population issues.

I am renewing especially for your attention to issues extremely important for the sustainability of human life on this planet.

Everyone who can envision even a few generations after we are gone needs to have some grasp of realities, or the next generations of humans might be scant indeed.

You do a great job of getting out good information on many useful and important things.

Thank you.

— *Bill*

Your articles on the subject of population seem to be part of an effort for government intervention. That is the only way population control will work—if the government is involved. Then "draconian" intervention will be mandated and human rights will be violated.

No amount of articles on your part will change the minds of people needed for population control to work. In one blow you have advocated government intervention and mocked Christian values.

— *Stacy*

Thank you, Mr. Welch, for being brave, independent and honest about the subject which appears to have offered your readership an interesting dilemma. Can you imagine? Who would have thought that a group of people that respect nature, admire conservation and the exploration of cutting-edge technologies, advances in "back to the land" movements and obvious open-mindedness could suddenly be unable to wrap themselves around this one?

You may not have been prepared for the response that has ensued because of your quiet suggestion that we *think* about population control. How opportune it is, now that we face this problem not on the population issue but on the actual economic front.

We are coming face to face with the issue which we may not fully understand and your article gives us the opportunity to put these two issues to the forefront. We can visualize success and now is the time. It is our evolutionary responsibility as a species. We have been presented a spiritual vision. Are we ready to see it?

— *Caryl*

I've been reading the ongoing discussion on population in your issues and I tip my hat to you for staying strong despite some disappointed readers out there. While I understand the sensitivity of the issue for many, to simply ignore the discussion and/or criticize those who participate is such an unproductive approach.

With so many elements to the issue and sources for opinion, I tried to elect one argument for myself to put forth in your ongoing dialog. I'm on the side of preserving the freedom of choice.

There is a real fear of regulation over something as personal as our reproductive rights, almost a kind of sci-fi scenario. The political argument against regulated action is the easiest for me to sympathize with, given my own disposition for Jeffersonian-style independence. But to that end, I feel it is all the more important that we make choices now that accept the potential for future problems. I work as an environmental educator, and I try to make choices in my own life that can prevent a future in which the limitation of resources and their distribution leaves us with a world that is forced into regulation and/or stratification.

Independence is one of our country's core values, and given the material, it's clearly dear to many *Mother Earth News* readers.

It is those choices that we make independently that can preserve the right for future generations to do the same. There is a bitter irony that the viewpoints often most dismissive of such a discussion can be the ones that could ultimately lead to their own worst nightmare.

— *Brendan*

You list population growth as one of the three mountains we as a society must climb to achieve worldwide sustainability. This time you have gone too far. The world was made for man's use, not vice versa. To teach that mankind itself is the problem is to subjugate the place of human life on this planet to fear. Not to mention that you're treading not-so-softly upon the ground of a belief that human life is a joy to be shared and that its proliferation is commanded by God—a god most of your readers believe in.

— *Cameron*

Thank you for addressing the most important issue of our time, overpopulation. Our local environmental group broke up over the issue years ago. But it is still true, only more so, that the environmental, social and health issues have only grown as populations have increased. No continent, no environment has been spared, yet in an economic downturn this issue still is swept under the rug.

— *Emma*

Having been born and raised in a religious family, it really ticks me off when people start picking and choosing which verses of the Bible they are going to quote to back up their personal views, while ignoring other verses they don't like.

Yes, God said "go forth and multiply." But he also gave us free will to see if we would do the right thing. The Bible is full of stories of people asking God why he allowed something bad to happen. The answer is often that it was a test to see if we used our free will to make the right or wrong decision. Read the Bible or ask your preacher if you doubt me.

Keep up the good work.

— *Gordy*

While I agree with most aspects of the idea of population control, I understand and can sympathize with others' views as well. My opinion on this article is not the point, though. I appreciate your boldness in broaching the subject and would continue to subscribe even if I did not agree with the article. Your magazine provides so much more, to cancel subscriptions over one article is truly wasting a valuable resource in itself, and juvenile to boot.

— *Sarah*

The world's human population is already well over what can be sustained in the long haul. One of the reasons is that we are eating food that is grown with the use of man-made nitrogenous fertilizer, manufactured using fossil fuels. Subtract out fabricated ammonium nitrate and half of the people on this planet would starve before year's end.

Folks, we are eating up our capital. We are living on the principal. We either voluntarily reduce our population or Nature will do it for us— which won't be pleasant.

— *Don*

I am writing to add my voice to those who have praised you for your comments on population reduction. The thoughts and suggestions that you put forward chime perfectly with my own feelings on this subject. None of us can hope for a sustainable and ecologically sound future without addressing the need to stabilize and gradually reduce our world population, and this is something that touches every one of us who chooses to bring children into the world.

It saddens me that whenever this thorny subject is raised, so many people start shouting, "You're playing god!" and, "What next, forced sterilization?" One thing's for sure, this issue will have to be tackled sooner rather than later if we are to inhabit a world worth living in. Education is surely the key, and I commend you for your brave and inspirational stance in choosing to get the debate out into the open.

— *Ian*

What I like about *Mother Earth News* is they promote a natural and healthy style of living.

The most common methods of population control are the pill and surgical sterilization. They are neither natural or healthy, so there seems to be a hypocrisy for *Mother Earth News* to promote population control when the current methods are so unnatural.

Natural Family Planning allows parents to be responsible and does so in a natural and healthy way. For more information, visit www.familyplanning.net.

— *Joyce*

I can conjure a dozen or so old sayings like, "You can't shake hands with a clinched fist," but I am too exhausted from reading the musings of people who seem to have deliberately and simply closed their minds to even a polite discussion of some of the more controversial issues you bring to the fore.

It is glaringly obvious that some people just quit learning at a certain point because they think their brains are entirely full-to-capacity with all the indisputable knowledge of what is true, right, natural and absolute in this experience we call life. Chances are good those people are even a bit smug about being the keepers of the ancient secrets of life. Why is it then that these same people will not admit that, from experiences in their own lives, what once was true isn't necessarily true anymore?

Death, taxes and change don't go away. Anyone with more than a couple of decades of experience in this journey would realize that change is the only constant. Jogging was good for me in my twenties. In my thirties, jogging was bad, because I blew out my knees in my twenties. In my forties, I approached business as a deadly-serious competition and learned to use all my competitors' weaknesses to my advantage to win contracts for my employers. In my fifties, I learned that winning business contracts wasn't everything when I lost my wife to cancer.

... Endlessly recanting stories about how perfect things were in the past isn't germane to solving any problems subject to the circumstances of the present.

Read everything that generates thought, good, bad and indifferent. If you don't agree with someone else's view just mentally file it away as the ramblings of a person who clearly has a different point of reference or experience than you.

It is important, however, that you know what other people are thinking and saying about your issues, because you never know when an opportunity will arise for you to intelligently and deliberately plant a seed of thoughtful change in their lives. A very bright man once said, "Don't raise your voice, improve your argument." Taking your ball home isn't an option for full-grown, thinking adults who have a responsibility to stand up, speak up and make this world a better place for the generations that follow.

— *William*

I just wanted to thank you for your essay called "Three Mountains...." The responses on the website and in the magazine are quite surprising.

I thought everyone was aware that the world is overpopulated and polluted. Just look around at how dirty and abused most people in the world are.

Birth control is a wonderful gift that lets a woman choose how many children she wishes to produce. Most women, if given the opportunity, would gladly take birth control.

If you don't have control over your body, you don't have control over your own life. I find it frightening that so many fundamentalist religions are trying to outlaw birth control, as if giving a woman choice threatens their control over people's lives.

Keep up the good work! I see from your archives that population control has been a subject since the magazine's inception. I will renew my subscription for the next 10 years.

— *Kris*

I had to reread the article that caused such vitriol. And re-agree with it. Those who purport the earth is here for humans are the same ones who butt in line, run water carelessly down the drain, only think of gas when it costs them a pretty penny, and overuse and overharvest for their all-important consumption. Lucky they weren't born in a third-world country, to die soon after or suffer horrendously through starvation or atrocity. Hopefully, they are old enough to die before water-rights wars, massive food-source extinctions (overfishing, overhunting) and mono-genetic crop failures create a cascading effect.

Has the idea, the very notion of overpopulation ever crossed their minds? And why does just the thought of it cause such outrage?

Keep up the good work!

— *Michele*

I agree with you that it is essential that we stabilize the population, but I disagree that socialism or communism are obsolete social systems. A system has to have been tried in the first place in order for it to be rendered obsolete.

The Scandinavian countries do a remarkable job with their socialistic programs. Their primary obstacle is competing in a world economic system ruled by American capitalism. Why does Al Gore never mention overpopulation as a contributing factor in global warming? Because he is a rich free-market guy who sees humans as consumers, and the less people there are the less people there would be to purchase fluorescent light bulbs with their mercury and Toyota Priuses, which still burn oil.

The only chance we have at all to reduce global warming if it's not too late is to reduce the amount of people contributing to it, which would entail a restructuring of our entire Darwinian economic system based on private profits. Our current economy functions on the need for consumers to buy, consume and buy more gadgets that eventually end up in a landfill.

— *Chris*

My husband and I are big fans of your magazine. We enjoy every issue and a variety of topics. We got the newest issue yesterday and I was very surprised that so many people are against population control.

I grew up in China and have seen firsthand what an important role population control in the form of the one-child policy has played in improving living standards and economic growth.

Although people may have different ideas on how it should be done, I hope more and more will at least realize that population control is an important step toward conserving our Mother Earth for the benefit of mankind.

By the way, I've baked many times the artisan bread by following the article from last issue. We love it! We'll have it for dinner again tonight. Thanks for all the good work.

— *Qin*

When I received my last issue of *Mother Earth News*, I quickly tucked it away without looking at it on purpose. I was getting my things ready to go to the hospital for four days and wanted to keep it to read during my stay.

I loved the crusty-bread article and couldn't wait to try it. Then I read the essay that talked about population control.

I couldn't believe my eyes. Here I was in the hospital having my fourth precious child and the magazine of my choice promotes population control! How could I be so deceived into thinking this magazine was worth my time, which is more and more precious with each child I have?

You are wrong. Would you have women subject their bodies to hormones, aka birth control? Abstain from the gift of sex? Have surgery to alter their bodies?

May I be granted with even more children that I can train to make a difference in this confused world. You should have stuck with gardening, living well and crusty bread. You're missing out on the good things in life. Merry Christmas!

— *Julia*

I have read your recent editorials on population control with great concern and apprehension. Since when did this planet become more important than those who inhabit it?

Thoreau once wrote, "There are a thousand hacking at the branches of evil to one who is striking at the root." The means of saving the Earth is not population control but a fundamental return to personal integrity and unselfishness.

You're just another one hacking at the branches. I refuse to support such stagnant and selfish values.

— *Quin*

After reading the many comments on the article regarding overpopulation, I came away with a slightly different outlook. I think it is wonderful that *Mother Earth News* is read and cherished by such a broad range of people. I find this comforting and enlightening. It had never dawned on me that the type of person who would become upset or defensive over the mention of overpopulation would be reading *Mother Earth News* to start with. I am glad that your magazine can provide information to such a diverse group and has helped to correct an apparently narrow view I have held regarding others.

— *Kristen*

Notes

1,2 Baltimore Monthly Meeting of Friends – Stony Run. *Faith and Practice: Quaker Queries.* http://www.stonyrunfriends.org/Queries.html. Sourced May 2, 2010.

3 Duane Elgin. *Voluntary Simplicity.* Second Revised Edition. HarperCollins, New York. 2010. ISBN 978-0-06-177926-8.

4 Blake Schmidt. *Ranchers and Drug Barons Threaten Rain Forest.* The New York Times. July 17, 2010.

5 Malcolm Gladwell. *The Tipping Point: How Little Things Can Make a Big Difference.* Little, Brown and Company, March 2000. First Back Bay paperback edition, January 2002, Page 7.

6 British Petroleum (BP). *Consumption by fuel, 1965 - 2008".* Statistical Review of World Energy 2009. http://www.bp.com/liveassets/bp_internet/globalbp/globalbp_uk_english/reports_and_publications/statistical_energy_review_2008/STAGING/local_assets/2009_downloads/statistical_review_of_world_energy_full_report_2009.xls. Sourced October 4, 2010.

7 U.S. Census Bureau. *International Data Base* (IDB). http://www.census.gov/ipc/www/idb/worldpop.php. Sourced October 4, 2010.

8 Enerdata. *Yearbook Statistical Energy Review 2010.* http://yearbook.enerdata.net/.

9 *Path to Freedom: The Original Modern Urban Homestead.* http://urbanhomestead.org/urban-homestead. Sourced August 16, 2010.

10 Parque Pumalin website. *History.* http://www.parquepumalin.cl/content/eng/index.htm. Sourced August 17, 2010.

11 Fairtrade Labelling Organizations International . *FLO International: Annual Report 2007.* 2008.

12 United Nations Development Programme. *UNDP and Biodiversity.* http://www.undp.org/biodiversity/about_us.html. Feb. 5, 2009.

13 *"Recession".* Encarta® World English Dictionary [North American Edition]. Microsoft Corporation. 2007. http://encarta.msn.com/encnet/features/dictionary/DictionaryResults.aspx?refid=1861699686. Retrieved on Feb. 10, 2009.

14 Joel E. Cohen. *Human Population: The Next Half Century.* Science Magazine No. 14. November 2003: Vol. 302. no. 5648, pp. 1172-1175. DOI: 10.1126/science.1088665

15 M. Werding, S. Munz and V. Gács. *Fertility and Prosperity: Links Between Demography and Economic Growth* (final report), Ifo Forschungsbericht No. 42, Munich: Ifo Institute for Economic Research. 2008.

16 *King James Bible.* Book of Genesis. Chapter 1, Verse 26.

17 FAO Agricultural Services Bulletin. *Renewable Biological Systems for Alternative Sustainable Energy Production.* http://www.fao.org/docrep/w7241e/w7241e05.htm#1.2.1. FAO Agricultural Services Bulletin – 128. 1997. Sourced Sept. 4, 2010.

18 Alden Whitman. New York Times obituary, August 19, 1969. *Mies van der Rohe Dies at 83; Leader of Modern Architecture.* http://www.nytimes.com/learning/general/onthisday/bday/0327.html. Sourced May 11, 2010.

19 Gregory Titelman. *Random House Dictionary of Popular Proverbs and Sayings.* Random House Reference. March 5, 1996

20 http://www.deere.com/en_US/attractions/worldhq/about.html. Sourced Jan. 4, 2010.

21 Agnes Bailllie Cunninghame Dunbar. *A Dictionary of Saintly Women: Volume One.* London. 1904.

22 A.H.M. Jones. *The Later Roman Empire 284-602.* Basil Blackwell Ltd. 1964. P. 647.

23 New World Encyclopedia. Census. http://www.newworldencyclopedia.org/entry/Census. Sourced May 12, 2010.

24 U. Dicke and G. Roth. "Intelligence Evolved", *Scientific American Mind.* (August/September 2008. pp. 75-77.

25 John Noble Wilford. *Lucy's Kin Carved Up a Meaty Meal, Scientists Say.* The New York Times. August 11, 2010.

26 Freeman, Scott; Jon C. Herron. *Evolutionary Analysis* (4th ed.)., Pearson Education, Inc. (2007). ISBN 0-13-227584-8 pages 786-788.

27 Elizabeth Pennisi. *Neandertal Genomics: Tales of a Prehistoric Human Genome. Science* issue 5916: pp. 866-871. doi:10.1126/science.323.5916.866

28 Paul Rincon. *Neanderthal Genes 'Survive in Us'.* BBC News. http://news.bbc.co.uk/2/hi/science/nature/8660940.stm. May 6, 2010. Sourced August 25, 2010.

29 M.P. Richards, P.B. Pettitt, E. Trinkaus, F.H. Smith, M. Paunović, I. Karavanić. *Neanderthal diet at Vindija and Neanderthal predation: the evidence from stable isotopes.* Proceedings of the National Academy of Sciences **97** (13): 7663–6. (June 2000) doi:10.1073/pnas.120178997. PMID 10852955

30 Jared Diamond. *Guns, Germs and Steel: The Fate of Human Societies.* 1999. P. 39. ISBN 978-0-393-31755-8.

31 Marc A. Carrasco, Anthony D. Barnosky, Russell W. Graham. *Quantifying the Extent of North American Mammal Extinction Relative to the Pre-Anthropogenic Baseline. Plosone.org.* December 16, 2009. Sourced August 29, 2010.

32 Anthony D. Barnosky, Paul L. Koch, Robert S. Feranec, Scott L. Wing, Alan B. Shabel. *Assessing the Causes of Late Pleistocene Extinctions on the Continents.* Science **306** (5693): 70–75. 2004. http://www.sciencemag.org/cgi/content/abstract/306/5693/70. Sourced August 29, 2010.

33 Gary Haynes. *The Early Settlement of North America: The Clovis Era.* Cambridge University Press. New York. 2002. ISBN 0521524636.

34 David A. Anthony. (2007). *The horse, the wheel, and language: how Bronze-Age riders from the Eurasian steppes shaped the modern world.* 2007. Princeton University Press. p. 67. ISBN 0-691-05887-3.

35 David V. Herlihy. *Bicycle: The History.* 2004. Yale University Press. pp. 200-250. ISBN 0-300-10418-9.

36 Ralph Stein. *The Automobile Book.* 1967. Paul Hamlyn Ltd.

37 Aviation History Magazine/HistoryNet.com. *St. PetersburgTampa Airboat Line: World's First Scheduled Airline Using Winged Aircraft.* http://www.historynet.com/st-petersburgtampa-airboat-line-worlds-first-scheduled-airline-using-winged-aircraft.htm/4. Sourced July 27, 2010.

38 Akash Kapur. *A Hindu Sect Devoted to the Environment.* The New York Times. October 7, 2010.

39 Michael E. Reynolds. *A Coming of Wizards: A Manual of Human Potential.* 1989. High Mesa Press. High Mesa Foundation. Taos, NM. ISBN 0-9614010-3-6.

40 www.earthship.com. Sourced Sept. 2, 2010.

41 Electric Drive Transportation Association. *2008 Hybrid Electric Passenger Vehicle Sales by Model (through December 2008).* http://www.electricdrive.org/index.php?ht=d/Articles/cat_id/5514/pid/2549. Sourced Oct. 22, 2009.

42 Brand Neutral White Paper. *The Prius Effect: Learning from Toyota; Engaging consumers, driving profit, and avoiding risk through environmental strategy.* Principal contributors were John Rego, Joshua Stempel and Richard Mintz. Copyright 2007, Brand Neutral, 8750 Wilshire Blvd., Suite 250, Beverly Hills CA 90211. www.brandneutral.com.

43 The International Energy Agency (IEA) reported that worldwide motor gasoline consumption in 2007 was 894,399,000 tonnes (http://www.iea.org/stats/oildata.asp?COUNTRY_CODE=29), or about 6.6 billion barrels (http://www.spe.org/industry/reference/unit_conversions.php), the equivalent of about 275 billion U.S. gallons. There are about 2 million Priuses on the highways worldwide, about three-tenths of 1 percent of the 600 million cars on the roads worldwide (http://www.sasi.group.shef.ac.uk/worldmapper/display.php?selected=31). If they save, on average, a third of the gas used by an average automobile then that's about one tenth of 1 percent of the gasoline used worldwide, or about 303 million gallons of gasoline each year.

44 Whole Foods Market website. http://www.wholefoodsmarket.com/company/history.php#1. Sourced April 3, 2010.

45 Michael Strong. *Be the Solution: How Entrepreneurs and Conscious Capitalists Can Solve All the World's Problems.* John Wiley & Sons, Hoboken, New Jersey, 2009. Page 364. ISBN 978-0-470-45003-1.

46 Gadsden Independent School District NMHSSA Test Scores, 2008. http://www.trulia.com/school-district/NM-Dona_Ana_County/Gadsden_Independent_School_District/. Sourced April 1, 2010.

47 Strong. Preface, p. xix.

48 Grameen Bank website. http://www.grameen-info.org/index.php?option=com_content&task=view&id=16&Itemid=112. Sourced April 3, 2010.

49 Jeffrey Gangemi. *What the Nobel Means for Microcredit.* BusinessWeek Magazine. October 13, 2006. http://www.businessweek.com/smallbiz/content/oct2006/sb20061016_705623.htm. Sourced April 3, 2010.

50 Emily Maltby. Small Biz Loan Failure Rate Hits 12%. CNNMoney.com/Small Business. February 25, 2009. http://money.cnn.com/2009/02/25/smallbusiness/smallbiz_loan_defaults_soar.smb/. Sourced April 3, 2010.

51 Dan Levy and David Henry. *Commercial Mortgage Default Rate in U.S. More than Doubles.* Bloomberg. http://www.bloomberg.com/apps/news?pid=20601206&sid=aExgk1dEfRrA. February 4, 2010. Sourced April 12, 2010.

52 Sean C. Keenan, Igor Shtogrim and Jorge Sobehart. *Historical Default Rates of Corporate Bond Issuers, 1920-1998.* Moody's Investors Service Global Credit Search. New York. January 1999.

53 Allison Fass. *Pickens Goes For The Grass Roots.* Forbes.com. http://www.forbes.com/2008/07/11/pickensplan-wind-energy-tech-science-cz_af_0710pickens.html. July 11, 2008. Sourced October 27, 2009.

54 Kambiz Foroohar. *Pickens Power Makes Al Gore Convenient Truth in U.S. Oil Policy.* Bloomberg.com. October 7, 2009. http://www.bloomberg.com/apps/news?pid=20601170&sid=agf9mm._YR4s. Sourced October 27, 2009.

55 Janet L. Sawin. *Wind Power Increase in 2008 Exceeds 10-Year Average.* Worldwatch Institute. May 7, 2009. http://www.worldwatch.org/node/6102?emc=el&m=239273&l=5&v=ca5d0bd2df. Sourced Nov. 1, 2009.

56 Elizabeth Rosenthal. *Ancient Italian Town Now Has Wind at Its Back.* The New York Times. September 28, 2010.

57 Jay F. Marks. *T. Boone Pickens Predicts Success for Plan.* Daily Oklahoman. October 30, 2009. http://newsok.com/pickens-predicts-success-for-plan/article/3413131?custom_click=rss. Sourced Nov. 1, 2009.

58 U.S. Department of Energy. *Technologies. Passive Solar Building Design.* http://www.eere.energy.gov/de/passive_solar_design.html. Sourced October 30, 2009.

59 REN21: Renewable Energy Policy Network for the 21st Century. *Renewables Global Status Report 2009 Update.* REN21 Secretariat. Paris.

60 California Public Utilities Commission. *CPUC Takes Another Step Toward State's Renewable Energy Goal with Approval of PG&E Renewable Contract.* http://docs.cpuc.ca.gov/PUBLISHED/NEWS_RELEASE/96710.htm. January 29, 2009. Sourced November 5, 2009.

61 Pvresources.com. *Large-Scale Photovoltaic Power Plants (Ranking 1-50).* http://www.pvresources.com/en/top50pv.php. Sourced November 5, 2009.

62 Reuters. *Desertec, a 400-billion-euro plan to power Europe with sunlight from the Sahara, is the world's most ambitious solar power project and would be a major example of concentrated solar power (CSP) technology.* http://www.reuters.com/article/idUSTRE57N01720090824?sp=true. August 23, 2009. Sourced September 12, 2010.

63 Felicity Barringer. *Solar Power Plants to Rise on U.S. Land.* The New York Times. October 5, 2010.

64 Ucilia Wang. *Stirling Redesigns SunCatcher, Plans 1.5MW Demo Project.* Greentechsolar: http://www.greentechmedia.com/articles/read/stirling-energy-systems-redesigns-suncatcher-plans-for-1.5mw-demo-project/. Sourced October 13, 2010.

65 DuPont Photovoltaic Solutions. *DuPont Expects Continued Revenue Growth in Global Photovoltaic Market.* http://www2.dupont.com/Photovoltaics/en_US/news_events/article20090317.html. Sourced November 5, 2009.

66 Thomas L. Friedman. *China's Sunshine Boys.* New York Times. Dec. 6, 2006.

67 City of Berkeley, California, Office of Energy and Sustainable Development. Berkeley *FIRST Financing Initiative for Renewable and Solar Technology.* http://www.cityofberkeley.info/ContentDisplay.aspx?id=26580. Sourced Nov. 5, 2009.

68 Greentech Media. *Power-Purchase Agreements to Spike.* http://www.greentechmedia.com/articles/read/power-purchase-agreements-to-spike-591/. Sourced November 5, 2009.

69 Japan National Institute of Advanced Industrial Science and Technology (AIST). *Converting ultraviolet light into electricity with transparent electronics.* http://www.aist.go.jp/aist_e/museum/science/12/12.html. Sourced November 5, 2009.

70 http://www.covalentsolar.com/. Sourced September 12, 2010.

71 T. H. Jordan. *Structural Geology of the Earth's Interior.* Proceedings National Academy of Science **76** (9): 4192–4200. 1979. doi:10.1073/pnas.76.9.4192. PMID 16592703. http://www.pubmedcentral.nih.gov/articlerender.fcgi?artid=411539. Sourced November 9, 2009.

72 J. Louie. "Earth's Interior". University of Nevada, Reno. 1996. http://www.seismo.unr.edu/ftp/pub/louie/class/100/interior.html. Sourced November 9, 2009.

73 D. L. Turcotte, G. Schubert. *Geodynamics* (second edition). 2002. Cambridge, England, UK: Cambridge University Press. pp. 136-137. ISBN 978-0-521-66624-4.

74 Chevron press release. *Chevron Deploys a Second Ultra-Deepwater Drillship: Next generation drillship has unsurpassed drilling capabilities.* http://www.chevron.com/news/press/release/?id=2010-03-11. March 11, 2010. Sourced June 20, 2010.

75 Árni Ragnarsson., *Geothermal Development in Iceland 2000-2004.* Proceedings World Geothermal Congress, Antalya, Turkey . April 24-29, 2005. Sourced November 11, 2009.

76 J. Lund, B. Sanner, L. Rybach; R. Curtis, G. Hellström. *Geothermal (Ground Source) Heat Pumps, A World Overview.* Geo-Heat Centre Quarterly Bulletin (Klamath Falls, Oregon: Oregon Institute of Technology) **25** (3): 1–10. September, 2004. ISSN 0276-1084, http://geoheat.oit.edu/bulletin/bull25-3/art1.pdf. Sourced March 21, 2009.

77 U.S. Department of Energy/Energy Efficiency & Renewable Energy. Energy Savers: Geothermal Heat Pumps. http://www.energysavers.gov/your_home/space_heating_cooling/index.cfm/mytopic=12640. Sourced March 23, 2010.

78 Ingvar B. Fridleifsson; Ruggero Bertani; Ernst Huenges; John W. Lund; Arni Ragnarsson; Ladislaus Rybach, (2008-02-11). O. Hohmeyer and T. Trittin. ed (pdf). *The possible role and contribution of geothermal energy to the mitigation of climate change.* Luebeck, Germany. pp. 59-80. February 11, 2008. http://iga.igg.cnr.it/documenti/IGA/Fridleifsson_et_al_IPCC_Geothermal_paper_2008.pdf. Sourced November 11, 2009.

79 Ronald DiPippo. *Geothermal Power Plants, Second Edition: Principles, Applications, Case Studies and Environmental Impact.* Butterworth-Heinemann. ISBN 978-0-7506-8620-4.

80 *Calpine Corporation - The Geysers.* http://www.geysers.com. Sourced November 11, 2009.

81 Declan Butler. *Energy efficiency: Super savers: Meters to manage the future.* NATURE: International Weekly Journal of Science. February 8, 2007. http://www.nature.com/nature/journal/v445/n7128/full/445586a.html. Sourced March 31, 2010.

82 U.S. Energy Information Administration Office of Coal, Nuclear, Electric and Alternate Fuels. *State Electricity Profiles 2008.* March 2010. U.S. Department of Energy, Washington DC 20585. DOE/EIA-0348(01)/2.

83 U.S.-Canada Power System Outage Task Force. *Final Report on the August 14 2003 Blackout in the United States and Canada: Causes and Recommendations.* Chapter 5. April 5, 2004.

84 Allan Chen. *Berkeley Lab Study Estimates $80 Billion Annual Cost of Power Interruptions.* Research News/Berkeley Lab. Feb. 2, 2005. http://www.lbl.gov/Science-Articles/Archive/EETD-power-interruptions.html. Sourced March 31, 2010.

85 U.S. Department of Energy Energy Efficiency & Renewable Energy. *The Green Power Network: Green Power Markets; Net Metering Policies.* http://apps3.eere.energy.gov/greenpower/markets/netmetering.shtml. Sourced April 1, 2010.

86 Todd Woody. *You'd Never Know He's a Sun King.* The New York Times. May 8, 2010.

87 Organic Valley website. http://www.organicvalley.coop/about-us/our-cooperative/. Sourced June 5, 2010.

88 Businessweek. *Smarter Corporate Giving.* http://www.businessweek.com/magazine/content/05_48/b3961607.htm. November 28, 2005. Sourced May 20, 2010.

89 Mondragon Corporation website. http://www.mondragon-corporation.com/language/en-US/ENG/Economic-Data/Most-relevant-data.aspx. Sourced June 6, 2010.

90 Organic Valley website. http://www.organicvalley.coop/newsroom/20years/fact-sheet/. Sourced June 5, 2010.

91 http://www.city-data.com/city/La-Farge-Wisconsin.html. Sourced June 5, 2010.

92 Chris Hubbuch. LaCrosse (WI) Tribune. *Organic Valley Adding Jobs; La Farge Gets Federal Grant for Future Growth.* http://lacrossetribune.com/news/local/article_ec303942-6945-11df-9bd1-001cc4c002e0.html. May 27, 2010. Sourced June 5, 2010.

93 Country Natural Beef website. http://countrynaturalbeef.com/index.php?option=com_frontpage&Itemid=1. Sourced June 6, 2010.

94 http://foodalliance.org/. Sourced September 12, 2010.

95 http://www.localharvest.org. Sourced June 6, 2010.

96 Doc Hatfield. Becky Hatfield Hyde. http://www.oregoncountrybeef.com/.

Our product is more than beef

"....it's the smell of sage after a summer thunderstorm,
the cool shade of a Ponderosa Pine forest.
It's 80 year old weathered hands saddling a horse in the Blue mountains,
The future of a 6-year old in a one room school on the high desert.
It's a trout in a beaver built pond, haystacks on an Aspen framed meadow.
It's the hardy quail running to join the cattle for a meal,
the welcome ring of a dinner bell at dusk."

97 http://www.native-languages.org/original.htm. Retrieved August 15, 2009.

98 Frederic C. Mish. Editor in Chief *Webster's Tenth New Collegiate Dictionary* Springfield, Massachuetts, U.S.A.: 1994--Merriam-Webster See original definition (definition #1) of "Aryan" in English--Page 66

99 "Civilization" (1974), *Encyclopedia Britannica* 15th ed. Vol. II, Encyclopedia Britannica, Inc., 956.

100 William H. McNeill. *The Rise of the West: A History of the Human Community*, University of Chicago Press, 1963, 1991. ISBN 0-226-56141-0.

101 http://news.nationalgeographic.com/news/2001/05/0518_crescent.html. Sourced August 30, 2009.

102 W. M. Denevan, *The Native Population of the Americas in 1492.* 2nd ed. Madison: University of Wisconsin Press. 1992 [1976].

103 S. Barry and N. Gualde. *The Biggest Epidemics of History: (La Plus Grande Epidémie de L'Histoire) L'Histoire* Magazine. 2006. pp. 45-46, say "between one-third and two-thirds"; R. Gottfried, "Black Death" in *Dictionary of the Middle Ages*, vol. 2, (1983). pp. 257-267, says "between 25 and 45 percent".
104 *The World at Six Billion,* United Nations Population Division.
105 http://www.census.gov/ipc/www/idb/country.php. Sourced 9.23.09.
106 David N. Weil. *Economic Growth.* Addison-Wesley. 2004. p. 111. ISBN 0201680262.
107 http://news.bbc.co.uk/2/hi/asia-pacific/7084749.stm. Sourced 9.24.09.
108 John Lie. *Multiethnic Japan.* Cambridge, Mass.: Harvard University Press, 2001 ISBN 0674013581
109 Lester R. Brown. *Plan B 3.0: Mobilizing to Save Civilization.* Chapter 7, "Eradicating Poverty, Stabilizing Population." W.W. Norton & Company. New York. 2008
110 http://www.migrationinformation.org/feature/display.cfm?ID=747. Sourced March 10, 2010.
111 Steven A. Camarota, Karen Jensenius. *A Shifting Tide: Recent Trends in the Illegal Immigrant Population.* Center for Immigration Studies. July, 2009. http://www.cis.org/IllegalImmigration-ShiftingTide. Sourced March, 2010.
112 http://tradingeconomics.com/Economics/Balance-Of-Trade.aspx?Symbol=JPY. Sourced October 3, 2009.
113 Robert Frank, Amir Efrati, Aaron Lucchetti and Chad Bray. *Madoff Jailed After Admitting Epic Scam.* The Wall Street Journal. http://online.wsj.com/article/SB123685693449906551.html?mod=djemalertNEWS. March 13, 2009. Sourced September 14, 2010.
114 Ibn Khaldun, *Muqaddimah.* Quoted in Dieter Weiss' (1995), "Ibn Khaldun on Economic Transformation", *International Journal of Middle East Studies.*
115 Julian L. Simon. *Population Growth, Economic Growth and Foreign Aid.* Cato Journal, Volume 7, No. 1 (Spring/Summer 1987) Copyright Cato Institute.
116 Migration Information Source. http://www.migrationinformation.org/Feature/display.cfm?ID=402. Sourced Oct. 2, 2009.
117 Center for Immigration Studies. http://cis.org/CurrentNumbers. Sourced Oct. 2, 2009.
118 United States Census Bureau. *U.S. POPClock Projection.* http://www.census.gov/population/www/popclockus.html. September 14, 2010.
119 Lester R. Brown. Plan B 4.0: Mobilizing to Save Civilization. W.W. Norton & Company, New York. 2009. Chapter 1, "Selling Our Future."
120 David P. Barash. *We Are All Madoffs: Our Relationship to the Natural World is a Ponzi Scheme.* The Chronicle of Higher Education. October 23, 2009.
121 Derrick Jensen. *Beyond Hope.* May/June 2006 issue of *Orion* magazine. Excerpted from *Endgame,* published in June 2006 by Seven Stories Press.

122 Daniel B. Smith. *Is There an Ecological Unconscious?* New York Times Magazine. January 27, 2010.
123 Rachel Carson. *Silent Spring*. Houghton Mifflin, Boston, 1962. Mariner Books, 2002, ISBN 0-618-24906-0
124 http://www.autofiends.com/index.php/2008/06/audi-r10-tdi-le-mans-racers-to-run-on-biowaste-diesel/ sourced in February, 2009.
125 http://www.greencarcongress.com/2008/06/audi-a4-20-tdi.html
126 The Associated Press. *With First Share Offering, Tesla Bets on Electric Car's Future.* http://www.nytimes.com/2010/06/28/business/28tesla.html?emc=tnt&tntemail0=y. The New York Times. June 27, 2010. Sourced June 27, 2010.
127 http://www.teslamotors.com/performance/acceleration_and_torque.php. Sourced November 22, 2009.
128 Tyler Hamilton. *Tesla CEO Following in Henry Ford's Tracks.* Thestar.com. http://www.thestar.com/iphone/article/Business/708847. October 12, 2009. Sourced November 27, 2009.
129 Claire Cain Miller. *Tesla Electric Cars: Revved Up, but Far to Go.* The New York Times. July 24, 2010.
130 Michael Belfiore. *Rocketeers*. HarperCollins, 2007. ISBN 978-0-06-114902-3 - see chapter 7 "Orbit on a Shoestring" pp. 166-195.
131 Sarah Lacy. *Entrepreneurs: Start. This. Company. Now.* TechCrunch. http://www.techcrunch.com/2009/11/19/entrepreneurs-start-this-company-now/. November 19, 2009. Sourced November 27, 2009.
132 Erica Gies. *Doing More While Using Less Power.* The New York Times. September 1, 2010.
133 Christopher Dickey and Tracy McNicoll. *The Flying Prius.* Newsweek. July 16, 2010.
134 Luis Locay. *From Hunting and Gathering to Agriculture.* Economic Development and Cultural Change, Vol. 37, No. 4 (Jul., 1989), pp. 737-756. The University of Chicago Press.
135 E.O. Wilson. *The Future of Life.* Alfred A. Knopf. 2002.
136 Wes Jackson. *Natural Systems Agriculture: A Radical Alternative.* 2002. Reprinted from *Agriculture, Ecosystems and Environment* Volume 88, pp. 111-117, 2002, with permission from Elsevier Science.
137 Rachel Carson. *Silent Spring. Fortieth Anniversary Edition.* First Mariner Books edition. Houghton Mifflin Company. 2002.
138 National Cancer Institute. *Agricultural Health Study.* Ongoing.
139 Felicity Lawrence. *Kate Barker: Not on the Label.* Penguin. 2004.
140 Jackson. 2002.
141 Luisa Kroll, Matthew Miller and Tatiana Serafin. *"The World's Billionaires".* Forbes. http://www.forbes.com/2009/03/11/worlds-richest-people-billionaires-2009-billionaires_land.html. March 11, 2009. Sourced Dec. 29, 2009.
142 http://www.communitygarden.org/learn/resources/research.php. Sourced Jan. 2, 2010.

143 Ben Macintyre. *"My Allotted Place in Our Green and Peasant Land."* TimesOnline. http://www.timesonline.co.uk/tol/comment/columnists/ben_macintyre/article5804558.ece. Feb. 26, 2009. Sourced Jan. 3, 2010.

144 http://www.jardins-familiaux.org/frameset/englisch/eoffi.htm. Sourced Jan. 3, 2010.

145 http://www.horsecouncil.org/nationaleconomics.php. Sourced Jan. 2, 2010.

146 Pliny the Elder. Gaius Plinius Secundus. *Historia Naturalis.* Book 18, Chapter 5. "*Majores fertilissium in agro oculum domini esse dixerunt.*" Sourced from http://www.bartleby.com/78/18.html, Jan. 4, 2010.

147 http://klt.org/. Sourced Jan. 3, 2010.

148 *"Many forms of Government have been tried and will be tried in this world of sin and woe. No one pretends that democracy is perfect or all-wise. Indeed, it has been said that democracy is the worst form of government except all those other forms that have been tried from time to time."* Speech in the House of Commons (1947-11-11) *The Official Report, House of Commons (5th Series), 11 November 1947, vol. 444, cc. 206–07.* Sourced from Wikiquote, http://en.wikiquote.org/wiki/Winston_Churchill, January 15, 2010.

149 Pandia Search Engine News. *Google: One Million Servers and Counting.* http://www.pandia.com/sew/481-gartner.html. July 2, 2007. Sourced April 24, 2010.

150 Eric Kuhn. *Google Unveils top Political Searches of 2009.* CNNPolitics. http://politicalticker.blogs.cnn.com/2009/12/18/google-unveils-top-political-searches-of-2009/?fbid=wYS5e7Dn-Cz. December 18, 2009. Sourced April 24, 2010.

151 Erick Schonfeld. *Google Processing 20,000 Terabytes A Day, And Growing.* TechCrunch. http://techcrunch.com/2008/01/09/google-processing-20000-terabytes-a-day-and-growing/. January 9, 2008. Sourced April 24, 2010.

152 Google Annual Report, 2009.

153 Ken Auletta. *Googled: The End of the World As We Know It.* Penguin Press. 2009. ISBN978-1-59420-235-3. Page 43.

154 *Googled.* Page 53, 226.

155 Google website. http://www.google.com/corporate/culture.html. Sourced May 17, 2010.

156 http://www.google.com/corporate/green/employee-benefits.html. Sourced May 17, 2010.

157 http://www.google.com/corporate/green/clean-energy.html. Sourced May 18, 2010.

158 http://www.google.com/corporate/green/datacenters/. Sourced May 18, 2010.

159 http://googleblog.blogspot.com/2009/01/powering-google-search.html. Sourced May 18, 2010.

160 Central Intelligence Agency. *CIA Factbook. Country Comparison: Electricity – Consumption.* https://www.cia.gov/library/publications/the-world-factbook/rankorder/2042rank.html. Sourced May 18, 2010.

161 Samantha Rose Hunt. *Top Google Executives Get a Fighter Jet.* TG Daily. http://www.tgdaily.com/trendwatch-features/39897-top-google-executives-get-a-fighter-jet. Friday, Oct. 24, 2008. Sourced May 18, 2010.
162 Fortune magazine/ CNNMoney.com. *Best Big Companies to Work For.* http://money.cnn.com/galleries/2010/fortune/1004/gallery.fortune500_best_employers.fortune/8.html. April 15, 2010. Sourced May 19, 2010.
163 Geoff Colvin. Fortune Magazine/CNNMoney.com. *What Makes Most Admired Companies Different?* http://money.cnn.com/2010/03/08/news/companies/admired_different.fortune/index.htm. March 9, 2010. Sourced May 19, 2010.
164 Clint Boulton. EWeek. *Google Users Concerned About WiSpy but Still Prefer Google.* http://www.eweek.com/c/a/Search-Engines/Google-Users-Concerned-About-WiSpy-But-Still-Prefer-Google-130784/. July 28, 2010. Sourced August 4, 2010.
165 Katie Hafner. The New York Times. *Google Options Make Masseuse a Multimillionaire.* http://www.nytimes.com/2007/11/12/technology/12google.html?_r=3&ex=1352610000&en=6166f2300d2e0283&ei=5090&partner=rssuserland&emc=rss&oref=slogin&oref=slogin. November 12, 2007. Sourced May 20, 2010.
166 Wikipedia. *Sergey Brin. Larry Page.* Sourced May 20, 2010.
167 Google.org website. *What is Google.org?* http://www.google.org/about.html. Sourced May 20, 2010.
168 Businessweek. *Smarter Corporate Giving.* http://www.businessweek.com/magazine/content/05_48/b3961607.htm. November 28, 2005. Sourced May 20, 2010.
169 Jeffrey Thomas. USINFO Staff Writer. *Charitable Donations by Americans Reach Record High.* America.gov. http://www.america.gov/st/washfile-english/2007/June/200706261522251CJsamohT0.8012354.html. Sourced May 20, 2010.
170 David Drummond. *A New Approach to China: An Update.* The Official Google Blog. http://googleblog.blogspot.com/2010/03/new-approach-to-china-update.html. Posted March 22, 2010. Sourced May 29, 2010.
171 http://www.google.com/governmentrequests/.
172 UN-Habitat. *Slum Dwellers to Double by 2030: Millennium Development Goal Could Fall Short.* Report on the Twenty-First Session of the UN-Habitat Governing Council. April 16-20 2007. United Nations Human Settlements Programme (UN-HABITAT) Nairobi, Kenya. www.unhabitat.org.

Index

Acknowledgements

It's impossible to give credit to the many, many persons who have contributed to this book. Any attempt to name you all would be futile. You know who you are. Thank you.

I want mention a few people specifically and thank them for their selflessness, their support and their affection.

Principally, my wife, editor and ranching partner Carolyn Welch, who long ago joined her dreams and visions with mine and made my life much richer for it.

Noah Welch, Caitlin Linscheid, Aaron Linscheid and Evan Welch gave me their affectionate support throughout the project and kept me interested. They are the inspiration for this work.

Several of my professional colleagues volunteered their time, advice and inspiration. In particular, Hank Will and K.C. Compton donated many hours and made the book much better. Hugh Delehanty and Barbara Graham lent a much-needed worldly perspective. Words can't express my gratitude.

My publishing partner and agent, Neil Salkind, was instrumental as was my book editor, Janet Majure and book designer Matthew Stallbaumer. Cheryl Long gave irreplaceable assistance in bringing my ideas to light. Bob Wright helped me focus my efforts and Alan Nichols provided a catalyst for me with his contribution of the "Destination Fixation."

All the inspiring leaders mentioned in these pages are owed a debt of gratitude, as well as those who offered kind feedback after it was finished.

I look forward to sharing a beautiful and abundant future with you all.

— *Bryan*

Advance Praise for Beautiful and Abundant

"We are in great need of an optimistic vision of the future. We have always been problem-solvers and pioneers of the possible. It is time to rediscover this core of the human experience. Bryan Welch is asking the right questions and points the way to a promising, beautiful and abundant tomorrow."

— Jurriaan Kamp, Editor-in-Chief, *Ode Magazine*

This is a book that invites us all to cut through the negativity of doomsday prophets and other 'progressive' thinkers and visualize a new and abundant future. Bryan Welch is that rare business leader who can run a successful company and at the same time write prose that is nuanced, eloquent and visionary. This luminous call to action will surely inspire you to join others in creating a better future for humanity. It happened to me."

— Wanda Urbanska, author of
The Heart of Simple Living: 7 Paths to a Better Life

"Why settle for anything less than beauty? In his compelling book *Beautiful and Abundant*, Bryan Welch challenges us to reframe our most pressing environmental challenges into a transformative, equitable vision of the future. His rich blend of practical strategies, poetic narrative, and deep curiosity will engage and inspire anyone intent on living a better life today—and creating a sustainable legacy for generations to come."

— P. Simran Sethi, Emmy award-winning journalist
and Associate Professor of Journalism, University of Kansas

"Bucking the gloom, doom and guilt-salving trends of the modern environmental movement, Welch grabs global sustainability by the horns and makes an eloquent case for proactively creating the future world we want. *Beautiful and Abundant* is a must-read for everyone with a stake in the future and offers an important paradigm shift to conventional thought. Environmental dooms-dayers, global-warming naysayers, policy-makers, scientists, financiers – you've been served!"

— Oscar H. Will III, PhD. Editor, *GRIT Magazine*